A Rainbow Book

"As I read *Balanced Living*, I became more and more wrapped up in the sense of it and realized what Dr. Mark Pitstick was trying to do in his book. He is incredible; I really appreciated his insights. As I read, I found myself wondering, 'When is he going to touch on . . .?' And then, wonder of wonders, he did. Many of the things Dr. Pitstick says have been said before, but he says them again forcefully and with many references to back them up.

"When I attended my Episcopal Sunday School, I remember the phrase: 'Let your light so shine before men that they may see your good works and glorify your Father Which art in heaven. To do good and distribute, forget not, for with such sacrifices, God is well pleased.' This was said just before they took up the offering, for which I sometimes contributed a nickel. Finally now, I think that I understand the message couched in those sentences. But I had to read Dr. Pitstick's book to get it.

"We in the nutritional field often claim that we are being wholistic when we suggest that someone take extra vitamins and change his/her lifestyle. But we do not know what that word wholistic (holistic) really means until we have read this book. Mark Pitstick has had the appropriate training to be a wholistic doctor. He has a degree in zoology, an M.A. in clinical psychology, and is a doctor of chiropractic medicine. To round all that out, he received graduate theological training and majored in pastoral counseling. When young people ask me to advise them what to take to become a truly helpful therapist, I tell them to get a degree in something (M.D., D.C., N.D., D.O.) so they will be credible and have a license to treat people, but also read about nutrition, and get involved with counseling. Dr. Pitstick went as far as he could to become a well-rounded therapist. He has developed skills in treating the body, the mind, and the spirit.

"This book, *Balanced Living*, is just what his title implies. He covers all aspects of body, mind, and spirit, and what therapy might best shore up any of those departments. Each, however, is dependent upon the others, like the legs of a three-legged stool.

If one leg goes, down goes the stool.

"Some readers may find that his doses of vitamins and minerals are not enough for their needs, but in the context of his wholistic approach, they may be plenty. I am sure that when I gave the doses of these nutrients to sick patients and they did not get well fast enough, I was not dealing with the other two parts of the patient. I assumed that megadoses of supplements would overcome any emotional tilt they had. Balance here in this book is the exact word for his approach. He has found that chiropractic evaluation and adjustments are very helpful in the total approach to the disabled patient.

"When I began to read about his relations with his God, I was beginning to get uncomfortable because I thought he was going to tell me to accept Jesus and everything would be just dandy. But he didn't do that. He did fill in many gaps in my perception of what religion can do for anyone, and even me. He helped to dispel some false ideas I have had about religion. He does make a belief in a higher being appear worthwhile.

"I was impressed with the hundreds of quotes he used, sprinkled throughout the manuscript from Gandhi, the Apostles, ancient Greeks and Romans. There is something in here for everyone. Although I am almost perfect, I am a better person for having read this book.

"Dr. Pitstick, you have done a wonderful job."

— Lendon H. Smith, M.D.
Author of *Feed Your Kids Right,*
Feed Yourself Right and other
bestselling books.

BALANCED LIVING:
REALIZING YOUR FULLEST POTENTIALS

Dr. Mark R. Pitstick

RAINBOW BOOKS, INC.

BALANCED LIVING: Realizing Your Fullest Potentials
by Dr. Mark R. Pitstick
$16.95

Library of Congress Cataloging in Publication Data

Pitstick, Mark R.
    Balanced living : realizing your fullest potentials / Mark R. Pitstick.
        p. cm.
    ISBN 0-935834-91-5 : $16.95
    1. Self-care. Health. 2. Health. 3. Holistic medicine.
    I. Title
    RA776.95.P58   1993   92-31432
    613—dc20   CIP

Recognizing the importance of preserving the written
word, Rainbow Books, Inc., by policy, prints all of its
first editions on acid-free (neutral pH) paper.

Warning/Disclaimer

Every effort has been made to make this collection of materials as complete and accurate as possible. Nevertheless, information
may change, there may be mistakes, both typographical and in
content. Important data may be omitted. Therefore, this book should
be used as a general guide only and not as a final source of information.

Further, all statements made by the author, Dr. Mark R.
Pitstick, are based on his own personal research and study; they do not
necessarily reflect the beliefs of all professionals. It should also be
noted that in no way is any information contained herein meant to take
the place of or to provide any kind of professional advice or treatment,
nor does it preclude the need to seek the advice of professionals on a
personal level.

CONTENTS

ACKNOWLEDGMENTS

To my family — Michelle, Faith, and Rae Lynn — for their love, support, and understanding in all my endeavors.

To my nuclear family — parents Bill and Virginia Pitstick, brother Tony, and sister Nancy — for the loving environment and stable home from which I could launch my explorations.

To my extended family, co-workers, educators, and friends who have helped me along the way.

To my patients who have taught me so much over the years.

Thanks to those mentors and colleagues whose teaching and friendship furthered my understanding of holistic health care: Paul Brown, Jim Elliott, Edward Flaherty, Steve Gold, Gary Greer, Ruth Grow, Jeff Hanes, James Hogg, Joe Hornberger, Richard Labarbera, Mike McConeghey, Jay Morgan, John Schott, Tim Skraitz, Judy Stillion, Mike Turner, and Jerry Walke.

To the staff and associates at the Balanced Living Chiropractic Center.

To publisher Betty Wright and the excellent staff at Rainbow Books, Inc.

To those authors and teachers whose works have helped me extensively. These include: Richard Bach, John Bradshaw, Eric Butterworth, Dale Carnegie, Norman Cousins, Ram Dass, Harvey and Marilyn Diamond, Wayne Dyer, Joseph Flesia, Jr.; Buckminster Fuller, Chuck Gibson, Bernard

Jensen, Charles "Tremendous" Jones, Elisabeth Kübler-Ross, Bob Love, Abraham Maslow, John McDougall, Earl Nightengale, Irving Oyle, Norman Vincent Peale, W. V. Pierce, Ken Ring, Robert Schuller, Hans Selye, Bernie Siegel, Jim Sigafoose, Lendon H. Smith, Gary P. Todd, Denis Waitley, Chester Wilk, and Zig Ziglar.

To God and Universe for being all caring, knowing, and present.

INTRODUCTION

At age 12, I was sitting alone in our kitchen, eating a bowl of cereal and reading the front page obituary of a prominent local man. Sunlight refracted through our beveled window panes and multicolored light shone into my peripheral vision. As I looked up into that light, an inner thought or voice that was calm and clear asked, "This man just ended his time on earth. Someday you will likewise die. What will you do with your time until then? Will you help others and leave the earth a better place? Or will you merely take up space?" This thought or voice was unlike any I had experienced prior to that time. The questions were not accusatory or judgmental but certainly were thought provoking. Similar experiences have inspired me to become all that I can and to encourage others to do the same.

I wrote *Balanced Living* to help as many persons as possible to reach their fullest physical, mental, and spiritual potentials. Holistic health education is a great idea but difficult for busy doctors to implement. This book covers the nuts and bolts of what I would emphasize for my patients and those of other health professionals. Finally, this book is part of *working on myself* — a lifelong and never-ending process; I'm continually looking for new ways to become transformed for the better. My purpose is to teach, heal, and help myself and others with a holistic approach to maximize our potentials and consciousness growth.

We each can become vitally healthy, productive, and at

peace with ourselves and our world. My commitment is to help us realize our *true nature* and vast abilities in all realms of life. Life on earth can be much happier, healthier, and more balanced than most of us dream. May this book stimulate dialogue, research, and personal experimentation until we are all *truly well* and discover our vast potentials.

I have studied a wide variety of health topics and have worked in health-related settings for 20 years. Work and school experiences include: certified respiratory therapist at two medical hospitals for six years; pre-medical bachelor of science degree in zoology; one year theological training majoring in pastoral counseling; two year masters degree in clinical psychology and five years practice in mental health centers and a college faculty position; Doctor of Chiropractic degree and eight years private practice. My wife, Michelle, is a licensed dietician who has helped me learn much about nutrition.

Thus, I have a unique perspective to offer. Buckminster Fuller stated that our world suffers from having too many *specialists* with their near-sighted viewpoints. I have purposely worked to become a *generalist* with a wider perspective. I am grateful for the opportunity to learn so much from so many persons. Now it is time to share my knowledge with others. As I've studied various disciplines, one fact is clear: even "the experts" don't agree with each other. Thus, I encourage a *synthesis* or sharing of views as we rationally discuss our areas of agreement and disagreement. I hope that in reading this book you will *find your true self* — and feel more joyous and trusting about life. Find your own balance and answers that work best for you.

Each of us is truly unique and different; as such, my recommendations are more *guidelines* than "carved-in-granite" laws. Use this book like a tool chest; choose those tools that make sense and work for you. Imagine that you are a sports car and your goal is to be as finely tuned as possible. As you read, highlight or underline areas of personal interest. A marked-up book is a compliment to an author and necessary for active reading.

Balanced Living is divided into several topics including: physical wellness, nutrition, rest, exercise, chiropractic, self-actualization, and spiritual enlightenment. These are the basic components necessary for true holistic health. These factors that contribute to total wellness are like pieces of a pie. Each piece contributes to the total picture of health or the lack thereof; true wellness involves a balance and harmony among these areas. The approach of *Balanced Living* is preventive as well as holistic. Consider the analogy of people falling through a hole in a bridge and into the river. The old, disease-oriented model was like having rescue teams save the drowning persons. The newer preventive and wellness approach is to fix the hole in the bridge so they don't fall through in the first place.

From years of personal and professional experience, I know that all persons can reach their highest potentials and enjoy vibrant living. These levels will be different for each person, but we all can enjoy *relatively* high levels of wellness. We can experience high levels of energy and endurance to meet the challenges of life. We can be completely or relatively free of disease and live a long, healthy, and vigorous life. We can have loving and nurturing relationships with many friends and family. We can fulfill our occupational dreams as we perform our life's work. We can experience a personal relationship with our Creator and walk with God along the journey of life. We can know an inner peace and joy that provides a bedrock foundation for times that test our faith.

This is the vision I have for myself and all other persons. There is, however, no such thing as a free lunch. We must want to change and be willing to put forth the time, energy, and money involved. The price we pay for vital health, however, is negligible compared to the many benefits we reap. As Zig Ziglar reminds us, we don't pay the price, we *enjoy the benefits* of living healthfully and in a balanced way. Try healthier lifestyle habits for six months and experience how much better you can look, feel, and be.

The blocks of wood that keep a stationary jumbo jet from rolling are only the size of a piece of firewood. By exerting a little power, however, the jet can easily roll over these blocks. Likewise, the factors that keep us from enjoying vital health are relatively small and can be overcome. These obstacles stop us only if we never try to better ourselves; any efforts toward positive change will result in eventual self-improvement.

Optimal growth is a lawful and predictable path when certain facts are understood and followed. We weren't created to live short, sickly, depressed, and tired lives. We were meant to be happy, healthy, enthusiastic, and successful. As George Burns, playing God in the movie *Oh God* said, "Tell everybody I set the world up so it can work . . . I gave you a world and everything in it. It's all up to you." Yes, we have everything we need, but some of us don't know that yet.

We need to *awaken* — become enlightened — to who we truly are and all we can achieve. A Hindu analogy describes people viewing a huge and exquisitely ornamented room by a single match flame. Due to the limited amount of light, they are unable to comprehend the vastness and beauty of their surroundings. Similarly, most humans have a *limited perception* of reality. Let us walk together, *sharing our match flames,* to enlighten our viewpoints and better appreciate the wondrous universe in which we live. By walking together and sharing our knowledge, dreams, and insights, we can achieve the collective wisdom necessary to solve our problems.

My message is one of hope. There is an accelerating evolution of consciousness going on right now that can lead to a virtual heaven on earth. Realizing heaven on earth is a result of salvation by grace *and* by works; God helps those who help themselves. With God's help — and God is always there to guide and assist us — we surely can reach greater heights. People are becoming increasingly interested in achieving their personal best in all realms of life. We are realizing that all persons on earth are part of one big family. Utopia can be a reality here and now as we all discover and express our physical, mental, and spiritual potentials. Let your light shine.

Recently, a school girl won first prize out of 16,000 youngsters for her upbeat predictions for the year 2010. Her vision included: No more wars anywhere; no child abuse; only healthy food; and cures for cancer, AIDs, and the common cold. Bravo! Why can't we? *When enough of us share this vision of heaven on earth, it will become a reality.* The possibilities and mechanisms for it are already in place. We need only ask for it in earnest and receive the gifts that our Creator has so generously supplied. Let's realize these truths, give thanks, roll up our sleeves, and start today — enjoying life, serving others, reaching our potentials, and remembering our Source.

A Native American story related to me by Rainbow Eagle of the Choctaw tribe tells of an eagle that thought it was a chicken. A baby eagle fell from its nest and landed near a chicken coop. A mother hen mistook the little eagle for one of her own. And so it was that the young eagle was raised by a chicken, with other baby chicks, and like a chicken.

But once in awhile, the little eagle would see a big eagle soaring overhead. The little eagle's heart was filled with awe and it felt confused, lonely, and unfulfilled. What's wrong with me? thought the eaglet. Why can't I be satisfied like the other chickens? And why do I stare so at the majestic eagles? But having been raised like a chicken, with chickens, and by a chicken, the little eagle continued to think it was a chicken.

One day, a big eagle looked down, saw the little eagle, and swooped down beside it. "What are you doing down here with these chickens?" asked the big eagle. "You're not a chicken; you're an eagle. Look at your size, shape, and feathers. You're like me — fly with me!"

But the little eagle still believed it was a chicken and was too afraid; the big eagle shook its head and said, "Spread your wings and do as I do." The little eagle watched his elder brother and began to spread his wings. Then it happened. At first, just an inch off the ground for a few seconds — then higher and longer in the air until at last — the little eagle could fly. *Realizing its true nature*, the eagle assumed its rightful place from that day on.

In the same way, all of us are like eagles — powerful, capable of attaining great heights, and full of marvelous potentials. But some of us think we're lowly chickens and settle for lower levels of achievement and satisfaction. How good it feels — a freedom like flying — when we discover and *really know* our true nature. We each are sitting on a literal gold mine of abundant health, prosperity, happiness, and success. We have all the tools needed for the job. We need only dig a little — discover our true natures and exert a little time and energy — to enjoy life's riches.

An alternate subtitle for *Balanced Living* is *Transformation to Heaven on Earth*. I believe that life on earth can be much like heaven or hell, depending on several matters under our control. I believe in an afterlife and progressively better inner and outer harmony for us all. We don't, however, have to wait until we die to experience heaven. We can increasingly experience that which we all desire — inner peace, love, joy, and total wellness. *Global change — one person at a time* is possible and starts with each one of us. Here are some steps to take and the road markers to look for.

PHYSICAL WELLNESS

"If you don't take the time in your life for exercise and health, then you have to take time later for illness and immobilization. The choice is yours."

— *Dr. Wayne Dyer*

Each of us is a living and breathing miracle. *The same Creative Intelligence that made the magnificent universe also designed the human body. This same intelligence that made the body can heal the body.* Call it Mother Nature, Innate Intelligence, homeostasis, or God — most scientists recognize an organized intelligence within the body. Any good physician will admit that healing is about 90 percent "Mother Nature." Voltaire said, "The art of medicine consists of keeping the patient in a good mood while nature does the healing." Thus, the person interested in total wellness works to assist these internal health maintenance and restorative mechanisms.

Benjamin Franklin said, "An ounce of prevention is worth a pound of cure." Former Surgeon General C. Everett Koop recently stated that doctors should concentrate on keeping people *well* rather than treating them after they are sick. What is needed, says Koop, is to work for the overall health of the nation through "an ethic of prevention . . . It is cheap. It is effective." The costs of staying healthy are negligible compared to the advantages of feeling and being well. Conversely, the costs — both financially and personally — of illness are staggering and often preventable. Yes, the saying is true: "Ignore your health and it will go away."

Some persons don't believe they can ever be healthy and feel great; they think that is only possible for others. My message to *each* of you is: You are a miraculous part of the creation. Your birthright is a healthy, happy, and successful life. Do you think the Creator made this wonderful universe, then — as an afterthought — threw some leftover scrap parts together to make humans? No, God created us magnificently and with forethought. Throw away your concepts that you were born unhealthily — that you have "sickly genes." Heredity is only one factor compared to many others over which we have control.

Self-responsibility is a major theme in the quest for true wellness. I vividly remember an extremely overweight patient who had just received her twelfth surgery for ankle, knee, and hip problems. Longterm obesity was the cause of her multiple joint damage. I remarked about the number of surgeries she had received, to which she replied, "Yes, I guess God just didn't put me together very well." She had not yet learned the important lesson of self-responsibility for her health and was literally paying for her lack of knowledge.

Your health is your responsibility; doctors can help some but can't make you healthy. I complimented Ida, an 80-year-old patient of mine, on her great health and how she takes care of herself. She replied, "Well, if I don't, nobody else is going to!" That's exactly right. Health cannot be bought and does not come in a prescription bottle. The saying, "If it ain't broke, don't fix it" isn't good for machinery or the human body. We each have only one body and should do our utmost to keep it 100 percent healthy. If we wait until "it's broke," it's often too late to regain complete wellness.

Many people spend the first half of their life making money and *ignoring* their health. In the second half of life, they spend this money trying to regain their health. Emmett Miller, M.D., author of *Feeling Good; How To Stay Healthy,* reminds us that we can be in control of our own health. Dr. Miller says we need to learn how to allow our natural, health-restoring abilities to work for us; we play a very important role in our own health, to the degree that we choose. The wise person recognizes early in life that good health is one of life's most valuable possessions and does everything possible to preserve it. *Please take the time to take care of yourself.*

When I first heard about *natural health care* — that didn't include drugs or surgery — my first reaction was, "What else is there?" Since then I have learned about many powerful natural treatments. Aruvedic healing techniques from India, as discussed by Deepak Chopra, M.D., in *Quantum Healing,* are thousands of years old. Early Greek and Roman healers recognized the power of the body to heal itself and the importance of preventive measures. Hippocrates taught that health was the expression of a harmonious balance among internal and external forces, involving mind as well as body. He stressed the healing power of nature and was opposed to treatments that might interfere with natural healing processes. His injunction "first do no harm" is still good advice.

Moses Maimonides, Jewish philosopher and physician, advocated preventive medicine as early as the 12th century, emphasizing the health benefits of proper exercise, nutrition, rest, and climate. Albert Schweitzer, M.D., stated, "We are at our best when we give the doctor who resides within each patient a chance to go to work." There are thousands of different named diseases. Are there really that many things that can go wrong or are there a relatively *few major causes* that influence the body to malfunction in many different ways?

The dangers of *invasive treatments* — drugs and surgery — have been well documented and make a strong case for conservative and natural healing approaches whenever possible. Dr. Virgil Slee and a medical commission found that 48,000 people *die annually* from among the four million unnecessary surgeries each year. The Yale-New Haven Hospital Study found that 1.5 million people are hospitalized and 100,000 die annually from prescription drug reactions. These figures clearly signal a need for conservative treatment whenever possible. Read *Medicine on Trial: The Appalling Story of Ineptitude, Malfeasance, Neglect, and Arrogance* by Inlander, Levin, and Weiner for some examples of what can go wrong with orthodox medical approaches.

Says Dr. Chopra, "About 80 percent of all the drugs that we use in western medicine are 'optional' or of marginal benefit, which means that if we didn't use them, it wouldn't make a bit of difference to the person except save money and prevent side effects . . . When we use drugs as indiscriminately as we do currently, we see some problems. There was a study in *The New England Journal of Medicine* in 1981, showing that 36 percent of 815 patients in a university hospital had a disease as a result of medical intervention . . . The No. 1 cause of addiction in the world is not street drugs from Columbia, but legal medicines — tranquilizers and sedatives — prescribed by doctors. There has been a 500-percent increase in addiction from prescriptions since 1962."

In *Health and Healing*, Andrew Weil, M.D., discusses illnesses and injuries most effectively treated medically. These include acute trauma, acute infections, and acute medical emergencies such as a heart attack. Acute surgical emergencies include twisted bowels, bile duct obstruction, inflamed appendices about to burst, and subdural hemorrhage. Says Dr. Weil, "I would look elsewhere than conventional medicine for help if I contracted a severe viral disease like hepatitis or polio or a metabolic disease like diabetes. I would not seek allopathic (orthodox medical treatment) for cancer, except for a few varieties, or for such chronic ailments as arthritis, asthma, hypertension (high blood pressure), multiple sclerosis, or for many other chronic diseases of the digestive, circulatory, musculoskeletal, and nervous systems. Although allopaths give lip service to the concept of preventive medicine, for practical purposes they are unable to prevent most of the diseases that disable and kill people today."

John McDougall, M.D., author of *McDougall's Medicine — A Challenging Second Opinion*, holds that medications are required in only a few cases and states, "Most medical treatments for long-standing diseases can honestly be called patch jobs and temporary fixes." He continues "Simple, sensible, safe, self-help approaches based upon a healthy diet and an equally healthy lifestyle are almost never mentioned by doctors. Instead, almost routinely, life-threatening drugs and dangerous surgeries are prescribed as if no other avenue of treatment were available."

I am not belittling the medical field; in certain cases, their results are miraculous. I regularly refer patients who may need drug or surgical treatment to medical doctors. However, the average medical specialist is too involved with these approaches to properly educate patients about *natural and preventive* measures. Health care consumers must also shoulder part of the blame, however, as they get what they ask for. Some persons want little or no involvement in their health care and want the doctor to quickly solve the problem with shots, pills, or surgery. Some patients become irate if their doctor doesn't send them home with a prescription.

A change in our health care approach is obviously needed. The U.S. has one of the most expensive health care systems among industrialized nations, yet ranks 17th in life expectancy and 20th in preventing infant mortality. The financial strain alone cries for a radical change in our health care delivery system. U.S. health costs are projected at $800 billion in 1992 and will double by the year 2000. The financial costs pale, however, when compared to the pain, suffering, and lost human potentials involved. The suffering of those with serious but preventable diseases is tragic. Even more common, however, are the people who suffer minor maladies and "just don't feel good."

Fortunately, more and more persons are becoming interested in preventive and natural health approaches. As this trend continues, a doctor can become a true *physician* — which means healer — instead of a *crisis care provider.* Norman Cousins stated, "Plainly, the American people need to be re-educated about their health. They need to know that they are the possessors of a remarkably robust mechanism. They need to be de-intimidated about disease . . . We are much stronger than we think. Much stronger." *Believe in health more than disease;* our body's healing potentials are formidable.

Julian Whitaker, M.D., author of *Reversing Heart Disease* , says: "Getting sick is neither natural nor unavoidable. We know that disease is often caused by the way we live, and by the food, water, and air we put into our bodies . . . And we're finding that there are things we can do to not only avoid illness, but actually reverse it! Your body is designed to *heal itself naturally* and then *keep* you healthy — IF you know how to help it!"

Make pursuing total wellness a personal goal of the highest priority. What can we become, how can we feel, and what will our world be like as more of us enjoy exuberant and energetic health? Let's find out. The following sections explore wellness habits that address the causes of common health problems and can help us reach utopia living.

Types Of Stress

Understanding the concept of *stress* is important for achieving total wellness. We often associate "stress" with psychological factors, but there are several types of stressors: emotional, physical, and chemical. Moderating *physical stress* requires sufficient rest, exercise, minimal thermal stresses, healthy work habits, proper skeletal alignment, and a normal nerve supply. *Emotional stress* consists of mental, spiritual, social, family, sexual, and financial emphases. *Chemical stress* includes what we put into our bodies: food, drink, air, and drugs. Monitor these factors especially during high stress times; for example, during weather changes (thermal stress) or after a loved one dies (emotional stress).

The "reservoir model" is useful for understanding the cumulative effect in many stress related phenomena. That is, various positive or negative factors *add up* over time to create wellness or disease. A container being filled with water can only hold so much before it overflows. Similarly, the various factors contributing to health or illness accumulate and eventually result in excellent health or an identifiable illness. Too many negative events can overflow into problems for you. *Balanced Living* discusses how you can best fill your life's container with positive factors.

Hans Selye, M.D., in *The Stress of Life*, defined stress as "the nonspecific response of the body to any demand." Stress is not inherently bad and a certain amount is desirable. A healthy person takes care to manage the various stresses of life since excess stress can make us more susceptible to illness and dysfunction. *Avoid overflowing your stress reservoir.* We each have different capacities for stress; listen to your inner signals and don't get "stressed out."

Some individuals thrive on a fast-paced existence; Dr. Selye termed such persons — who are challenged and fulfilled by a busy schedule — "race horses." Thus, what constitutes "excessive stress" is a relative matter. A healthy and balanced person finds time for leisure, family, and self as well as occupational, financial, and social pursuits. Find your balance in life and meet your own unique needs and goals. Aristotle considered temperance and moderation to be among the highest virtues; pursue balance and moderation in all these areas.

Proper Elimination

Proper elimination of body waste products is crucial for total wellness. Just like homes and industries, our bodies produce waste products — garbage — daily. *Eliminative processes — bowel movements, urination, sweating, and breathing —* are the sanitation mechanisms of our bodies. A natural health maxim holds, "There is but one disease, congestion. And there is but one cure, circulation." This certainly holds true for eliminative processes; open circulation of these channels is vital for good health.

The bowels should move easily and at least once per day. Hard, well-formed stools that require straining are not normal and can cause many problems. We should urinate often throughout the day; with sufficient fluid intake, you will probably have to void at least once during the night. Sweating flushes wastes through the pores. Finally, our breath eliminates carbon dioxide from our bodies. These four eliminative routes — bowel movements, urination, sweating, and exhalation — should be sufficient for waste removal in the healthy person. Problems can occur, however, when waste products are removed insufficiently or with a chronically poor diet.

Certain bodily signs indicate whether waste products are being *removed* efficiently. (Causes of excess waste *formation* from poor diet will be discussed in the nutrition chapter.) The *tongue's appearance* is the most observable estimate of the digestive system's health. The tongue should be pink, smooth and glistening; if your tongue is covered with crud, your intestines may be in the same decrepit state. Mold-like coverings on the tongue reflect bacterial growth and accumulation of waste products in the body. A total package of good diet and inner cleanliness is required to correct the underlying causes.

The *appearance* of our *bowel movements* (BM) is another indication of our internal hygiene. BM's should be light brown, large, and soft. If your stools are hard, well-formed, and dark, you are constipated. I'm not suggesting you become obsessed with your BM's but do check these signs periodically. Changing bowel habits is easy and of the utmost curative and preventive importance. In *The Save Your Life Diet*, David Reuben, M.D., lists common diseases associated with constipation: high blood pressure, colon cancer, stroke, hemorrhoids, appendicitis, varicose veins, and diverticular disease. I would add spinal problems, specifically, intervertebral disc strain and bulging, to this list.

Achieving healthy bowel habits is a matter of proper diet, exercise, mental attitude, and proper nerve supply. Obtain sufficient fiber and water with a diet that emphasizes fruits, vegetables, whole grains and their products. Minimize meat, dairy, junk food, and processed food consumption to decrease internal waste production. Regular exercise and deep breathing aids peristalsis that pushes digesting matter through the bowels. Our mental attitudes about BM's are important; as we accept that eliminative processes are natural, these functions proceed more smoothly. Those who are embarrassed or uptight about their toilet habits are more likely to "hold it in" and become constipated. Finally, the digestive system must receive a normal nerve supply to function correctly.

Urination eliminates both soluble and particle wastes. Urine should be pale yellow in color and odor free; if your urine is dark yellow and has a noticeable smell, this system is being overloaded. Parenthetically, multivitamin supplementation that includes thiamine, a B vitamin, can cause the next urination to be a brighter yellow than usual. Drinking lots of water flushes the kidneys and may prevent common disorders such as kidney stones and bladder infections. Urinate as soon as possible after you feel the urge. This reduces bladder and urinary sphincter pressures that contribute to stress incontinence problems.

Our *skin*, with its millions of pores and sweat glands, is the largest eliminative organ in the body. Exercise, saunas, hot baths, sunbathing, and steamrooms open and cleanse the pores. Don't clog sweat glands in the armpits with "antiperspirant" deodorants that prevent sweat glands from self-cleansing. That's one reason why rashes, pimples, infected hairs, and swollen lymph nodes sometimes occur in the armpits. Sweat regularly, eliminate wastes properly, practice inner hygiene principles, and use more "natural" deodorants, if necessary, to prevent body odor.

In addition to showering or bathing regularly, *skin brushing* is an excellent way to remove dead cells and dry wastes secreted by pores. Use a dry "skin brush" or "loofla" sponge with water to vigorously scrub the skin, especially the underarms, groin, buttocks, and outer thighs.

Exercise and deep breathing aid efficient removal of waste products from the lungs. Breathe with the entire volume of your lungs to allow ventilation of all airspaces. *Diaphragmatic breathing* uses the bellows-like diaphragm muscle to aid inhalation and exhalation. As you *inhale*, let your abdomen gently bulge *out*; as you *exhale*, gently pull *in* the abdominal area. Take ten cleansing breaths three times per day; inhale, hold, and exhale to the count of four, later increasing the count to seven, if possible. With practice, you can use this technique during walking or other mild exercises.

Having discussed the four *normal* eliminative routes, let's examine some of the *abnormal* routes the body may have to use. If too many wastes are produced or if the usual four routes are not functioning properly, backup mechanisms are used. These include sinus drainage, sneezing, coughing, diarrhea, vomiting, and, in severe cases, excess menstrual flow.

Sinus drainage, sneezing, and coughing are common backup routes for waste removal. Thin mucous secretions are produced to keep sinus cavities moist and trap inhaled particles. Temporary and occasional sinus drainage, sneezing and coughing to remove dust, fumes, and smoke is normal. But if the body is consistently overloaded with these irritants or is *toxic* because of excessive waste products, chronic congestion may develop. Sensitivities to substances such as grass and dust might be better tolerated if the sinuses weren't already in a congested and bacteria-laden state.

Diarrhea and vomiting are other obvious ways that the body can quickly flush itself of waste products. Finally, excessive *menstruation* is another secondary route that may be necessary in an unhealthy eliminative situation. Periods may become excessively long, heavy, or both.

"Doris" had only one BM *per week,* drank very little water, and didn't exercise — and her body showed it. She experienced heavy menstrual flows with cramping for a week at a time. Despite regular bathing, she also had blemishes, body odor, and bad breath. Proper diet, increased water intake, exercise, and chiropractic adjustments allowed her bowels, urine, sweat, and breath to remove bodily waste products. Within two months her various problems cleared up — she has daily BM's and her periods are symptom free with a normal four-day flow. She looks, acts, feels, and smells better!

The Cleansing Crisis

A "cleansing crisis" — like a cold or flu — is another way the body can rid itself of wastes. The body conducts this internal "spring cleaning" to prevent more serious health problems in persons who don't take care of themselves properly. Accumulated waste products in the body can allow increased bacterial growth and illness. Remember, excess wastes occur when we eat a poor diet or we don't eliminate wastes efficiently. If the body has enough energy to expend, it will *purge* itself of excess wastes and initiate various healing mechanisms. That is, the body purposely creates or allows these inner changes despite the unpleasant symptoms involved. Nature's wisdom places survival and proper functioning over pleasure. If the body becomes excessively toxic and full of wastes, it simply cleans itself out.

We come in contact with pathogenic or disease-causing microorganisms on a regular basis without contracting disease. Three factors that determine whether or not an infectious process or cleansing crisis will occur include the *number* of microorganisms, the *virulence* or strength of the germs, and the overall health or *resistance* state of the person.

Bacteria are everywhere; microorganisms are all around and inside us. In a healthy person, good bacteria called "normal flora" are in a state of balance with "bad" or pathogenic bacteria. Normally, the majority of microorganisms are helpful and keep pathogenic germs in check and at a *relatively low population level.*

Pathogenic microorganisms and their illness-causing potentials are like rats in a garbage dump. If you keep lids on trash cans and dispose of garbage regularly, you won't have rats. However, if you have garbage strewn in or around your house, chances are good that rats will be attracted and will *multiply.* You could trap individual rats but *that wouldn't get to the cause or root of the problem.* A more efficient way to solve the problem would be to clean up the garbage. The first factor, then, is the *number* or proportion of "good" to "bad" bacteria.

Microorganisms vary in their *virulence* or infection-causing potentials; some bacteria are harmful while others are readily infectious. Certainly you should avoid direct contact with anyone who is temporarily overwhelmed with virulent microorganisms. But pathogenic microorganisms play an important role and, at a limited population, are helpful. These "bad guys" play a role in digesting dead matter — old cells, mucous, and other microorganisms. Ralph Von Aling, 93-year-old health enthusiast and author of *Well-Being Through Conscious Evolution,* considers germs, viruses, flies, buzzards, possums, and maggots all in the same category. All are *scavengers* — nature's way of disposing of dead or decaying material.

The third major factor in whether a person might contract an infection is *host resistance.* French physiologist

Claude Bernard said illnesses constantly hover above but do not set in unless the terrain is ready to receive them. The body is a *host* for many indwelling microorganisms; if you are healthy and strong, with all bodily processes working as designed, you will rarely become ill. In football language, "the best defense is a strong offense."

Healthy people rarely get sick; unhealthy persons with low immunity or resistance "catch" many illnesses. With a strong resistance, the other two factors are relatively less important. If the number and virulence of microorganisms were the most important factors, doctors would be ill all the time since we're always exposed to patients who have lots of virulent germs. *The crucial factor in not getting infections, then, is to increase your resistance and become vibrantly healthy.*

Drainage, congestion, inflammation, fever, and fatigue characterize most cleansing crises or infections. *Drainage* involves the outward flow of unwanted substances; for example, lung or sinus drainage in which mucous is expelled from the body by coughing or sneezing. Other examples of drainage are found in eye, ear, skin, genito-urinary, tooth and gum infections. As mentioned, diarrhea and vomiting can be viewed as a drainage or flushing of the digestive system. All of these examples involve a *catharsis* or release of unwanted or excess wastes.

Congestion, for example, in the sinuses or lungs, occurs when secretions are too thick or plentiful for the body to expel them. *Inflammation* involves extra blood and specialized cells to fight and contain the infection, thus the redness, warmth, swelling and soreness. Common examples include infected sinuses, arthritis, and inflammation around infected wounds.

Fever is another sign that the body is fighting off an infection. *Fever is created by the body* to help fight excessive and virulent microorganisms. The body's inner wisdom operates by *a law of conservation of energy*. Any bodily change or process — including a fever — occurs for a lawful reason. Disease-causing microorganisms usually have a narrow range of temperatures in which they can survive. Mother Nature takes advantage of this weakness by slightly raising the body's temperature and killing or weakening these pathogens.

More pediatricians are encouraging their patients to allow a fever below 104 degrees Fahrenheit to run its course. Dr. Phillip Brunell, chairperson of the Committee on Infectious Diseases of the American Academy of Pediatrics, says of fevers: "It is one weapon the body uses to protect itself. Moderate fever is not an enemy. It can usually be allowed to run its course."

Lowering a fever of less than 104 degrees with drugs or cool baths may interfere with natural healing processes. Fever-related convulsions usually result from a *rapid* rise in temperature and brain damage seldom occurs below 107 degrees. With good health habits and extra rest, a mild fever will often be sufficient to fight off an impending illness. The vast majority of fevers are self-limiting within one to five days and helpful. Discuss these ideas with your doctors while you and your family are healthy; prior preparation can reduce anxiety associated with fevers.

The last component of infectious or cleansing processes is *fatigue*. When faced with an impending health problem, the body conserves and prioritizes its energy for healing and survival. It's natural to feel tired when your body is fighting off an illness or cleansing itself. Your body is telling you to rest and lay low for a time. I sometimes hear patients complain they have been tired lately but "are too busy to slow down." Then a severe cold or flu — with unpleasant symptoms and lost work time — *makes* them take a break.

Now you understand why colds, flus, and other infectious processes commonly occur and how we can prevent or limit them. The symptoms are predictable and logical when you understand the body's adaptive processes. You are now acquiring potent knowledge to prevent many common illnesses and maintain excellent health.

Minimizing Prescription Drug Use

A "line of time" model makes a case for being wary of any drug use. A 38-foot length of rope represents the time since earth began, approximately 4.6 billion years ago. In comparison, the Dinosaur Age was 200 million years ago (20 inches), the first humans existed about 5 million years ago (1/2 inch), and the Declaration of Independence was signed 215 years ago (.00001 inch). *Synthetic drugs are even more recent,* having been used widely only in this century. These powerful substances are very new in comparison with the slow and cautious tests of time. *My position is against illicit drugs and for extreme moderation with prescription and nonprescription drugs.*

Our bodies contain the world's most amazing pharmacy. Says Bernie Siegel, M.D., "I will guarantee you that in five to ten years, we will be treating most major illnesses with products that are normally made in the body." Our body can produce every chemical substance needed, in the right amounts, and without appreciable side effects. It can produce a wide array of amazing chemicals to control pain and make us feel good naturally. Consider the amazing pain-killing properties of endorphins and the natural euphoria from aerobic exercise. Acupuncture also aids the release of natural pain blockers and can be used for anesthesia during surgery.

Thus, whenever feasible, rely on internally produced

chemicals instead of immediately popping a pill. The wisdom of the body has been shaped by eons of evolution *and* by the genius of our Creator. The use of synthetic drugs is in its infancy and potentially dangerous. *Drugs are big business,* a primary reason they are used so commonly and as a first approach. Says David L. Schiedermayer, M.D., author of *Life and Death Decisions*, "With one rep for every 15 physicians, about $3 billion ($5000 per U.S. physician) is spent yearly on drug detailing, more than on raw materials to make the drugs. Advertising costs top 25 percent of sales."

Our body's elaborate biofeedback system can be impaired by drugs; pain and other symptoms are best understood as "signals" produced by the body for a reason. Taking drugs may decrease symptoms, but important questions should be considered: "Why did my body report this symptom? What is causing or creating the problem behind the symptom? Is there some habit I need to change? Do I need to consult a physician for a more serious health problem?"

Deepak Chopra, M.D., states, "We have the idea in the U.S.A. that there's a pill for everything. If you can't believe you ate the whole thing, then have a couple of Alka Seltzer. If you can't go to sleep, take a tranquilizer. If you have an infection, there's an antibiotic. If you have cancer, there's chemotherapy . . . None of this gets to the basic cause of the disease. It's merely treating the symptoms. The reason people get ill is something very simple: how they think, how they interact with their environment, how they behave, and what they eat. And if we address these simple problems of lifestyle and nutrition, then we can handle about 80 percent of all disease."

Irving Oyle, D.O. and author of *The Healing Mind* and other excellent books, is a leader in wellness and holistic health care. He uses the analogy of sitting on a tack. The resulting pain could be temporarily relieved with stronger and stronger painkillers until the person has a drug problem or drug tolerance renders this approach ineffective. Surgery to cut the nerves reporting pain sensations to the buttock region could be performed. Counseling might help the person better cope with the pain. Or, more simply and effectively, one could pull the tack out of one's behind. Prescription drug use can delay exploration of the real causes of health and disease. Getting to the cause of the problem is always the preferable approach.

Shutting off symptoms also gives the patient a false sense that the problem has been solved and the cause is understood. If you were driving your car and the red "oil warning" light came on, you would immediately stop your car until the cause of the signal was determined. Continued driving could cause serious and expensive engine damage. You wouldn't think of covering the warning light so you wouldn't see it. Nor would you cut the wires to cause the warning light to disappear. Consider, however, that these ludicrous suggestions are exactly what is often done in response to our body's warning signals!

So far we've discussed three negative aspects of prescription drug use: decreased reliance on the body's natural chemicals, impaired biofeedback, and an overemphasis on relief versus correction of causes. Drug use also has many potentially harmful side effects, an average of two dozen per drug. People are more aware of these dangers thanks to widespread distribution of the *Physicians Desk Reference* and other drug education books such as *The People's Pharmacy* by Joe Graedon, R.Ph. Recall the statistic of *100,000* deaths annually from prescription drug reactions. That's more people than died in Viet Nam or who die each year on our nation's highways. Finally, prescription drugs may actually slow recovery by interfering with the body's internal healing mechanisms.

Medications are needed for *some* conditions; "some" is a key word, however. Natural health approaches have not been sufficiently utilized or researched to know when medications are really needed. For example, consider a 29-year-old male who was overweight, highly stressed, and who did not exercise or observe basic dietary recommendations. He had no family history of high blood pressure, yet a local physician put him on blood pressure medication after only one moderately high reading. He was not given any other recommendations or lifestyle counseling. Is this state of the art health care and appropriate use of prescription medications?

Antibiotics are a miracle drug under certain circumstances, but there can be potential problems. In my practice, I see four- or five-year-olds who have already been on antibiotic therapy dozens of times. Could this be a case of too much of a good thing? Dr. Stuart Levy, professor at Tufts University Medical School warns against the dangers of antibiotic overuse: "In this country, antibiotics are prescribed for everything, including ailments such as the common cold."

Antibiotics are powerful aids in fighting harmful infections; when used indiscriminately, however, they lose their effectiveness and stronger dosages or types must be subsequently used. They have potential side effects and can upset the normal balance of microorganisms in the body. Most parents have not been educated about the underlying causes of illness; many think that proper health care involves waiting until their child is ill, then going to the doctor for antibiotics. Believe me, there is a better and less expensive approach to health care and maintenance.

Work with your doctor to minimize use of antibiotics. Lendon H. Smith, M.D., author of *Encyclopedia Of Baby And Child Care* and other excellent books, maintains that antibiotics and ear tubes are not needed for childhood ear infections and, in fact, can increase recurrence and eardrum scarring. Dr. Smith says ear infections are commonly caused by allergies (most commonly to cow's milk), infection, mechanical obstruction, and nutritional deficiency. Regarding a medical article recommending antibiotic usage, he remarks, "I could almost cry that not a word was mentioned about breastfeeding and about building up the immune system with vitamin C, essential fatty acids, and time. Are all these doctors tools of the pharmaceutical industry? Shame."

Medications may be prescribed inappropriately, too quickly, for too long, or in improper combinations. For example, patients are sometimes given diuretics or water pills for minor or first-time swelling. Swelling can occur for a number of reasons and sometimes is the result of *insufficient* water intake. If a person habitually drinks too little water and is dehydrated, the body may store water much like a desert animal. Donald S. Robertson, M.D. and co-author of *The Snowbird Diet*, states: "Drinking enough water is the best treatment for fluid retention. . . . Diuretics offer a temporary solution at best."

Prescription drugs can't *cure* disorders caused by poor lifestyle habits; doctors should educate more about nondrug treatment alternatives. Minimize prescription drug use and be aware of potential side effects. Whenever possible, address root causes of the problem instead of using a drug cover-up or quick and temporary fix. Communicate your concerns about medications with your doctor and increasingly rely on the body's wondrous internal pharmacy and healing potentials.

Minimizing Nonprescription Drug Use

Nonprescription or "over-the-counter" drugs include the many preparations that can be bought in drug or discount stores without a prescription. As with prescription drugs, these can alter our bodies' signals, interfere with natural healing processes, and foster false impressions that the *cause of the problem* has been addressed. A 13-year study completed in 1986 by the U.S. Office of Public Health found that two-thirds of all "over-the-counter" drugs fail to do what their manufacturers purport. All nonprescription drugs have potential side effects, albeit less dangerous than those of prescription medications.

Americans swallow nonprescription *painkillers* and anti-inflammatories for chronic and severe arthritis by the *tons* every day. Painkillers are occasionally helpful during severe aggravations of arthritis, fibromyalgia, and other chronic or permanent musculoskeletal disorders. During severe colds or flus, symptom-relief preparations can temporarily reduce miserable feelings. For example, cough syrup may be less damaging than coughing all night and not resting.

But be aware that decongestant preparations can interfere with the body's efforts to cleanse the sinuses. Think about it. Mother Nature has decided the sinuses need cleansing and begins a drainage process. But these drugs work to dry up sinuses and stop drainage. Granted, some relief is experienced but at what cost? More frequent or severe illnesses may occur later as the body takes additional measures to perform necessary cleansing functions.

Laxatives can actually worsen constipation and the bowels can become dependent on artificial preparations. The best "laxatives" are proper diet, adequate water intake, exercise, and a proper nerve supply. *"Weight loss"* pills may temporarily reduce appetite, but have you ever known any-one who maintained weight loss using diet pills? Perma-nent weight loss is only possible with a lifestyle change that you can live with over the years. Last but not least on this list of questionable health aids are *indigestion* preparations that cost Americans two to three billion dollars each year. I discuss *natural* ways to cure common indigestion symptoms in the nutrition chapter. For now, I'll give you a hint: the way to indigestion-free living is not by ingesting antacids.

We have been falsely led to believe that it's normal to have headaches, upset stomachs, sinus conditions, and a myriad of other preventable ailments. Who are the culprits reinforcing these erroneous messages? In large part, drug industry commercials advertising the "remedy" that the manufacturer wants you to buy. Fill in the blank: "How do you spell relief? For tension headaches, most doctors recom-mend ________. Cold season is coming, you need ________." Notice how we are *programmed* by advertising to think of one or more brand names for these common but often pre-ventable symptoms.

The underlying assumption of symptom-relief commer-cials is: "It is normal and common to have these symptoms. The solution? Buy our product to temporarily relieve the symptom." What about the *cause* of the problem? Why did it occur in the first place? What can we do to prevent these common maladies and become truly healthy? The answer is not in indiscriminately taking powders, pills, and potions; health cannot be swallowed, snorted, or rubbed on.

Our current "health care" system still overemphasizes outer or external sources of healing whereas real healing occurs from *within*. The body often doesn't need any help; it just doesn't need any interference. By now, you're hopefully seeing the shortcomings of symptom-relief approaches.

Twenty-first century health care will treat the causes of

disease and focus on natural and lasting sources of wellness. Symptom-relief drugs have little to contribute toward this holistic approach. Someday we will look back at our present-day treatments much as we now view 19th century quack remedies. Use over-the-counter relief aids only when absolutely needed and, whenever possible, use one of the more natural products. Health consumers, save your money and your health with positive lifestyle habits that address the underlying causes of health and disease.

Alcohol and Illegal Drug Abuse

Illegal "recreational" drugs include marijuana, cocaine, downers, uppers, psychotropics such as LSD, and newer derivatives of these. Webster defines "recreational" as "creating anew or refreshing in body or mind." There is nothing refreshing or renewing about recreational drug use. I have observed drug use firsthand and the results are clear. "Just say no!" is the best and wisest approach — it's better to never start or try "just once." Some persons who are "just going to try it once" become psychologically and physiologically addicted. Drug use and abuse causes accidents, murder, suicide, domestic violence, child abuse, and lost potentials. My recommendation is to definitely steer clear of all illegal drugs.

Alcohol has powerful addictive and destructive potentials and approximately ten percent of our population are alcoholics. Signs and symptoms for being at risk for alcoholism include: morning drinking, blackouts, regrettable actions while intoxicated, trouble stopping, five or more drinks per day, if friends and family are concerned, if you drive under the influence, and a family history of alcoholism. Additional warning signs are physical symptoms after drinking that include headaches, weakness, nausea, stomach pain, insomnia, or depression. If you choose to use alcohol, wait until legal age and *don't drive while drinking!* At least 50 percent of America's fatal traffic accidents involve alcohol.

If you're not an alcoholic, you can enjoy moderate and responsible drinking but remember the potential hazards involved. Alcoholics, either by genetic predisposition or acquired addiction or both, cannot drink socially. The trouble is, most persons don't know they are alcoholics until it's too late. All persons associated with the alcoholic suffer; Al-Anon and ACOA (Adult Children of Alcoholics) can help the families of alcoholics. Family members often experience negative psychological effects that include shame, low self-esteem, and difficult interpersonal relationships. These harmful emotional factors contribute to "dysfunctional" family traits so common in our society. For the problem drinker, AA (Alcoholics Anonymous) is the most effective approach, especially in conjunction with an intensive in-patient "drying out" and education program. Help is available.

Pressures to experiment with drugs can be powerful, especially during adolescent years. However, there are better ways to feel good; artificial approaches to getting high are temporary, illegal, dangerous, and expensive. Heavy alcohol users often become alcoholics. Marijuana users may develop amotivational syndrome, befuddlement of mind, and chronic lung conditions. Downer users fall asleep while upper users become nervous and have insomnia. Cocaine users snort up a lot of psychological and physical problems at a significant personal and financial cost. Crack and other drug derivatives can addict or kill instantly. LSD and psychedelic users may have great insights but usually can't explain or remember them. Are we having fun yet?

The chemicals in all drugs are powerful, often cumulative, and their longterm effects largely unknown. Marijuana, once considered by some to be "a harmless herb," has

400 different chemicals in it. When smoked as a joint, the burning paper and marijuana combination releases over *2000* chemicals. Some of these fat soluble chemicals accumulate in organs and can cause short- and longterm impairments. Drug use of any kind can cause significant personal, family, and societal problems.

Wise and mature youth of today can learn from the experience of others and not waste another second at this roadblock. We need only watch the news to see the disastrous events that regularly accompany drug use. For the person who "only occasionally" smokes a joint or snorts a little cocaine, I see several potential problems. First, your activities are illegal and you subject yourself to legal penalties that can ruin your life. Paranoia and an "us versus them" attitude that accompanies outlawed activities may be subtle but emotionally unhealthy. Even *only occasional use* brings with it the *occasional chance* of auto accidents or other injuries. Finally, it directly supports and condones the activities of drug smugglers and pushers.

Using drugs to feel better engenders the false notion that we need an external source to "get high." In fact, the best way to get and stay high is to become vitally healthy and happy in all areas of life. Some persons use drugs or excess alcohol because it gives them a *glimpse* of inner peace or heaven. Why not pursue a natural path that helps you reach these sublime states and *stay there* most or all of the time. The last 30 years of drug experimentation in America has left a clear conclusion: there is no safe, legal, or effective way to get and stay high on drugs. God knows that enough persons have tried and paid a tragic price for the experiment. Need we keep "reinventing the wheel?"

Education and focusing on other ways of feeling good are the best ways to minimize substance abuse. Young persons, please don't make the same mistakes that prior generations have. Visit mental hospitals or chemical dependency units and see firsthand the results of chemical and alcohol use.

During my pastoral counseling practicum in a psychiatric hospital, I met Jim, a 16-year-old boy who had "just tried" PCP once. Despite a year of psychiatric treatment, he was a walking vegetable and will be a mental invalid the rest of his life. Can the rest of us learn from Jim's experience? Haven't we individually and collectively suffered enough? Let's focus on natural ways of altering and improving consciousness. Only then can we truly realize who we are and express our amazing potentials.

Tobacco Products

I purposely discuss tobacco use (cigarettes, chewing tobacco, "smokeless" tobacco, cigars, and pipe smoking) after illegal drugs because they both take a tragic and preventable toll on human life. *Each year* in the U.S., over *400,000 persons* die from diseases attributed to cigarette smoking: emphysema, lung and oral cancer, asthma, bronchitis, heart and blood vessel disease. These *yearly* deaths exceed the total number of U.S. battle deaths in World War II. In fact, according to the U.S. Surgeon General, smoking kills more persons in the U.S. *each year* than do crack, cocaine, heroin, alcohol, AIDS, fire, murders, and car accidents combined!

We are saddened by occasional plane crashes that kill many persons. The number of Americans who die from cigarette smoking *every day*, however, is equivalent to two full jumbo jets crashing with no survivors! Where is the public outcry and front page headlines over this deplorable and preventable situation? Our government vows to catch terrorists who bomb one plane and rightfully so. Why and how, then, can our government subsidize an industry that kills nearly a half-million persons each year?

Cigarette smoking doesn't make sense from a purely economic standpoint either. The latest government estimates for smoking related health costs are *100 billion dollars per year*. The greatest cost, however, is the pain and grief experienced by smokers and their loved ones. Cost estimates cannot begin to reflect the suffering of smokers, their families, and friends. How many tears, smothering spells, and premature funerals will occur before we all come to our senses about this lethal habit?

The temperature of cigarette smoke as it enters the body is approximately 200 degrees Fahrenheit. No wonder chronic lung and sinus changes occur as the smoker *literally cooks* sensitive tissues. Cigarette smoking interferes with the lung's normal removal of mucous and foreign particles. Thus, trapped mucous and debris collect and contribute to development of lung diseases. We all try to minimize our exposure to radiation from various sources. But if a person smokes two packs per day, he or she is receiving the radioactive equivalent of more than one chest X-ray EACH DAY! Is it any wonder that cells mutate over time and become malignant?

Research verifies the danger of "secondhand," "passive," or "side stream" smoke exhaled by the smoker or as the cigarette burns. The American Heart Association reports nearly 53,000 American deaths by passive smoke, the third leading preventable cause of death. Children of parents who smoke are more likely to contract wheezing, asthma, pneumonia, and bronchitis than children of nonsmokers. Infants of women who smoke are 30 percent more likely to die before or soon after birth due to low birth weight, shortened gestation period, respiratory distress syndrome, or related diseases. These babies face a 400 percent greater risk of "crib death" or Sudden Infant Death Syndromes (SIDS). Choosing your own premature illness and death is your right; however, no one has a right to harm family members, fellow workers, and others who deserve better. If you smoke, please don't expose others in the same room, car, or office.

Smoking is a deadly habit that's on the way out. Smokers pay higher health insurance premiums and are not hired by some companies. Many businesses and public places have banned smoking on the premises. Smokers develop a tolerance to the noxious fumes released by a burning cigarette so it's hard for them to realize how irritating cigarette smoke is to the nonsmoker. Smokers, remember how you felt after your first cigarette? Most people experience dizziness, coughing, watery eyes, headache, and burning of the throat and lungs. Your body was telling you how offensive a habit smoking is.

The powerful addictive hold of nicotine and tobacco on the smoker cannot be disputed. Have you ever seen a smoker nearly cough their guts up and then immediately light up another cigarette? I realized the severity of tobacco addiction during late night rounds of patients on oxygen and respirators. A 38-year-old patient hospitalized for severe mouth and throat cancer had smoked two packs per day for 20 years. After surgery, he had to breathe through a permanent tracheotomy or hole in his throat. I found him SMOKING A CIGARETTE THROUGH HIS THROAT the night before he died! This and other examples of human suffering have led me to educate others about cigarette smoking.

Tobacco companies must spend $17 million *each day* to recruit new smokers to replace the more than 1000 persons who die *daily* from smoking. It's unbelievable that we allow ridiculous and glamorized cigarette advertisements in any form. Many health consumers and parents are rightfully outraged at advertisements contributing to this fatal addiction. The American Medical Association has joined the battle and taken its stance *against* tobacco products. Most cigarette ads show young, beautiful, and healthy persons having lots of fun; sexual connotations are strong and frequent. Our young people are a vulnerable population for this powerful appeal.

In reality, cigarettes are a sure ticket to premature aging, disease, disability, and death. Several ex-"Marlboro men" have contracted early cancer and lung diseases. Mary Wells — once a Motown great with hits like "My Guy" — recently died at age 49 from lung and throat cancer. She blamed her old two-pack-a-day habit and secondhand smoke for her condition. Temptation's singer Eddie Kendrick just died at age 52 of lung cancer. He said the disease was caused by 30 years of smoking, and he urged all persons, especially children, not to smoke. A recent Ann Lander's column listed famous actors who have died from a smoking related disease: John Wayne, Sammy Davis, Jr., Lucille Ball, Yul Brenner, and Nat "King" Cole, among others.

Advertisers should be required to provide equal time coverage of the *aftereffects* of cigarette smoking. Full color action shots would show terminal lung disease patients as they hook up their oxygen masks and struggle for a breath. How about a group of longterm smokers — "the beautiful people revisited" — having coughing jags and receiving breathing treatments together?

The former U.S. Surgeon General C. Everett Koop, M.D., vociferously attacked nicotine as a drug with an addictive potential similar to that of *heroin*. This is why some persons have such difficulty getting off cigarettes. We have methadone treatment clinics for heroin addicts and recognize them as seriously ill persons. But *our* government spends *our* tax money to subsidize tobacco growers and companies that directly contribute to premature death and destruction of our friends and relatives! Does this make any sense to you?

If you detect anger through my words and exclamation points, you are correct. I have worked directly with thousands of persons as they suffered and died horrible deaths from cigarette smoking. How many of you have seen someone die from advanced emphysema or lung cancer? Visit any VA or hospital pulmonary ward and observe our brothers and sisters going through a *living hell* as they slowly and progressively suffocate to death. Please don't let this happen to you!

Speaking of sisters, "you've come the *wrong way*, baby" with increased cigarette consumption. In the past, women smoked much less than men and had lower lung cancer rates to prove it. Women have recently achieved a dubious sign of equality as the most common type of cancer deaths for males *and* females is now lung cancer. Women who smoke and use oral contraceptives increase their risk of stroke and have a ten-fold greater risk of coronary heart disease. Tobacco companies that increase profits with appeals to female psyches and women's lib themes clearly aren't concerned with women as people.

You can experience what it's like to suffer from a terminal lung disease. Cover your mouth with one hand and pinch off your nostrils with the other hand. Now breathe. Go ahead, do it for a couple of minutes. You can't, right? What a relief to be able to remove your hands. Chronic lung disease patients can't remove their hands! They constantly struggle to keep one breath ahead of suffocation. As a respiratory therapist, I often tried to keep terminal patients as comfortable as possible while they died. Breathing treatments, oxygen therapy, postural drainage, and respirators gave only temporary relief to these patients.

Many patients have begged me to warn others about

the dangers of cigarette smoking. Only in the last several decades has the vast increase in death and disease among smokers been proven. In the 1940s, some advertisements showed doctors recommending cigarettes to help a so-called "T zone" over the trachea and bronchi. I remember a patient named Mary, crying as she sat up late at night, trying to breathe just before she died. She looked at me with eyes already glimpsing the next realm and implored me to warn others: "We didn't know how dangerous cigarettes were when I started smoking in the 1930s. Please tell others so they won't have to go through what I have."

I'm doing my best, Mary; I hope your suffering was not in vain. *The dangers of smoking are clearly known now.* It's way past time to change our habits and laws to escape the damage brought about by cigarette smoking. Another patient, Harold, was a bear of a man in his fifties who loved to fish and hunt. He slowly lost weight and was eventually wheelchair-bound as his emphysema progressed. He told me about his secret fishing places and his eyes filled with tears as I told him about the big ones I caught. Our goal was to get him healthy enough that he could fish for a little while from his car while breathing oxygen. He never made it.

Sam suffered from severe emphysema but was always so appreciative of the little things in life. A widower, his loneliness was obvious, and I visited him at the hospital whenever possible. I visited him at home once; he was waiting in his wheelchair by a window where he spent so many hours watching life go by.

Ted, a 62-year-old, had just retired before being diagnosed with lung cancer. Ted lost 60 pounds, aged 30 years, and lost all his hair during the six months before he died. Some retirement. Weeks before he passed on, he wrote these words for me to tell others: "My message to young people —

if you haven't started smoking yet, *DON'T.* And to all people young or old, if you do smoke — *PLEASE QUIT.* Cancer is miserable and deadly." Well put, my friend.

Knowing these individuals has vividly illustrated the horrible toll exacted by a *preventable habit.* Remember, over 400,000 U.S. deaths are directly attributable to smoking each year. Statistics sometimes lose their meaning and our hearts and minds can become numbed by the pain we see and the hopelessness we feel. Knowing just one of these "statistics" — a Mary, Harold, Sam, or Ted — however, aids our empathy and activism. We *can* change this particular tragedy via increased education, proper legislation, prevention, and smoking cessation programs.

Write your government representatives and demand an end to tobacco subsidies and advertisements. President Bush wanted a war on drugs; that's greatly needed, but let's include *the most common addictive drug — nicotine in tobacco.* Remove cigarette machines that allow minors to purchase cigarettes. Don't patronize events or publications sponsored by cigarette companies. Let's form a national organization — similar to MADD — called *PACK: "People Against Cigarettes Killing."*

I'm well aware of the economic issues involved, having lived in North Carolina tobacco country. But what about the financial costs of lost worker hours, increased insurance premiums, and care taking costs for the illness and premature death produced by tobacco use? The $100 billion price tag *each year* didn't include the cost of death and disability incurred by tobacco use. Other crops can be grown on that land; even paying farmers for *not* growing tobacco would be an improvement.

Tobacco industry officials, you and your family members and friends are suffering and dying from cigarettes, too. Increase your diversification into other markets and prepare to phase out tobacco operations. Government, help the tobacco industry, if need be, in restructuring business applications. Economic considerations are insignificant compared to human costs.

Consider the recent fiasco of test-marketing a cigarette brand aimed toward blacks. Men and women of all racial and socioeconomic groups, don't be conned by deceptive advertising. No age, sex, ethnic, or income group needs more death and disease. And let's not "solve" the problem by sending tobacco overseas. That's like dumping garbage into the ocean and pretending the problem is solved. Our international friends don't deserve junk food and destructive products like tobacco. The world is too small to make financial profits at the expense of other persons. Remember, we're all children of the same God.

The *good news* is that our lungs have a remarkable potential for rejuvenation. In mild and moderate smokers, much of the airway damage is reversible after a year of not smoking. Thus, it is important to quit as soon as possible and stay away from cigarettes. The desire to quit is the most important factor for success. Reread the many harmful effects including radiation and cancer formation, increased heart and lung disease, and effects on loved ones. Consider whether the temporary buzz and enjoyment of smoking is worth it. Clearly it's not; if you can't see that, it's because of your physical and psychological addiction to tobacco.

Have compassion for other smokers and for yourself if you're fighting this habit. Nicotine is a powerful drug that may interact with genetic predispositions toward addiction. That's why some persons can't quit or start again soon after quitting. If family members or co-workers are trying to quit, give them your full support and don't smoke in front of them. Stop-smoking programs are available through the American Heart, Lung, and Cancer Associations. Other recommended programs include: *Control from Within: A Nine-Step Program to Stop Smoking* by Dr. Wayne Dyer; the *SMOKENDERS Program* and *You Can Stop* by Jacquelyn Rogers; and the *LifeSign* minicomputer and education program.

Recommendations for stopping smoking include:

- Set a date and stick to it.
- Enlist a friend or relative to quit with you.
- Write down and review daily your reasons for wanting to quit.
- Focus on quitting *one day at a time.*
- Drink lots of fluids — especially water — to flush your system.
- Throw away all cigarettes, matches, lighters, and ashtrays.
- Keep busy with new hobbies, exercise, or other activities.
- Use gum, mints, toothpicks, and carrot or celery sticks instead.
- Phone an ex-smoker friend for support when needed.
- Keep a positive mental attitude and reward yourself for success.
- Change old habits, for example, walk after a meal versus smoking.
- Take deep breaths with long exhalations to resist cravings.
- Ask friends, relatives, and co-workers for their support.
- Exercise regularly and enjoy fresh and healthy air.
- Keep your hands busy with a pencil, paper clip, or marble.
- Frequent places such as a library or movie where you can't smoke.
- Meditate or relax daily to release tensions naturally.
- Ask God to help you quit.

You may feel mentally and physically uncomfortable for awhile after you stop smoking. If you smoked one pack per day, you inhaled smoke more than 60,000 times in one year. You have had plenty of practice being a smoker; *give yourself some time to become a nonsmoker.* Learning any new habit is tough at first, but the psychological addiction decreases with time. Physical symptoms of irritability, fatigue, and depression are short-lived as the body goes through withdrawal from nicotine. If necessary, consult your physician for a "nicotine gum" or skin patch prescription to help you through withdrawal, especially if you have failed in previous attempts at quitting.

Some smokers rationalize their behavior by pointing to the weight gain they experience after quitting smoking. This is like saying, "I'm going to eat arsenic — just a little each day — because it helps control my appetite." Weight gain is not inevitable after smoking cessation and is partly the result of increased appetite as the sense of taste returns. With effort and awareness, weight gain can be prevented or minimized. The metabolism does change for about six months after stopping smoking but most ex-smokers return to their former weight in time. Don't replace cigarette smoking with overeating; control your diet and exercise. Remember that a few extra pounds are harmless compared to the longterm effects of smoking. Consult your physician or psychologist if weight issues, anxiety, or other factors interfere with your efforts to quit smoking.

Once you have successfully quit, try to never pick up that first one again. Especially during times of increased stress, don't let yourself be fooled into thinking that you'll smoke "just one." That is how many persons fall back into the habit. Much like the alcoholic, you are better off by never having "just one." The worst is over one week after quitting; don't make yourself go through that again.

If you do start smoking again, try and try again to stop. Most ex-smokers eventually succeed by starting and stopping several times before finally quitting and sticking to it. If you find yourself smoking again, don't feel guilty or criticize yourself. Forget it and start over. Tell yourself, "I *am* becoming a nonsmoker! I enjoy breathing only fresh and healthy air."

Remember, the bottom line is: *You can really quit smoking if you want to!* Our minds and spirits are more powerful than any addictive habit. You do have control over your actions. With help from above, within, and from others, you can let this destructive habit go and experience a quantum leap in physical and mental wellness.

Techniques for Healthy Muscles

At rest, muscles are normally soft and pliable. However, *chronic tension, occupational and postural stresses, and skeletal misalignment* can contribute to tight and spastic muscles. The most common sites for muscle tension are the neck and shoulders; "muscle tension headaches" in the back of the head are often due to these chronically tight muscles. Muscles move the bones of the skeleton and hold them in place like "guy wires." To function correctly, muscles must be sufficiently strong, receive periodic rest and stretching, and be balanced. Muscles work in pairs; if one muscle is too weak or too spastic, the other muscle undergoes excessive strain as it tries to maintain balance in the system.

J. B. Watson, founder of behavioral psychology, stated that for every psychological thought there is an accompanying muscular contraction or glandular secretion. This is one reason why mind and body are so intimately connected;

what affects one affects the other. A body language of tensed muscles and strained posture often accompany negative emotions of anger, worry, and fear. Over time, a habit of tightening certain muscle groups leads to chronic muscle tension and spasm. Eventually, painful fibrotic tissues called "trigger points" form within the muscle.

Occupational and postural demands can also strain muscles and set up muscle spasm cycles. Thus, proper posture and habits while sitting, standing, and working are important. Persons with jobs requiring detail work — secretaries and accountants, for example — often bend over close to their work. Heavy material handlers may have to repetitively lift, twist, and bend. These stresses can cause chronic muscle problems over the years.

Finally, misalignment of the skeleton can affect muscle balance in two ways. First, misaligned bones cause abnormal biomechanical stresses on muscles. Bones act as anchors or originating points for muscles; thus, changes in skeletal positioning can stress muscles. Second, misalignment or "subluxation" (less than a dislocation) of bones can slightly compress or irritate nerves. This is especially important in the spinal column where slight pressure can disturb normal nerve supply or nerve functioning. Since nerves connect the brain to all parts of the body, muscles are affected if they do not have proper communication with the brain. A "pinched" nerve can weaken or overly contract certain muscles, contributing to chronic muscle disorders.

Whatever the cause, overly tight and spastic muscles are common problems that cause discomfort and contribute to chronic musculoskeletal conditions. A syndrome variously termed "fibromyalgia, myofibrositis, or myofascitis" refers to chronic inflammation and tightness of muscles and underlying soft tissues. The causes of fibromyalgia are not clearly understood but can include: chronic anxiety, traumatic injuries, sleep disruption, skeletal misalignment, cold damp weather, insufficient exercise, smoking, and excessive animal product intake. The recommendations below are of particular importance for fibromyalgia patients as no totally effective treatment is currently available.

It is important to identify and correct the underlying causes of muscle spasm. Address the origin of the problem rather than simply taking muscle relaxants or pain pills (medication to aid sleep, however, may help fibromyalgia). Those who specialize in neuromusculoskeletal problems are best trained to sort out the various causes. These include chiropractors, physical therapists, physical medicine specialists (physiatrists), or osteopaths who practice manipulation. Seek a second opinion if you haven't significantly improved after a few months of treatment. Fortunately, there are a number of effective and natural treatment approaches.

Try the various self-help techniques described below:

• *Relax* your body at least twice daily; with practice, you will learn the difference between tension and relaxation. Some persons become tense without even knowing it. Relaxation techniques help *focus your awareness* so you become more aware of when you tense up. All of us have events or thoughts that temporarily tense us; the key is to realize *what* has upset or worried us and deal with it then and there. This prevents a "snow-ball" effect of cumulative negative emotions and muscle tension.

• *Exercise* at least four days per week to rid the body of muscular tension on a regular basis. Use *stretching* and strengthening exercises to better handle job and daily living demands.

• *Hot soaks* in a tub or whirlpool are excellent for muscle relaxation and tension release. Soak 30 minutes to allow sufficient heat penetration into soft tissues. Consult your doctor first if you have heart problems or if you develop dizziness or headaches after soaking. A moist heating pad for 30 minutes over the area of muscle tightness is also helpful.

• *Inadequate nutrients* — especially calcium, magnesium, potassium, and vitamin E — can cause muscle spasms, particularly in the legs. Nutrients required for proper muscle function may become depleted by chronic muscle spasm, thus the need for low dosage and balanced multivitamin and mineral supplementation.

• *Reflex points* on the body correspond with specific muscles and organs. The reflex points for the neck and upper trap muscles — those most often chronically tense — are at the base of the skull, under the middle of the collar bones, and on the front top portions of the arms. These *accupressure* points respond to brisk rubbing; rub each point firmly for 60 seconds, three to four times per day. Feel for and rub areas that are most tender or knotty. This technique can aid muscle balance, relaxation, and lymphatic drainage. Read *Touch for Health* by John Thie, D.C. or contact a physician trained in *Applied Kinesiology* for additional information.

• *Massage techniques* can improve or prevent chronically tight muscle areas. Parents can gently massage young children; this is especially relaxing and comforting for newborns. Make a healthful and mutually beneficial habit of massaging each other. For those who live alone, find a friend or relative who wants to trade massages. We're here to help each other; touching each other is one of the oldest healing approaches. We all need and want to be touched, hugged, and loved.

Contact a *licensed massage therapist* (LMT) for advanced treatment; these therapists are highly trained, licensed by their state medical board, and their practice is strictly professional. Massage therapists in the USSR, Germany, China, and Japan work in hospitals as members of the health care team. Certified *reflexologists* massage the feet and work on specific reflex points. Reflexology treatments are immensely relaxing and a natural way to alleviate tensions. Both massage and reflexology improve circulation, relax muscles, and stimulate reflexes that can aid bodily balance.

A Japanese massage technique called *Nimmo* can be effectively and safely used at home. With the "patient" lying face down, apply a general relaxing stroke — like kneading bread dough — to sore muscles. This technique is most helpful over the upper traps, along the spine, over the shoulder joints, and at the base of the skull. After relaxing the area, instruct the patient to breathe slowly and deeply as there is some discomfort involved with the next step.

Apply firm pressure with the ends of your thumbs over the muscle area. With practice, you will be able to feel *trigger points* or myofascial tension areas. These feel like lumps or knots ranging in size from a "BB" to a quarter. When you feel such an area, it will usually be somewhat painful. Ask the patient to let you know when you push on a "hotspot." Push firmly and steadily over the knotty area for about ten seconds. Occasionally apply the relaxing or kneading stroke to give the patient a break and mobilize the metabolic by-products of chronic muscle spasm. This simple but amazingly effective procedure can reverse long-standing muscle spasms but only if done consistently over a period of months.

Aging Gracefully

Our geriatric population is increasingly well-educated and health-minded. This "graying of America" movement is rewriting many of our erroneous notions about what senior citizenry is all about. This is only the beginning of a trend in which older persons will live longer, more actively, and healthfully. Growing older is a special time that can bring much wisdom and peace to one's self and others. As Robert Browning put it: "Grow old along with me! The last of life, for which the first was made." Here are some recommendations for increasing the quality and quantity of the "golden years."

Remember that chronological age is, to a large extent, a relative matter. As Freda, a bouncing 83-year-old, put it, "Don't worry about your age — it's only a number." Yes, there are physical changes and aging processes, but one's mental outlook is paramount for vital living. Some 80-year-olds act like they're 30 and some 30-year-olds act like they're 80. So forget the clichés that it's all downhill after age 30 or 40. *It's all downhill when you think it is.* The human body was designed to last about 120 years. We are just beginning to realize that our potentials include a long, healthy, happy, and active life. Vital persons in their 80s and 90s should be the rule rather than the exception.

Read *Ageless: Living Younger Longer* by Ben Douglas, M.D., who states, "You can live younger longer; we can all choose to age less and enjoy a longer, healthier life." Peter Kelder, author of *Fountain of Youth*, writes, "If an old person truly wants to grow younger, they must think, act, and behave like a younger person, and eliminate the attitudes and mannerisms of old age."

Wise younger persons will benefit by respecting and learning from their *elders*. Persons at all stages in life have real and important talents to share. Senior citizens, you are a growing political and economic power; use your clout accordingly. Become more active in obtaining benefits and products that serve your needs. Younger persons should assist this process for a number of reasons; we too will be seniors in a blink of an eye. All segments of society should better serve older persons who have conferred so many benefits to future generations.

As aging progresses, it may be necessary to adjust to bodily changes and modify some habits. *Aging gracefully* and adapting to life changes can be a natural and beautiful process. There is a time for every season and lessons to be gained from all of life's experiences. Don't fight or begrudge the changes but don't give in to them too quickly either. Do all you can to live optimally; treat your body like an antique car that needs a little extra care and maintenance. A growing number of "retirement villages" offer recreation facilities, security, social and leisure offerings, and adjacent health care facilities. As one 75-year-old — who became a patient after a biking injury — put it, "There's so much going on that no one wants to die and miss out on everything."

Remember the spiritual truths and insights discussed later in the book. Our *enduring self* or spirit is eternal. The body is only a vehicle that gets us around for a while. We all will leave our body eventually; senior citizens are just taking the long and scenic route. Don't get too caught up with bodily changes and remember who and what you really are. Just as there are cycles in every aspect of nature, so aging is an important and beautiful phase in the great design of life.

Environmental Issues

Native American Chief Seattle warned, "Humankind has not woven the web of life. We are but the thread of it. Whatever we do to the web, we do to ourselves. All things are bound together. All things connect. Whatever befalls the earth befalls also the children of the earth." An ancient Navajo prophecy states: "If we dare to pollute the land and water, we will all suffer the consequences." But the *I Ching* encourages us: "What has been spoiled through man's fault can be made good again through man's work."

A young boy once tried to trick a wise man with this question: "Is the bird in my hands alive or dead?" The wise man knew that if he said "alive," the boy would crush and kill the bird. If he said "dead," the boy would open his hands to show the still living bird. Thus the wise man replied, "The bird is alive *or* dead, as *you would have it to be*." Similarly, answers to many questions about the future are in our hands. Our individual actions are very important. Do whatever you can to improve the environment and stop further damage to our incredibly beautiful and complex ecosystem.

We have only one body and thus should care for and respect it. Likewise, we should nurture our physical home, the planet Earth. Our planet is a living and dynamic entity — not a huge inert sphere that we can endlessly abuse without penalty. The health of our planet directly affects our individual health statuses and quality of life. The time has passed for thoughtless or profit-oriented pollution and abuse of our planet. Total wellness includes healthy environmental habits so that future generations have a healthy world in which to live.

Take heart in the 1990 Earth Day slogan: "Who says you can't change the world?" The ecosphere has several corrective measures that can help remedy problems if we give it a chance. Respected scientists such as Andrew Solow caution that our knowledge of the overall picture is limited and that dire predictions may never arrive. So it's not hopeless; *our immediate and unified responses can work.* Technology, people, and nature *can* work together without doing each other harm. The next step beyond "high tech" can be "clean tech" as new technologies become more sophisticated and environmentally sensitive.

TIME writer Greg Easterbrook notes: "It would be nice to think that salvation for the environment lies in forsaking civilization and getting back to nature. It would also be nice to think that tapping our feet together takes us to Kansas. Naysayers believe that technology grows ever more damaging and inhumane. That need not be. Truly advanced technology should grow cleaner, safer, more responsible toward its masters."

Learn and follow recommendations for a healthy environment. Each of us *can* make a difference. Edmund Burke said, "Nobody made a greater mistake than he who did nothing because he could only do a little." Read *50 Simple Things You Can Do To Save The Earth* by The EarthWorks Group, *How to Make the World a Better Place* by Jeffrey Hollender, *Empty Harvest* by Mark Anderson and Bernard Jensen, D.C., Ph.D., and *Your Heart —Your Planet* by Harvey Diamond.

Risk Reduction Strategies

Balanced Living discusses physical, mental, and spiritual approaches for preventing and treating various ailments. Some conditions additionally benefit from specific techniques discussed in this section. Keep in mind — as we'll discuss in the Chiropractic chapter — that the vertebral subluxation complex (VSC) and nerve interference can play a role in the cause or progression of any disease.

Cardiac Risk Reduction

Cardiac Risk Reduction refers to modifying factors that significantly reduce one's chance of developing heart and blood vessel diseases — the #1 cause of death in the U.S. The major factors involved in the development of heart disease are sex (male or female), family history of cardiac problems, weight, exercise, diet, stress, diabetes, blood pressure, age, and cigarette smoking. You can't control your age, family history, or gender. But remember that the factors contributing to any disease are like pieces of a pie; modify the factors that can be controlled:

- If you have a family history of diabetes, have your blood glucose level checked regularly.

- *Have your blood pressure checked regularly.* Some cases of high blood pressure can be successfully treated with weight loss, a semivegetarian diet, salt reduction, chiropractic adjustments, cessation of smoking, exercise, and stress management. Some patients may, however, require medication as well.

- *Minimize fat intake.* For each extra pound of fat, the heart has to pump blood through an extra MILE of small blood vessels. Excess fat can increase blood pressure and hardening of the arteries.

- Use *aerobic exercise* to tone the heart and blood vessels.

- Read *Reversing Heart Disease* by Julian Whitaker, M.D., and *Dr. Dean Ornish's Program For Reversing Heart Disease* by Dean Ornish, M.D. See *Resources* for information about the educational and treatment opportunities. These holistic approaches are excellent for the prevention and treatment of many organic disease processes.

- Manage your stress levels and enjoy a balanced

lifestyle.

- Don't smoke!

Cancer Risk Reduction

Cancer occurs due to a variety of factors including: hereditary predisposition, excess exposure to radiation and chemicals, poor diet and lifestyle, cigarettes, excessive alcohol, decreased immunity, and an unhealthy emotional state. Much research suggests there are significant ways we can minimize our risks of contracting cancer. Small numbers of cancer cells routinely form during cellular growth and repair; only in certain individuals do these malignant cells survive and spread to cause detectable cancers. The best strategy in preventing cancer is to minimize risk factors while strengthening the immune system:

- Minimize radiation; moderate sunlight exposure.
- Avoid fumes, dusts, and inhaled sources of chemicals.
- Most importantly, *avoid smoking*. The National Academy of Sciences reports that smoking accounts for 50 percent of male cancer deaths and an increasing number for females. (An additional 30 to 40 percent of male and 60 percent of female cancers are due to diet. Thus, diet and cessation of smoking could prevent 90 percent of cancer deaths.)
- *Consume alcohol moderately or not at all* since excessive alcohol consumption increases several types of cancer.
- *Minimize fat intake and increase dietary fiber*. Eat more fresh fruits, vegetables, and whole grains and their products while decreasing intake of meat, fried foods, and dairy products. The *cruciferous vegetables* — broccoli, cab-

bage, cauliflower, and brussels sprouts — seem most effective in preventing cancer formation. Also eat lots of yellow and dark green leafy vegetables for an increased beta-carotene intake. Obtain sufficient vitamin A, C, E, selenium, and zinc since these *anti-oxidants neutralize free-radical formation* involved in some malignancies.

• Minimize smoked, smoke-cured, or pickled foods that can increase cancer by irritating the stomach and esophagus.

For an excellent summary on the natural prevention of cancer, read *Nutrition, Health, and Disease* by Gary Todd, M.D. Dr. Todd describes viewing white blood cells or lymphocytes with phase light photography. Lymphocytes are a primary component of our bodies' defense system that periodically inspect cells for abnormalities. They entered normal cells and left without any change in the cellular structure. When a cancerous cell was encountered, however, lymphocytes assumed a torpedo shape and exploded inside the malignant cell. This "Star Wars"-like event is miraculous and inspires hope.

Don't underestimate your amazing bodily defenses; focus on optimizing your inner healing powers instead of fearing cancer. Says Dr. Todd, "It would appear that cancer is the result not so much of carcinogenic substances producing cancerous cells, as the failure of normal immune mechanisms to eliminate those cells."

Modify the factors that increase cancer incidence, strengthen your immune system, and live each day without fear. Live and eat healthfully, believe in your body's healing powers, and trust God. Utilize the powerful physical, emotional, and spiritual approaches that can help prevent or heal cancer formation.

Hiatal Hernia

The upper stomach and esophagus can become wedged *against* or above the diaphragm; most cases can be prevented or treated conservatively. Heartburn sensations may travel toward the throat and are often worse after a large meal, when bending forward, or when lying down after a meal. Obtain a medical opinion to rule out other problems since hiatal hernia symptoms may mimic signs of a heart attack.

For *prevention,* avoid conditions that push the stomach against the diaphragm. These include: obesity, constipation, excessive bending forward at the waist, and eating or drinking an excessive amount at any one time. These recommendations especially hold true for pregnant females who already have extra pressure against the abdominal contents.

Early treatment includes strict adherence to the above suggestions for prevention. In addition, elevate the head of your bed about six inches, allowing gravity to lower the stomach while you sleep. Daily diaphragmatic breathing to improve the flexibility of the diaphragm is important since a fixed or restricted diaphragm can contribute to hiatal hernia development.

An old medical technique involves drinking one to two quarts of water, then jumping off a low chair or stool several times. The water's weight in the stomach can pull it down and away from the diaphragm. Finally, some chiropractors and osteopaths are trained to adjust the stomach and esophagus downward. This is a simple, safe, and painless maneuver that often quickly corrects early conditions.

Varicose Veins

These can sometimes be conservatively prevented and treated. Several conditions can cause excessive pressure on the veins and cause them to swell and develop varicosities.

• *Chronic constipation* with straining is the most common cause.

• *Postural factors* include excessive standing and sitting; these cause pooling of blood in the legs due to gravity and lack of muscular activity.

• Systemic *dehydration* due to inadequate water intake can result in thicker blood and make venous return more difficult.

• One-way valves in veins can become congested or calcified after years of the above causes.

Recommendations for prevention and early treatment include:

• Adequate water intake;

• Vitamin E, vitamin A, and bioflavonoid supplementation;

• Sit or recline with the feet and legs propped up;

• Aerobic exercise to strengthen the circulatory system and aid the return of blood from the legs to the heart;

• Change occupations or modify your job if necessary; break the routine of sitting and standing by changing positions, walking, and moving around on the job.

• Massage strokes that "milk" venous blood up the legs are helpful but shouldn't be used on persons with a history of phlebitis or blood clots. With the "patient" lying face down, rub lotion or oil on the back of the thighs and calves. Use the thumbwebs to slowly push *upward* toward the buttocks. Perform ten to 20 strokes per leg once per week for prevention and maintenance of healthy veins. Do more often but gently if varicosities or tender and swollen valves have begun to develop.

Visual Well-Being

Vision therapy or "behavioral optometry" incorporates eye exercises and the selective use of corrective lenses for vision fitness. This is different from the orthodox approach of putting strong corrective lenses on a person and leaving them on all the time. Crutches may be needed initially when we sprain an ankle; however, if we continue to walk on crutches all the time, the ankle will not be challenged to strengthen and improve on its own. Similarly, continuous use of strong corrective lenses, especially with children, does not challenge vision to adapt naturally. If lenses correct vision to 20/20, why should the eyes improve on their own? Opthamologist William Bates, M.D., began this approach in the 1940s; read *Seeing Beyond 20/20* by Robert-Michael Kaplan, O.D., and *20/20 Is Not Enough* by Arthur Seiderman, O.D. See *Resources* for addresses of the *Program for Better Vision* and doctors who use vision therapy.

Genito-Urinary Information

Since these two systems are open to the outside environment, the potential exists for infection and irritation. Simple hygiene and common sense measures can prevent many common afflictions:

• Drink plenty of water to regularly flush the kidneys, ureters, and urethra.

• Wash daily, especially before sexual activity. After a bowel movement, women should wipe from front to back — away from the vaginal opening. Avoid touching the vaginal area after any anal contact to prevent genito-urinary infection by bacteria found in the intestinal tract.

- Avoid soaps that irritate the vagina or urethra.
- Empty the bladder at regular intervals, especially just before and after sexual intercourse.
- Cranberry juice, one to two quarts per day, can combat bladder infections by increasing the acidity of the body.
- Minimize caffeine since it may irritate the urinary system and increase bladder infections.
- *Kegel exercises* strengthen sphincter muscles and can reduce stress incontinence problems. Some senior citizens and females after childbirth experience urinary leakage, especially after coughing, sneezing, or laughing. Tighten the muscles between the anus and genitals with a maneuver similar to that of holding in a bowel movement. Hold that position for ten seconds, five to ten times and repeat several times throughout the day.
- Avoid birth control pills; use a diaphragm or condom in conjunction with safe and responsible sex.

Upper Respiratory Infections (URI)

Remember, during a "cleansing crisis," the body tries to heal itself via sinus drainage, productive cough, fever, fatigue, and other mechanisms. Avoiding a bacterial and waste-product laden state is the best strategy to escape common URIs and colds. Our immunity is increased by stress management, not smoking, proper rest, healthy diet, and other healthy lifestyle habits. True prevention of URIs, therefore, focuses on the same factors that are important for total wellness.

Even with the best preventive and holistic health lifestyle, some persons contract an occasional illness. Fortunately, with continued adherence to natural health principles, such illnesses are rare and minor in severity and duration. When symptoms first appear, mentally focus on quickly and naturally reversing the illness; *you don't have to become sick.* Here are several techniques for aiding the body when a URI or cold seems imminent:

• Avoid or minimize dairy products that, for many persons, increase mucous in the body and trigger allergic reactions.

• Minimize sweets and junk food. Eat fresh fruits and vegetables for increased vitamins, minerals, water, and fiber.

• Drink lots of water to flush your system.

• If you feel like skipping a meal or eating only light fare, that's fine. Energy normally used for digestion can be used instead to aid the immune response.

• Increase Vitamin C intake to about three grams to bowel tolerance per day for adults (maintenance dose 500-1000 milligrams per day); for children give 10-15 milligrams per pound of body weight (when healthy, give 5 milligrams per pound). Lendon Smith, M.D., author of *Vitamin C As Fundamental Medicine*, recommends pushing the vitamin C until the bowels get a little soft (bowel tolerance). He also suggests taking vitamin A, zinc, and Echinacea to help fight infection. Take partial dosages several times throughout the day or use "time-release products" to ensure maximal absorption and utilization. Vitamin C is water soluble and the body will flush out any extra through the kidneys. Two-time Nobel Prize winner Linus Pauling, Ph.D., recommends up to ten or more grams per day while fighting an impending illness; thus, a few extra grams of vitamin C is a conservative dosage that may help prevent an impending URI.

• The *thymus thump technique* may stimulate the thymus gland and its production of immunity-boosting blood cells. If you remember the old Tarzan movies, you already know the technique. Lightly thump over the upper breast-bone for one minute several times each day. The jungle cry is optional.

• Tell your body that you *hear* the messages it is sending. Promise that you'll improve your lifestyle habits so the body doesn't have to go ahead with a full-blown URI. This approach can conceivably work with any illness but make sure you keep your word.

• A *sinus massage* technique can mobilize congested secretions and relieve sinus pressure. Rub over the frontal sinuses (above the eyes) and maxillary sinuses (between eyes and mouth) for one minute. Then feel for tender or swollen areas and apply pressure for ten seconds. Finally, lightly tap over these sinus areas for another minute. These three procedures — *massage, pressure, and tapping* — increase blood flow, aid drainage, and achieve reflex benefits. Use this procedure several times each day or as needed.

• The *saltwater nasal douche* technique is a safe and effective way to cleanse the sinuses. Contact your local pharmacy for an inexpensive glass tube called a "nasal douche." Mix one half cup of lukewarm water with one half teaspoon of salt and pour some solution into the glass tube. Tilt your head back and slowly release saltwater solution into one nostril. Tilt your head from side to side and let the solution bathe the sinus cavities for about one minute. Let the solution drain out and repeat in the other nostril. Saline mist spray bottles help some but don't irrigate and cleanse the sinuses as well.

Saltwater kills pathogenic bacteria, thins congested deposits, and helps reduce swollen nasal membranes. Be prepared for sinus drainage afterwards. Consult your physician before using this technique if you have any sinus abnormalities; generally, however, it is safe and effective.

Use once or twice a day until you notice a significant improvement. Then wean off the program and use as needed to maintain benefits and prevent reoccurrences.

ACTION STEPS

* Review highlighted information and make "to do" list.
* Read the books listed for further information on any topic.
* Choose the most important areas that need improvement and start changing those habits this week.
* Invite a doctor who specializes in natural healing to speak to your church, club, or other organization.
* Resolve to improve your lifestyle habits.

REST AND SLEEP

"The beginning of health is sleep."
— *Irish Proverb*

Getting sufficient rest and sleep is necessary for balanced living, but sleep requirements vary widely. Circulate fresh air in your sleeping area; even in winter, occasionally crack your bedroom window to provide plenty of oxygen. Extra rest is needed during times of increased stress and illness. Let's examine how rest and sleep relate to total wellness.

How Much Sleep?

Two geniuses, Albert Einstein and Thomas Edison, differed greatly in their need for sleep. Edison required only four hours per night plus short naps during the day. Einstein, on the other hand, preferred ten to 11 hours sleep each night. Similarly, each of us have unique sleep needs. The best way to estimate how much sleep you *need* is during a time when your life is about "normal." That is, don't try this during times of abnormal stress or during a vacation. Go to sleep the same time each night for one week and keep track of when you *naturally* awaken. How long do you sleep before you open your eyes and realize it's morning? This is the approximate amount of sleep you need. Get the amount you require on a consistent basis for optimal functioning. Chronic fatigue, irritability, lowered resistance to disease, inability to concentrate, and other impairments can result from insufficient sleep.

Some individuals, on the other hand, get *too much sleep*. Excessive sleep wastes precious time that could be used for other pursuits. We may oversleep because we're bored or it's a handy escape from the stresses of life. Many of us can thrive on less sleep than we think. Our need for sleep usually decreases as we age. Some persons report needing less sleep when they consistently exercise, eat a vegetarian or semivegetarian diet, and properly combine their food.

How much would you sleep if you didn't have a clock or other external influences? How much sleep would you need if your life were extremely happy, healthy, interesting, and creative? Self-actualized individuals enjoy many things in life instead of "sleeping their life away." There are many interesting pursuits and much work to be done for those on the path. *Balanced Living* techniques can minimize the amount of sleep you need to be healthy and active.

When to Sleep

The old saying, "Early to bed, early to rise, makes a person healthy, wealthy, and wise." is good advice for most of us. Natural Hygiene teachings hold that the hours of sleep before midnight are the most restful and beneficial. Unhealthy habits such as excessive eating, drinking, and watching TV often occur late at night when other activities are more limited. Early to bed and early to rise helps reduce these habits that are best kept minimal for one seeking a balanced and full life.

Sleep Positions

We spend about one-third of our lives in bed so *sleep postures* or positions are important. Sleep on your back or on either side with regular changes in these positions throughout the night. Avoid sleeping on your stomach and on your side with your arm raised above your head; these positions cause chronic twisting of the vertebrae in the upper back and neck. You wouldn't spend eight hours a day with your head turned to one side or arm above your head; avoid these positions at night as well. Program your brain to awaken and remind you if you assume an improper sleep position.

Newborns should sleep only on their sides since they don't have sufficiently developed "gag reflexes" and could breathe in vomit or mucous while sleeping on their backs. Dr. Smith cites an increased SIDS risk if newborns sleep on their stomachs. Dr. Hal Huggins, dentist and author of *Why Raise Ugly Kids?*, states that children who sleep on their stomachs are more likely to develop dental and facial structural problems due to chronic pressure on these bones. Teach your children about good waking *and* sleeping postures so they'll escape chronic skeletal stresses.

The type and number of *pillows* you use is another consideration for sleep positions. Use only one pillow with a thickness of the distance between your ear and shoulder. This allows the head to be in a *neutral position*, that is, not bent forward, backward, or to one side. Sleeping on two or more pillows cocks the head in an altered position throughout the night. Some persons, especially those with neck trauma, have abnormal curves of the neck. These individuals often can't get comfortable with any pillow arrangement and have tried one, none, more than one, and a rolled up towel. For these persons, I recommend corrective chiropractic adjustments and a specially designed pillow that supports and gently tractions the neck during sleep.

Avoid saggy mattresses that strain the spine and cause back discomfort. *Firm* conventional mattresses or water beds are good sleeping surfaces for most individuals. Some persons benefit from a very firm sleeping surface that only a conventional mattress and box springs will provide. Avoid the original water beds; these lack firm support and can strain unstable backs. The best way to find which mattress is optimal for you is to sleep on different ones. How do you sleep throughout the night and how do you feel the next morning?

Improper rest and sleep positions can contribute to spinal strain. Don't prop just your head up while watching TV or reading on a couch or bed; rather, use several pillows to elevate your entire upper body. Position the pillows from the shoulder blades up to sufficiently elevate the entire upper torso. Specially designed cushions with arms are available for reading and watching TV in bed. Propping your head up on the arm of a couch can misalign and strain neck vertebrae. Neck strain can also occur when a person falls asleep sitting up. The head jerking back and forth causes minor whiplashes that contribute to neck problems.

Certain sleep positions may be helpful if you suffer from low back problems. When lying on your back, put a pillow under the knees, thereby keeping both knees slightly bent. When on your side, bend your knees slightly and put a pillow between them. Lie on your back on the floor and rest your calves on a couch or chair. These positions can relieve strain on the low back and nerves that supply the legs and groin.

Naps

Naps are useful for maintaining peak energy and reducing stress. Naps have been successfully utilized over the ages by highly productive persons such as Thomas Edison, Winston Churchill, and Napoleon. While being visited by three American presidents and Henry Ford, Edison curled up on the grass and snoozed while they looked on. The benefits of a nap by far exceed the time involved. Whenever possible, try to arrange a nap to break up your day. Even a short nap gives our computer-brain a rest from eye strain, midday fatigue, and the demands of the day. For those who can't sleep during the day, "resting the eyes" with your head down on your desk or with a relaxation technique is the next best thing.

Rest and Illness

Rest is one of the most underestimated and powerful healing tools at our disposal. Extra rest and sleep allow the body to make adaptations and work internal miracles. When ill, animals often "hole up" and rest completely, reappearing only when they have recovered. Humans need to increasingly listen to their innate intelligence; follow the example of animals in nature and get extra rest when you just don't feel right. Lighten your schedule; go to bed earlier, cancel social engagements, and fit in a nap. This extra rest may mean the difference between just feeling under the weather for a day versus getting a full-blown illness.

As you reach optimal well-being, you will feel great nearly all the time. Then, when you have a minor symptom or don't feel quite right, you can quickly analyze what you need. Some persons feel tired and crummy all the time; thus, they have no reference point for wellness and miss subtle cues that healthy persons detect. It's normal to feel tired for awhile after surgery, illness, physical trauma, or psychological stress. This is your body's way of telling you to get extra rest. Some persons ignore these messages and keep pushing themselves, perhaps with the aid of chemical stimulants like nicotine, caffeine, and sugar. Then, as a last resort, the body may collapse and go into a serious illness.

Insomnia

Insomnia refers to an inability to sleep as desired, either getting or staying asleep. As you increase in mental, physical, and spiritual well-being, your sleep habits will likewise be more balanced. The following techniques should enable you to fall asleep easily and rest deeply. Wind down for an hour or two before bedtime by reading, watching a nonstressful show, taking a warm bath, or doing some relaxing activity.

Waking and decreased alertness cycles occur approximately every 90 minutes. Listen to your body and catch the next cycle. Many regular exercisers report an increased ability to fall asleep; decreased tension, increased physical fatigue, and release of relaxing brain chemicals are possible reasons for this phenomena. Avoid exercising within a few hours before bedtime as this may overstimulate you.

Sleep expert June Fry, M.D., Ph.D., recommends the following home therapy techniques:

• Change of diet. Excess caffeine, alcohol, or smoking can cause insomnia. Don't go to bed hungry or stuffed.

• Adjust your inner clock. Set your alarm for the same time every day, regardless of when you fall asleep. Avoid naps.

• Use the bedroom only for sex or sleep. If fitful sleepers associate the bedroom with their inability to sleep, they may get caught in a vicious cycle.

• Don't stay in bed if you can't sleep. If you're awake for more than 20 minutes, get up and leave the room.

Engage in some activity. Write a letter, read, or do a nonstimulating task. You'll feel yourself getting drowsy again as the next sleep cycle approaches. Don't fight insomnia or worry about it. Avoid becoming dependent on sleeping pills for getting to sleep. Rather, address the various factors discussed here and see which ones are affecting you. Use the relaxation exercises for natural ways of promoting sleep. Avoid protein-rich, late evening snacks as these help form alertness chemicals. Valerian root, tryptophan, and carbo-hydrate snacks — like fruit — help form *calming* brain chemicals and may be as effective as a sleeping pill in inducing relaxation.

Finally, insomnia may be due to vertebral subluxation complex (VSC), particularly misalignment of bones in the upper neck. Subtle pressures on the spinal cord or upper cervical nerves can cause irritability, chronic tension, and an inability to relax. Sleep positions may further aggravate spinal misalignment thereby making sleep more difficult. Patients frequently enjoy improved sleep habits after a series of corrective chiropractic adjustments.

A Time for Creativity

Geniuses like Einstein and Beethoven have reported creative flashes and insights just before, during, or after sleep. Paul McCartney wrote "Yesterday" after awaking with the song in his head. Our amazing computer-brain processes information during times of rest. The wise person, therefore, uses this time to enhance their creativity and productivity. Bedtime prayers have long been recommended as an end of the day activity; this attunes our thoughts and spirit with the Creator and reminds us of the eternal and unified nature of all life.

The time just before sleep is also excellent for listening to or reading affirmations and goals. Keep a tape recorder or pencil and paper by your bed so you can record creative ideas as they occur just before, during, or after sleep. We all receive flashes of genius from our deep centers of wisdom and the collective unconscious. Getting these insights on paper aids evaluation and follow through. Record dreams to allow fuller recollection and analysis. The brain sweeps out cobwebs in the attic of the mind as we sleep. Worries, fears, and past concerns can be ventilated and catharsis can occur as we dream.

Bedtime is also an excellent opportunity for optimal learning and memory work. Alpha brain waves that predominate just before sleep are well-suited for rapid and lasting memory storage. The book *Superlearning*, by Ostrander and Schroeder, describes this technique of enhanced learning that I taught to over a thousand graduate students. Designed primarily for use while awake, accelerated learning can also occur during the initial stages of sleep. This is also a good time to listen to tapes for self-improvement and cessation of destructive habits such as smoking or overeating.

Parents, read to your children each night for several reasons. Reading to them for just fifteen minutes enhances their vocabulary and comprehension while you spend quality time together. As my children fall asleep, I remind them how smart, beautiful, creative, talented, and beloved they are. Imagine the positive net effect on the child's self-image with such quality parent-child interactions.

ACTION STEPS

• Obtain sufficient rest and naps, if desired.

• Observe proper sleep postures and other recommendations.

• Use sleep periods for prayer, enhanced creativity, and learning.

WELLNESS AND EXERCISE

"The wise for cure on exercise depend."
— *John Dryden, circa 1675*

"If you don't use it, you lose it!" is certainly true of exercise and total health. Everyone knows we should exercise, but only 17 percent of our population does so on a regular basis. *The benefits by far exceed the time and energy involved.* Follow the example set by 90-year-old Strom Thurman, the oldest member of the U.S. Congress. His secret? A good diet and daily exercise including calisthenics, lifting weights, and riding a stationary bicycle. Says Senator Thurman, "If a person follows that, then they will have a chance to live a happier life and help humanity."

A construction worker named Joe opened his lunchbox and cursed. "Tuna fish sandwiches again! I get tuna all the time. Look at these other guys. They get roast beef, turkey, ham — something different every day. Me? Always tuna fish!" This went on day after day until finally the foreman talked to Joe: "Look, the other guys are getting tired of hearing about the tuna fish. Why don't you ask your wife to pack something different tomorrow?" Joe looked at him with surprise and replied, "What do you mean my wife? I pack my own lunch!"

As far-fetched as this story sounds, *we all pack our own lunches when it comes to lifestyle choices and health habits.* We directly determine what we get out of life by our thoughts, words, and deeds. We each are responsible for our health, success, happiness, quality, and quantity of life. Exercise is a prime example of how we can positively alter our lives with a little time and effort. Proper exercise need not be time-consuming, difficult, or expensive to be beneficial. Moderate exercise on a regular basis has amazing benefits in so many ways — it is truly one of the "secrets" to long and vital health.

As we grow in self-love and appreciation of our marvelous bodies, we naturally want to take better care of ourselves. Motion is life. My healthiest senior citizen patients keep active and exercise regularly. As 90-year-old Alfred said, "You gotta keep moving. The best way to get old and die is to sit around and do nothing."

Kenneth Cooper, M.D., reports that, according to longevity projections, you'll gain four years of life by exercising regularly. As a side note, we gain three to eight years by not smoking and two to eight years by controlling our weight. That's between nine and 20 years gained by lifestyle changes in just three areas. An eight-year study of more than 13,000 persons by the Institute for Aerobics Research found that even moderate exercise significantly reduces the risk of death from virtually all causes including cancer and heart disease.

Why Exercise?

Our ancestors didn't have to worry about getting enough exercise; walking, lifting, stretching, and other physical movements were part of their activities of daily living.

Many of us, however, now lead a sedentary lifestyle that directly decreases the length and quality of our lives. Let's examine each system of the body and the positive effects of exercise on it:

• *Heart and Circulatory System:* The heart and blood vessels can be gradually and safely strengthened with an exercise program. Regular aerobic exercise can develop "collateral circulation," alternate blood vessel routes, for those with existing coronary artery blockage.

• *Musculoskeletal System:* Exercise strengthens muscles, tendons, and ligaments and increases their flexibility and balance. Repetitive musculoskeletal movements allow intervertebral discs to absorb necessary fluids and thereby minimize degenerative changes. *Bones* are strengthened by weight-bearing exercises — running, walking, stair-climbing, aerobic dance, skiing, and lifting weights. This is important for all of us but most critical for postmenopausal females who are prone to developing osteoporosis or bone fragility. The benefits of calcium supplementation are unclear, and estrogen therapy only *maintains* bone mass. Exercise can *maintain* and *increase* bone density, thus increasing resistance to fractures.

According to Gail Dalsky, Ph.D., exercise can cause significant increases in bone density after just nine months of consistent exercise. She states that most women can progressively increase their walking distance to three miles per day, four or five days a week. One study of women with an average age of 84 showed increased bone mineralization from 30 minutes of light exercise three times a week.

• *Nervous System Conditioning:* Exercise improves coordination, balance, and reflexes. As a person improves in physical prowess, there is often an accompanying emotional growth and mastery in other areas of life. Ismail and

Trachtman state that the brain functions more imaginatively and thoughtfully in a physically fit person.

• *Brain and Body Chemistry:* Exercise promotes healthy brain and body biochemistry by increasing production of chemicals that help us feel good and live more energetically. Endorphins and other internally produced chemicals act as natural painkillers, tranquilizers, mood elevators, and antidepressants. Richard Sternbach, Ph.D., a specialist in pain management, states: "The inactive person tends to have less tolerance for pain compared with those who exercise regularly."

Regular exercise produces the chemicals needed for nerves to fire quickly and often. Exercisers reflect this in their abundant energy and euphoric feelings; this is termed the "runner's high" although it can be reached with any aerobic exercise. Working with men who had a history of anxiety-tension problems, researchers found a 15-minute walk brought more relief than a mild tranquilizer. Griest et al found running to be as effective as psychotherapy in improving moderate or neurotic-reactive depression.

• *Elimination Processes:* Exercise increases the amount of sweat and excreted wastes removed through the pores of the skin. Exercise also completely aerates the lungs, thereby eliminating carbon dioxide wastes and excess mucous. Repetitive muscular movements of exercise aid optimal lymphatic circulation and waste removal. Finally, exercise aids the movement of digesting matter through the intestines, preventing constipation and promoting regular and easy bowel movements. For those who cannot exercise, practice exaggerated diaphragmatic breathing — an old yoga technique — to achieve the same effect.

• *Weight Loss:* Exercise assists weight loss and helps maintain a desired weight by burning calories with preferential utilization of fat. Our metabolism — the rate at which we burn calories — increases for 12 to 24 hours after aerobic exercise. Thus, we continue to burn calories at a faster rate *during* and *after* exercise. Aerobic exercisers often report decreased appetite. Says Joel Henning, author of *Holistic Running,* "Although scientific explanations of this phenomena differ, they do seem to confirm that a strenuous workout has the effect of suppressing appetite." No wonder regular exercise, combined with eating the right amount of healthy foods, results in optimal weight.

• *Stress Reduction:* Exercise helps reduce mental tension and excessive stress. Any good stress reduction program will include regular exercise as a primary component. Some exercises foster a Zen-like state of mind similar to that achieved during meditation. An improved ability to sleep deeply and easily is probably a function of this general relaxation and stress reduction. Thaddeus Kostrubala, M.D., author of *Joy of Running,* describes an exercise-produced state of consciousness alteration as being "very positive, creative, less conscious, and an insightful interlude."

As you can see, the advantages of exercise are many and far-reaching when compared to the time and effort involved. Please get motivated to regularly exercise throughout your life. Jack LaLane is a remarkable example of how we can look, feel, and function throughout our lives. On his 70th birthday, he swam one mile while pulling 70 small boats containing friends and local residents. After showing film footage of his latest feat, the TV host gushed, "Jack, you're amazing — I don't know how you do it!" Jack replied, "You're missing the whole point! *I'm* not amazing. This is how we *all* can be if we take care of ourselves and exercise!"

I know it's hard to get motivated sometimes: feelings of fatigue or embarrassment may make getting started seem difficult, *but make up your mind to be all that you were meant to be.* Be a healthy animal and exercise so you can enjoy the many facets of life. Get going! You'll feel, look, and *be* better for it. Joel Henning said it well: "Running is a powerful paradigm for many of life's activities; it reminds us that most things are accomplished only slowly and with effort, step by step."

Which Exercise?

Which exercise you do depends on a number of factors including your age, current physical condition, and fitness goals. In *Healthy Pleasures,* Sobel and Ornstein list different exercises and activities of daily living and the number of calories they burn. Trying to exercise too much too quickly is a common reason that exercise programs fail. After overdoing it, the person feels sore, tired, and unwilling to suffer again. Build yourself into shape *slowly* and *steadily* using graduated steps. Kenneth Cooper, M.D., considers aerobic exercise very safe for all ages if six basic guidelines are followed:

• Get a complete physical examination within a year of starting an exercise program — within three months if you're over 40.

• Watch your diet and control weight, blood sugar and cholesterol levels. Wait at least two hours after a heavy meal before exercising vigorously.

• *Warm up* with stretches and slow walking.

• Don't overexert and stop exercising if you experience chest pain, severe shortness of breath, dizziness, or nausea.

• *Cool down* or taper off exercising during the last five minutes. This helps prevent nausea, cramps, and soft tissue strains.

• Avoid gaps in your program. Stick with your exercise

schedule, especially during the first ten weeks of a new program.

The three major components of exercise are stretching, strengthening, and cardiovascular conditioning. Different exercises vary in the extent to which they meet these goals. As discussed, weight-bearing exercise increases bone density while soft tissue flexibility and strength increases with stretching and strengthening exercises. Cardiovascular benefits are derived by *aerobic conditioning*. The word "aerobic" refers to exercise done "with oxygen," that is, avoiding oxygen debt or an anaerobic state. Some persons avoid exercise because of past erroneous notions of "No pain, no gain." We can gain all the benefits we need with moderate and enjoyable aerobic exercise.

Understanding basic terminology used in exercise programs is helpful. *Duration* refers to *how long* the exercise session lasts. *Frequency* means *how often* you exercise and is usually expressed in sessions per week. *Intensity* refers to *how strenuously* you work out. Most guidelines recommend aerobic exercise three to four times per week for 30 minutes. This frequency and duration meet the basic exercise needs for optimal health.

There are three basic ways to monitor the *intensity* of your workout:

• You should be able to *chat comfortably* with another person as you perform your workout. You are not exercising aerobically if you are too winded to converse.

• *How do you feel?* Stop exercising immediately if you feel dizzy, out of breath, nauseated, or develop a headache. These all are signs that you are exceeding the ability of your body to handle the intensity of the workout. Consult a physician or exercise trainer if these symptoms persist or recur.

• Measure your pulse or *heart rate* by lightly feeling an artery on your wrist or neck; count the number of beats per ten seconds and multiply by six. An equation to find your *target heart rate* is: (220 - your age) X 70 percent. That is, 220 minus your age is your approximate *maximum heart rate*. Multiplying your maximum heart rate by a percentage gives your *target heart rate*. For example, if you are 50 years old: (220-50) X 70 percent = 119. Thus, a 50-year-old would be reaching 70 percent of his or her maximum heart rate when exercising with a pulse of 119.

Maintain your target heart rate for 20 minutes for optimal cardiovascular benefits. With a warm-up and cool-down period of five minutes each, this requires a 30-minute exercise session. Most authorities recommend exercising at 70 percent of your maximum heart rate. Depending on your age, health, and fitness goals, you may want to exercise at 60 to 85 percent. Consult your doctor or fitness trainer regarding the best target heart rate for you.

With this basic understanding of exercise terminology, let's look at some common ways of exercising. There are many types of exercise to choose from; select those *you enjoy* and get started!

• *Walking* is the best overall exercise for most persons. It can be done anywhere, at any time, and provides necessary musculoskeletal and cardiovascular benefits. To reach your target heart rate, walk briskly and swing your arms and legs. Walk with *hetero-lateral* coordination, that is, the *opposite* arm and leg going forward at the same time. Persons with dropped arches or "flat feet" may benefit by putting arch supports in their shoes. Have someone observe your gait and foot strike: are both legs and feet moving at roughly the same distance and angle? Observe the wear patterns on your shoes; the areas and degree of wear should be similar — primarily on the heel and ball of the foot. Vary your walking route and enjoy the beauty of nature and the diversity of life around you.

• *Jogging* is okay for many persons when done *moderately* and *correctly*; I include these qualifiers because jogging isn't for everyone. The benefits are many and include superb cardiovascular conditioning, muscular strengthening, and mental relaxation. My primary concerns about jogging are the cumulative stresses and jarring forces on the joints. If you choose jogging as part of your exercise program, do everything possible to minimize this impact. As often as possible, jog on soft surfaces such as dirt trails, sand, grass, and high school tracks. Wear good jogging shoes with shock absorbing inserts.

Mileage covered per week is another consideration in cumulative shock absorption. Premature osteoarthritis or degenerative joint disease (DJD) can occur with high-mileage jogging especially if improper biomechanics are involved. In a study of Finnish long-distance runners, researchers found only a four-percent incidence of hip DJD versus 8.7 percent among nonrunners. However, most running in Finland is done on soft surfaces and forest paths. The reviewer of this article stated that recent U.S. data suggests arthritic tendencies in runners who train at high mileage on paved roads or when injured. In my experience, other increased risk groups include those with heavier frames, one short leg, weak or injured joints, or misaligned skeletal structures.

Olympic team physician, Leroy Perry, D.C., considers *jogging* the worst thing you can do to your body. Jogging usually involves an upright posture with foot strike on the heel or the entire sole of the foot. *Running* is done with a forward lean at the waist and foot strike on the ball of the foot. Thus, running usually does not cause the cumulative jarring forces that accompany jogging. Brisk walking, interspersed with runs or sprints, is a reduced impact alternative to jogging. If you want to jog, limit yourself to about nine to 15 miles per week and observe these recommendations.

• *Swimming* is the ideal nonimpact exercise for optimal muscle strengthening, stretching, and cardiovascular conditioning. The obvious drawbacks for swimming are that it requires a swimming pool and an ability to swim reasonably well. Younger persons need to swim continuous laps to obtain aerobic benefits. Senior citizens may be able to raise their heart rates sufficiently by walking or doing exercises in the water.

• *Biking* is another nonimpact alternative to jogging for those who want an intense muscle and cardiovascular work out. Biking allows fitness training for all age groups as speed and terrain allow varying intensities. Helmets are a must and caution should be used when biking on roads. Some persons prefer handle bars that allow an upright sitting position rather than a slumped-over posture. Biking with the wrists *hyperextended* or bent backwards can cause "carpal tunnel syndrome" symptoms. This can be minimized by keeping the wrists straight and varying the position of your hands. Minor misalignments of the wrist bones can contribute to this syndrome and are usually correctable with chiropractic extremity adjustments.

• *Aerobic Dance* is a fun way for all age groups to enjoy workouts of varying intensities. Aerobic dance instruction is available on TV, videotapes, and at local exercise programs. Varying amounts of impact and intensity are available. Use caution in snapping the head back and forth while dancing; this can cause neck problems or aggravate pre-existing ones.

Astanga yoga is a fitness yoga that involves vigorous and continuous stretching, strengthening, and breathing postures. This form of exercise combines the traditional benefits of yoga with a pace similar to aerobic dance.

• *Weight Lifting* is one of the best ways to strengthen bones, muscles, tendons, and ligaments. Weight training can be performed at various difficulty levels and is thus suitable for all age groups. Weight lifting stimulates red blood cell production and thus helps build the blood system. Weight training can be an aerobic exercise if the heart rate is kept sufficiently high during the work out by going quickly from set to set.

Start with a weight that can be lifted eight to ten repetitions (reps) with moderate difficulty. Perform these reps twice, that is, in two sets. Avoid cheating or using other body parts when exercising a particular set of muscles. For example, don't throw your back and hips up or outward to gain momentum for biceps curls or bench presses. This can strain other body parts and doesn't really strengthen the area being exercised. When training with free weights, have others nearby. I especially recommend weight training for:

• Those with congenital or acquired defects of the spine, for example, moderate or severe scolioses.

• Those whose job demands exceed their strength limitations.

• To fully rehabilitate musculoskeletal traumas due to auto accidents, industrial injuries, sports injuries, or falls.

• *Racquet Sports* — tennis, racquetball, handball, and squash — can elevate and sustain your pulse rate if you keep moving between points and games. Chase the ball and minimize delays in the action to obtain aerobic benefits. Check your pulse rate periodically to ensure you're within the target heart rate. Wear eye protection (except tennis) and avoid diving and wall collisions.

• *Aerobic Machines* provide an intense but nonimpact aerobic workout. These include treadmills, ski and rowing machines, stationary bicycles, and stair-climbing devices. All these can raise and maintain your heart rate into the target area and allow exercise during inclement weather.

• *Other Exercises* — push-ups, sit-ups, pull-ups, and other strengthening exercises — can be done nearly anywhere and during spare moments. Sit-ups should be performed with the knees bent and by just raising the shoulder blades off the floor. This leaves the low back on the floor and prevents low back strain that can occur with other forms of sit-ups. With the shoulder blades off the floor, you can hold it there or do "crunches" or repetitive abdominal flexions. For the abdominal obliques or "love handles" on the side, rotate your torso to either side and hold or crunch.

Back extensors are performed while lying face down. Simultaneously raise the head, arms, chest, and legs — leaving only the pelvis on the floor. Hold for several seconds and repeat. This exercise strengthens muscles that surround the spine and aids proper posture and vertebral alignment.

Leg raises strengthen lower abdominal muscles and complement sit-ups. Lying on your back, raise your legs up and hold or move the legs up and down or back and forth. *Reverse sit-ups* strengthen the low back and are done lying face down with your upper body hanging over the edge of a bed, bench, or top of the stairs. Have someone hold your legs down or strap them down with a belt around a bench. Raise your upper body up, then lower yourself slowly.

• *Minitramps* or rebounders are a useful addition to any exercise program. Jogging or bouncing on a minitramp firms muscles, increases circulation, and is an excellent way to start the day. Those persons with joint injuries or degeneration can enjoy rebounding without incurring additional joint stresses. For a more efficient exercise program, jog on the minitramp while lifting dumbbells. This strengthens the upper body while providing whole body benefits of jogging. See *Fit for Life II: Living Health* by the Diamonds for additional information on this exercise approach.

   • *Exercise Alternatives* exist for those who are immobilized by age, handicaps, or even paralysis. *Cross crawl* exercises can be done lying on the back by raising the opposite arm and leg up at the same time, then alternating. If paralyzed, have another person raise your arms and legs so that circulatory, breathing, and body movement benefits are obtained. Bicycling-like movements can be done while lying on your back with the legs in the air. For those who can't sit on a stationary bike, a set of pedals and handle bars can be used while sitting in a regular chair. Isometrics for the whole body can be performed by alternately contracting, holding, then relaxing different muscle groups. Various stretches can be done by those who are bedridden. Remember, where there's a will, there's a way.

   As you can see, there are many different ways to exercise. Best results are obtained with *cross training*; combining two or more exercise programs provides a total body workout and change of pace. Choose exercises you enjoy and change if they become too routine.

Stretching

   Stretching is a natural and important component of total health. Observe a dog or cat after a long nap; their first movement is a long, deep stretch, arching the back, then stretching each leg. Stretching should be a pleasant habit and need not be strenuous or painful. *Yoga* is, in part, an age-old Eastern science of stretches designed to improve flexibility and alignment of musculoskeletal structures. Yoga classes, books, and TV programs are an excellent way to increase your knowledge about stretching.

Fountain Of Youth, by Peter Kelder, describes ancient *rites* or postures used by Tibetan Lamas to aid longevity and vital functioning in all areas of life. Moshe Feldenkrais pioneered body movement and awareness work with his "Functional Integration" technique; W. Reich, F. M. Alexander, Ida Rolf, Fritz Perls, and Alexander Lowen are other early teachers of the mind-body link. Your chiropractor may teach you specific stretches that *reprogram* healthy neuromuscular patterns while *deprogramming* aberrant ones. Recommended techniques include Flesia's Neurological Re-Integration Movements, Aragona's ASBE maneuvers, Harrison's Biophysics, Pettibon's spinal remodeling, and Hornberger's prescriptive exercises.

Astronauts showed early arthritic changes after only seven weeks of joint immobilization. Degenerative and arthritic changes occur primarily when joints are injured, out of normal alignment, or not used. Regular stretching can prevent or minimize the effects of all these factors. Stretching takes only a few moments and pays many dividends, including:

- increases joint and soft tissue flexibility and strength.
- relaxes tense muscles and decreases cumulative muscle tension.
- prevents or slows arthritis formation. Decreases the stiffness and soreness that often accompany existing arthritic conditions.
- muscles, tendons, and ligaments that have been stretched are less likely to be injured by unexpected strains.
- helps mobilize fixated or misaligned vertebrae and other bones. Have you ever noticed a "pop" or "crack" sound of bones moving as you stretch, exercise, or turn over in bed?

Follow these guidelines when stretching:

• Perform stretches slowly and gently; bouncing or jerking movements don't stretch as well and could strain.

• Stretch just to the point of slight pulling or tightness.

• If pain or limited range of motion persists, consult a chiropractor or other specialist trained in biomechanics of the musculoskeletal system.

• Stretch just before exercising or starting any strenuous labor.

• Stretch two or three times per day when initially starting, especially if recovering from an injury. Do this for several weeks until significant changes are noted in flexibility; eventually, once per day will suffice for most persons. Persons with arthritic conditions can benefit from more frequent stretching, even in the middle of the night.

With practice, a thorough stretching program can be performed in a few minutes. Stretches can be done while watching TV, listening to music or educational tapes, or talking to family members. All athletes stretch before a game; start your day with stretching before you begin the game of life. Here is a basic stretching program that quickly covers the entire body:

• *The Tree* stretch counteracts gravitational forces and can be done standing or lying on the back. It tractions the spine with an action much like hanging from an inversion table or boots. With arms and hands high above the head, stretch the entire body until you feel a slight pull along the spine.

• *Neck range of motion* stretches include moving your head forward, backward, looking over each shoulder, and bending to both sides. I don't recommend rolling the neck in circles; the joints in the neck are best designed to move in the six directions described above.

• *Trunk twists* stretch the thoracic spine or midback. Keep the lower body stable while twisting the upper torso back and forth to each side. Keeping your arms outstretched facilitates full range of motion of this area.

• *Side bends* stretch the lumbar spine, sacroiliac joints, and hip sockets. While standing, bend to either side and run your fingertips along the outside of the leg.

• *Back bends* help maintain the normal low back curve and alignment of lumbar vertebrae. While standing, place your hands in the small of your back and stretch backwards.

• *Hamstring stretches* benefit muscles on the back of the thigh. These are often overly tight and can pull the pelvic bones out of position. Lie on your back and raise one leg up, keeping the knee joint straight. Grab behind the knee with both hands to assist stretching of the hamstring muscles.

• *Calf stretches* stretch the hamstrings as well as the calf muscles. This is the commonly seen "runner's stretch." Hold onto something while standing with one foot out-stretched behind you. Keep up on the toes and ball of that foot as you stretch the heel toward the ground.

• *Quadriceps stretches* aid the muscles on the front of the thigh. While standing, stabilize yourself with one hand and grab your ankle with the other hand. Pull your heel toward your buttocks and feel the quadriceps stretch.

• *Groin stretches* are for the inner thigh and groin muscles. I also call this the "Indian Sit" because of the position. Sit with both feet near the crotch and let your knees stretch down toward the floor. This is a simpler ver-sion of the half or full lotus position that rests one or both feet on the opposite inner thigh.

• *Knee-chest* pulls stretch low back muscles and are

done while lying on your back. Pull first one, then the other, then both knees to the chest as far as possible. Then, with both knees near the chest, gently rock back and forth on the back.

• *Cat stretches* are done on your hands and knees. Let the small of the back drop down, then arch up — much like a cat or dog stretches after a nap.

• *Shoulder stretches:* With arms outstretched, do circular rolls one way and then the other. Move your arms forward and backward, then above your head and down to the sides. Do shoulder shrugs in four directions — up, down, forward, and backwards.

• Other stretches — the knees, ankles, or wrists can be put through range of motion stretches if needed. Simply move these joints in every possible direction several times.

ACTION STEPS

For the many reasons discussed, *start today,* and make stretching and exercising a regular part of your lifestyle program.

BALANCED LIVING
WITH CHIROPRACTIC

"The Doctor of the future will give no medicine, but will interest his patients in the care of the human frame, in diet, and in the cause and prevention of disease."
— *attributed to Thomas Edison*

Chiropractic is a nondrug and nonsurgical healing profession that is gaining rapid and widespread popularity. Chiropractic fills a vital niche left vacant by orthodox medical treatment. Most persons know when to consult medical doctors (M.D. and D.O.), dentists, eye doctors, foot doctors, and psychologists. However, many persons — including doctors of all types — don't know what chiropractic is and how it can help. Chiropractors are much more than just good "bad back" doctors — they are *nerve and spinal specialists.* State-of-the-art chiropractic treatment can dramatically aid the prevention and treatment of many ailments.

What is Chiropractic?

B. J. Palmer, co-founder of chiropractic, defined it as "a philosophy, science, and art of things natural; a system of adjusting the segments of the spinal column by hands only, for the correction of the cause of dis-ease." Chiropractic utilizes the inherent recuperative powers of the body with emphasis on the relationship between the nervous system and the spinal column. Another definition is "the science which concerns itself with the relationship between *structure*, primarily the spine, and *function*, primarily the nervous system, of the human body as the relationship may affect the restoration and preservation of health."

Perhaps the best definition I've seen states, "Chiropractic is a health science built on the premise that within man there is an intelligent, constructive force operating through clearly defined channels. It is this *life force* which generates, develops, and maintains our bodies from conception to grave."

The word chiropractic comes from two Greek root words meaning "done by hand." This refers to the chiropractic *adjustment* of misaligned bones, originally accomplished only by the hands of the doctor. Chiropractic is a more *specific* version of an age-old practice of restoring misaligned bones to their normal position. Evidence of "bone setting" or "manipulation" in Egypt and China goes back at least five thousand years. Hippocrates, the Father of Medicine, stated, "In all disease, look first to the spine. . . . Get knowledge of the spine, for this is the requisite for many diseases." Galen, the Greek "Prince of Physicians," said, "Look to the nervous system as the key to maximum health."

This form of treatment went through cycles of popularity and relative disuse until 1895 when Daniel D. Palmer discovered chiropractic in Davenport, Iowa. Of synchronous interest is the multitude of related discoveries in 1895. In nearby Missouri, Andrew Taylor Still founded "osteopathy" which focused on impairment of blood circulation by bony misalignment. In Europe, Roentgen discovered the X-ray, making direct observation of skeletal structures possible. It seems the time was right for realizing that *structure governs function.*

Rather than using gross or general manipulations, Palmer's "chiropractic adjustment" sought to specifically move a single bone. Palmer theorized that misplaced vertebrae or other bones could "pinch" or put undue pressure on adjacent nerves, thereby affecting changes in health and body function. A misaligned or displaced bone is called a *subluxation* (less than a dislocation) or, more accurately, vertebral subluxation complex (VSC).

The VSC is not just a theory; it has been confirmed by chiropractic and medical researchers and consists of five components: *spinal kinesiopathology* (abnormal position or motion of spinal bones), *neuropathophysiology* (abnormal nervous system functioning), *myopathology* (abnormal muscle function), *histopathology* (abnormal soft tissue pathology), and *pathophysiology* (abnormal function of the spine and body). These five components occur spontaneously and can be treated with appropriate chiropractic care. Yes, the existence of the vertebral subluxation complex has been well documented by independent researchers and is recognized by knowledgeable doctors of all types.

C. H. Suh, Ph.D., a University of Colorado expert in biomechanics, has stated, "The vertebral subluxation is very real. We have documented it again and again. . . . The vertebral subluxation complex changes the entire health of the body . . . (and) causes not only structural dysfunction of the spine and adjacent tissues but also causes nerve dysfunction."

Medical and neurological specialists of the spine recognize the subluxation and resulting health consequences. These include Calliett, Mennell, Jackson, Kirkaldy Willis, Farfan, Nachemson, Sunderland, Epstein, Kovacs, Shmorl and Junghans, Lindbloom and Rexed, Hadley, Korr,

Sharpless, Och, Sjostrand, and Luttges. Joseph Flesia, Jr., D.C. — co-founder of the Renaissance chiropractic education program — lists 496 research articles documenting the various aspects of the VSC.

The nervous system is the master system and controls — directly or indirectly — every cell in the body. The first organ system that forms in a developing fetus is the nervous system. From that time on, as *Gray's Anatomy* states, "The nervous system controls and coordinates all organs and structures of the human body." *Complete health is only possible, then, when you have a normally functioning nervous system.* Nature protects vital organs with bone, for example, the heart and lungs by the ribs and the brain by the skull. Similarly, the vertebral column protects the brain stem, spinal cord, and nerve roots. However, there is not much extra room in the human body for *misalignment* of bony structures. Excessive misalignment or immobility of spinal bones can exert pressure on nerves, blood vessels, and other vital tissues.

Anyone who has worked with engines or mechanical devices is familiar with the concept of *tolerance.* Moving parts must be within an acceptable tolerance or distance from each other. If they are closer together or further apart than they should be, problems will eventually occur. The same interrelationship applies to the various parts of the human body. If any of the bones of the skeleton — especially the spine — are out of normal alignment, the health and proper functioning of adjacent body tissues can be affected. Chiropractors are trained to detect and correct skeletal misalignments that may exert slight pressure on the nervous system.

Again, normal spinal structure and alignment is crucial for optimal functioning of the nervous system and consequently the entire body. This simple principle has numerous important ramifications for reaching and maintaining health. As is often the case with new viewpoints, these ideas were initially met with skepticism; they sounded too simple and too good to be true. Chiropractic has grown steadily since those early years — primarily because of clinical successes, often when other approaches had failed.

There are over 65,000 D.C.'s and students worldwide, making chiropractic the largest natural healing profession and second only to M.D.'s among primary care physicians. D.C.'s are licensed to practice in all 50 U.S. states; 36 countries worldwide have practicing chiropractors and belong to the World Federation of Chiropractic. There are chiropractic colleges in the U.S., England, Australia, Japan, France, Russia, and Canada. A Doctor of Chiropractic (D.C.) degree is granted after a minimum of seven years of college. The graduating chiropractor must pass two sets of National Boards as well as State Board Exams for individual states.

Having spent *four years* studying the spine, chiropractors are the only *spinal specialists* among health professionals. Expertly locating and adjusting the vertebral subluxation complex is a difficult *art* that requires years of practice and dedication to attain. Chiropractic *science* is the ever-increasing research and improvement of nearly 100 years of clinical expertise. Chiropractic *philosophy* contributes to its unique position in the health care field; many of the holistic ideas in vogue today have been principles of chiropractic since its inception.

Chiropractic philosophy, in a nutshell, holds that the intelligence that created the body still resides within the body; *"The power that made the body can heal the body."* Lewis Thomas, M.D., in *The Medusa and the Snail*, writes of "a kind of super-intelligence that exists in each of us, infinitely smarter and possessed of technical know-how far beyond our present understanding." This amazing inner intelligence has been termed God, homeostasis, "Meditrix Naturae" — the healing power of nature, and Innate Intelligence. Anyone who studies the human body is aware of a marvelous and still largely incomprehensible intelligence that harmonizes all internal processes. Chiropractic works *with* this intelligence; "Nature doesn't need any help, it just doesn't need any interference."

The Doctor of Chiropractic understands that getting well is always an *inner* process and seeks to remove interferences that hamper nature's healing mechanisms. D. D. Palmer labeled these potential interferences as *structural, chemical, autosuggestive*; he recognized that our diet and mental state can profoundly affect our health. Chiropractic's *unique contribution*, however, is correcting the VSC to allow optimal functioning of the nervous system and entire body.

What is the Vertebral Subluxation Complex?

A basic anatomy and physiology lesson is necessary for understanding the VSC. The brain is connected to all parts of the body via the spinal cord and nerves. The spinal cord and nerve roots are encased inside and protected by bones of the spine. The spinal cord sends off spinal nerve roots that branch into nerves leading to all parts of the body. These nerves supply muscles, organs, blood vessels, lymphatic tissues, and — directly or indirectly — every cell of the body.

Spinal nerve roots exit through small openings between two adjacent vertebrae; misalignment of these vertebrae can alter the size and shape of the opening, thereby exerting slight pressure on the sensitive nerve roots. Just 25 mm Hg pressure can decrease the transmission of normal nerve supply from the brain to the tissue cell by 60 percent. The lay term for this condition is a "pinched nerve;" in reality, *slight compressive pressure* or irritation of the nerve can disturb normal nerve function and cause different health problems. Most doctors know that loss of bowel, bladder, and leg control can occur if a ruptured or bulged disc presses on the spinal cord or nerves in the low back. The VSC (vertebral subluxation complex) — slight nerve pressure due to misaligned bones — is a less severe but much more common problem.

If nerve pressure exists, optimal control and coordination from the brain may not be transmitted; the body area supplied by the "pinched" nerve then could not function or work properly. This may cause immediate symptoms or may start a degenerative process that eventually results in disease. Since nerves supply all muscles, organs, and other tissues, many different health problems can be caused by an improper nerve supply. Symptoms of the VSC may include pain, numbness, tingling, burning, hot or cold sensations, itching, aching, cramping, weakness, or other abnormal sensations. Nerves supply the entire body; thus, these symptoms can occur anywhere. However, the VSC may be a silent process — like high blood pressure — so *we can't rely on symptoms to know whether VSC exists.*

Disorders caused by nerve pressure can be roughly divided into two categories: musculoskeletal (Type M) and organic or visceral (Type O). Most persons recognize that chiropractors treat Type M problems; these include back and neck pain with possible radiation of symptoms into the head, arms, and legs. Chiropractic can also help Type O dysfunctions; these include organ symptoms such as asthma, high blood pressure, gastric conditions, bowel problems, and others described below.

Nerves from the upper *neck or cervical spine* supply the head and neck and — if pinched — can cause nerve pressure symptoms (pain, numbness, tingling, burning, etc.) to these areas. They also supply the eyes, ears, sinuses, and other tissues in the head and neck. The most common Type O symptoms caused by nerve pressure in this area are headaches, migraines, sinus conditions, visual disturbances, allergies, loss of hearing, ringing of the ears, and dizziness.

The first two bones of the neck protect the lower portion of the *brain stem*, as it forms the spinal cord. Thus, misalignment of these two spinal bones can exert slight pressure on the rest of the nervous system and cause any of the symptoms listed for the entire spine. Symptoms such as numbness or weakness in both hands and feet or on one side of the body can be due to slight brain stem or spinal cord pressure. The upper cervical spine is so important that some D.C.'s adjust only this area yet aid correction of many ailments from head to toe.

The *lower* neck and upper *thoracic or chest* areas supply the shoulders, arms, and upper trunk. Pain, numbness, tingling, and burning radiating down the shoulders, arms, or chest are common Type M symptoms of nerve pressure in this area. The primary organs supplied are the heart, lungs, and thymus gland; thus, impaired immune function, heart palpitations, lung disorders, and other conditions associated with these organs could occur due to improper nerve supply. Granted, there are other causes of disease and symptoms in all these areas. Improper nerve supply due to VSC, however, is a common cause that is often not diagnosed and therefore is not treated properly.

The thoracic spine — the middle of the back — sends nerves between the ribs to the front of the chest. This explains the pain and other symptoms that sometimes occur in this area despite normal heart and lung diagnostic testing. These nerves also supply the upper abdominal organs. The most common Type O complaints caused by nerve pressure in this area are indigestion and gastritis.

The *lumbar* or low back area emits nerves that supply the lower abdomen, groin, legs, and feet. Pain, numbness and other symptoms in these areas are often due to nerve pressure. Organs supplied by this area include the intestines, bladder, and reproductive system. Disorders that commonly respond to chiropractic care — if the cause is improper nerve supply — include bowel disturbances (constipation, diarrhea, excess gas, spastic or irritable bowel syndromes), bedwetting and other bladder problems, and dysmenorrhea (painful menstrual periods).

These are the most common symptoms and ailments caused — at least in part — by nerve pressure. Improper nerve supply can be the primary or a secondary cause of any disease process; thus, this common cause of dysfunction should always be considered when formulating diagnostic and treatment plans.

Selecting a Good Chiropractor

During my twenty years in various medical, psychological, theological, and chiropractic settings, I have tried to maintain objectivity in my observations. Each field has its strengths and weaknesses and each has treatments or philosophies ranging from conservative to liberal. Each profession has great practitioners whom I would trust implicitly; conversely, each has those who shouldn't be in the health care field. There are a few rotten apples in every bushel and — unfortunately for their patients — this also applies to doctors.

To find a good chiropractor, select one who examines and X-rays the spine before adjusting; without films, there is a certain amount of *guesswork* involved and competent D.C.'s want to *know* — not guess — about their patient's spinal conditions. "Rare earth" film and screens should be used to minimize radiation exposure. Choose a D.C. who performs *re-examinations* and *post-treatment X-rays* to evaluate your progress.

The use of a skin temperature reading instrument (dermathermograph) each visit is also highly recommended. A chiropractic physician who treats persons of all ages — *especially children* — is another good sign. A top-notch chiropractor will use tapes, lectures, and educational materials to educate patients about the VSC — vertebral subluxation complex.

The *technique* or method a chiropractor uses is also important; find a D.C. who has scientific criteria for how, where, when, and when not to adjust. I recommend *full-spine adjusting* although the cervical or neck area is the most important. *The area of pain is not always where the problem is*; thus, I examine and film the entire spine. "Motion films" reveal vital information; the ultimate is the *spinal videofluroscopy or visualizer unit* that shows the spine in motion while requiring very low radiation levels. D.C.'s using the most advanced methods have these units. I highly recommend the following techniques: Pierce, Pettibon, Stillwagon, Harrison Biophysics, and ASBE. Other useful techniques include Thompson, Kale upper cervical specific, Sweat, Grostic, Gonstead, Activator, Applied Kinesiology, SOT, Cox, Nimmo, and motion palpation.

I also recommend a chiropractor who practices *corrective care*, not just relief or crisis treatment. That is, some D.C.'s give only a few adjustments until the pain is gone and then release the patient. This "chiropractic aspirin" approach gives only symptom relief: the vertebral subluxation complex still exists and symptoms will return in a matter of time. Meanwhile, degenerative joint changes and dysfunction due to silent *nerve pressure* can have major negative effects on the patient's health. Select a chiropractor who is willing to discuss these topics *before* starting treatment. See *Resources* for additional information about how to find D.C.'s with advanced training and technology as described above.

What does a Chiropractor do?

Most chiropractors utilize a *holistic approach* to prevent disease and restore and maintain optimal health; proper nutrition, rest, exercise, and positive mental attitude are emphasized. Some chiropractors use physical therapy modalities to aid the healing process. These can be useful in certain cases but shouldn't be needed every visit on every patient. Correcting the vertebral subluxation complex to restore normal biomechanics and nerve functioning should be the primary focus of a chiropractor.

There are a number of ways that the Doctor of Chiropractic detects the VSC. A *history* is taken and a chiropractic exam that includes orthopedic and neurological tests is performed. *Palpation* with the fingertips is one diagnostic tool to feel misaligned or fixated vertebrae. *Clinical signs* such as areas of tenderness, muscle spasm, and other visual clues are noted. *X-ray studies* of the spine are necessary for measuring vertebral malposition in four dimensions. X-rays also allow the D.C. to identify spinal abnormalities, contraindications to adjusting, and conditions that require a medical referral. As mentioned, *heat sensing instruments* called dermathermographs provide further data regarding the existence, location, and degree of the VSC.

If vertebral subluxation complex exists — and it does in the vast majority of persons — spinal adjustments are needed to remove nerve interference and restore normal joint relationships. A *series of adjustments* is needed to strengthen and correct the VSC. Patients are instructed about proper work habits and strengthening exercises to aid rehabilitation. The D.C. leaves the use of drugs and surgery to the medical profession and focuses on assisting powerful internal healing mechanisms. The practice of chiropractic is very rewarding as many persons can be helped safely and conservatively.

Who Should See a Chiropractor?

Everyone should receive a chiropractic examination and, if necessary, spinal adjustment. I'll explain why this is obviously true and vitally important.

Cars periodically need a front end alignment because of road wear and mechanical stresses; tires wear unevenly when the front of the car is out of alignment. Similarly, the moving parts of our bodies can become misaligned as we encounter the *chuckholes of life.* Just like a car, the skeleton — especially the spine — needs an occasional alignment. The body is our temple and we only have one. Unlike a car, we can't overhaul or trade-in our body if it becomes a junker. Thus, it behooves us to keep ourselves vitally healthy and address the *causes* of ill health. A major cause of health problems — *the vertebral subluxation complex* — is still not well understood by many persons. *People are suffering needlessly and dying prematurely because of spinal misalignment and nerve interference.*

The human body is marvelously designed for each system to interact harmoniously. Each body part has certain requirements to function normally; these parts can become slightly malpositioned and cause dysfunction. *Structure governs function.* Most persons know that displaced organs, such as a prolapsed bladder or uterus, can cause health problems. *Similarly, the bones of the skeleton, especially the spinal vertebrae, can become slightly misaligned and cause health problems.* I am emphasizing this because it is new information to many lay persons and doctors alike.

Causes of skeletal misalignment are either traumatic or cumulative. *Traumatic causes* include auto accidents, falls, sports injuries, birth trauma, and other forceful injuries. Auto accidents, even minor "fender benders," involve *whiplash* forces that subluxate vertebrae, especially in the neck. The most common falls are down stairs, in the bathtub, on ice, and after misjudging a curb. Watch an infant learn to walk and observe the frequent falls directly on the tailbone. Recall childhood bike wrecks, sports injuries, and falls off the monkey bars. Almost falling but catching ourselves can be worse than free falling if we twist and wrench body parts in an effort to stay up. Birth trauma — involving vacuum or forceps delivery, an abnormal presentation, and surgical or forceful delivery — can misalign tiny vertebrae from day one.

When you think about all the minor and major traumas we suffer, it's not a question of how bones can become misaligned. It's a better question to ask how any bones can still be in the correct position. Once trauma has damaged the supporting structures of the spine, recurrences or aggravations can occur more easily.

Cumulative or *chronic* causes involve nontraumatic stresses that accumulate over the years. These include occupational stresses, poor posture, muscular tension, and improper musculoskeletal habits. Every job has its own particular set of occupational stresses; any job that requires prolonged sitting, standing, twisting, lifting, or bending can eventually cause various spinal, muscle, and skeletal disorders. Poor posture is common and cumulatively stressful so observe proper sitting, standing, and sleeping positions.

Chronic muscle tension often occurs in overly tense individuals and can pull vertebrae slightly out of alignment. This is why "worriers" often have shoulder, neck, and "tension headache" problems. Finally, improper habits in our activities of daily living can inordinately stress musculoskeletal balance.

Thus, most of us are subjected to traumatic and chronic stresses that misalign vertebrae and cause neuromusculoskeletal (nerve, muscle, and skeletal) problems. The medical profession is increasingly addressing these needs with physical therapists and physical medicine specialists. Chiropractors, however, have *unique* training and experience with a 100-year history that makes them a valuable part of the health care team.

This is why everyone should consult a chiropractor for a spinal examination, especially those with the symptoms and causes discussed above. Twenty-first century prevention and wellness care will include routine chiropractic visits. Babies should have their spines checked to ensure a subluxation-free start in life. Children and adults should be checked by a D.C. soon after any significant injury. It's time to increasingly utilize this effective health care approach so we all can enjoy optimal health and well-being.

More About Chiropractic Treatment

A common question about chiropractors is why a series of adjustments is necessary. Some persons complain that with chiropractic care, "once you start, you have to keep going back again and again." A series of adjustments is analogous to taking a pill daily for years. Chiropractic adjustments can also be compared with orthodontic techniques that straighten crooked teeth. Orthodontists require one or more years of braces followed by a retainer to maintain the correction. Similarly, chiropractors are realigning "crooked" spines — a more difficult job since we can't use braces or even directly touch or see the vertebrae. Many patients have had subluxations for decades and have developed degenerative spinal changes. This is why *correction* of the VSC requires time, expense, and multiple adjustments.

The *number of adjustments needed* depends on several factors including age, duration of problem, general health, severity of trauma, muscle tone, exercise history, mental attitude, occupation, and patient cooperation. The "ideal" patient would have the following attributes: young, physically and mentally healthy, exercises, follows treatment schedule and home rehabilitation recommendations, seeks treatment immediately after the injury or at the first sign of a problem, and has an occupation that doesn't delay improvement. Obviously, few patients meet all these criteria; thus, some persons need more care than others.

Bones are held in place by "soft tissues" — muscles, tendons, and ligaments. When bones are misaligned for extended periods of time, these restraining tissues adapt to the *altered* position. Thus, for spinal correction and strengthening to occur, these tissues must *re-adapt* to hold bones in the correct position. If trauma is involved, these soft tissues may be slightly torn or degenerated; this further disrupts structural integrity and extends correction time. This is a major reason why a series of adjustments are needed for significant and lasting change.

Another factor is *what kind of treatment does the patient want*? Three different stages or options of care available from the Doctor of Chiropractic are relief, correction, and wellness care. *Relief* or crisis treatment involves just the number of adjustments necessary to relieve the symptom. Some patients equate removal of the symptom with removal of the problem but removing pain or other symptoms is only the tip of the iceberg. Chiropractors can often provide rapid pain relief, but if a patient stops treatment at that point, the symptoms are likely to return later.

To reiterate, relief — the first stage of treatment — requires only a few weeks or months until a patient's symptoms are decreased or gone. D.C.'s are interested in giving their patients symptomatic relief as quickly as possible. However, relief is only the initial stage of *correcting the cause* of the problem.

Symptoms from a recent and minor misalignment are usually relieved quickly. A chronically or severely "pinched" nerve is like having your hand slammed in a car door; your hand won't immediately feel better when removed from the car door. Similarly, a significantly pinched nerve requires time for complete pain reduction. A nerve may become swollen, bruised, and irritated to varying degrees depending on the severity and duration of the nerve pressure. Hence, it may take time for nerve injury to heal completely and for alleviation of all pain and other symptoms.

The second stage of chiropractic care takes longer and involves correcting, strengthening, and rehabilitating the spine. *Correction* may require treatments over the course of a few months to a few years. Young children may require only a relatively few adjustments before they're ready for wellness care. Severely traumatic or chronic cases may require adjustments over a several year period before correction is achieved. Remember that these numbers vary widely, but repetition is essential for structural change. When joint alignment and motion improve, the patient is ready for longer intervals between adjustments. If nerve pressure has caused muscle or organ dysfunction, time and repetitive adjustments are needed to restore normal nerve supply and healthy body functioning.

I ask my patients which type of care they want — relief

or correction — but recommend correction for all cases. Most patients want *real and lasting changes*, not just temporary relief. Correction has been reached when previously misaligned bones maintain optimal alignment and flexibility and nerve interference is removed. Correction involves improving the abnormal conditions as close to 100 percent as possible.

The last stage of chiropractic treatment, wellness care, is concerned with maintaining the correction and assisting optimal body functioning. This stage of care is similar to wearing a retainer after braces are removed from the teeth. Occasional checkups are required to ensure that misaligned bones don't revert back to an improper position. Bones that were significantly misaligned usually require an occasional adjustment to maintain the normal state. What constitutes *occasional* varies among patients. Some persons, especially after severe trauma or chronic problems, need adjustments at least once per month; others can go three months between adjustments if they stretch, exercise, and observe proper spinal habits. Wellness visits can *reduce* health care costs and allow us to reach our full potentials.

The human body is superbly designed but structural integrity may never be the same once bones and soft tissues are injured or degenerated. Statistically, the chances of a recurrence double after each back injury or symptom episode. Thus, a person who has had back problems twice has a four times greater chance of a reoccurrence than someone with no prior problem. This is why it's essential to care for your body and prevent major problems in the first place. Chiropractic care and healthy lifestyle habits are doubly important when a patient has a prior history of neuromusculoskeletal problems.

Examples of Chiropractic Patients

Low back pain, often accompanied by leg symptoms, is the most common presenting symptom in a chiropractor's office; 80 percent of our population will experience a significant low back problem during their lifetime. The patient is often bent forward or to one side and muscle spasms may occur secondarily. Sedentary lifestyles, excessive sitting, and insufficient exercise pose problems for the lumbar spine. Chiropractic has much to offer in both prevention and treatment of low back disorders.

Mary, a 60-year-old farm wife, had suffered with moderate low back and leg pain for 15 years. Her medical doctor had told her — without taking any X-rays — that she had arthritis and would have to live with her pain. Family and friends convinced her to try chiropractic; her films revealed misalignment of her lower lumbar vertebrae and her sacrum or tailbone. She experienced significant relief after several adjustments and only needs a wellness check-up every month or so. Over 65 years old now, she did have some low back soreness after falling down while chasing a cow!

Susan, a 28-year-old aerobics instructor, had experienced low back and left buttock pain for a month. She was also infertile, having unsuccessfully tried to conceive children for nine years. Her back pain quickly subsided as I adjusted her lumbar vertebrae and pelvic bones. She finished the correction process to ensure a strong spine and optimal neuromusculoskeletal health. One year later, while practicing in a different state, I received a phone call from Susan. She wanted me to know that she was three months pregnant. Recall that the low back area emits the spinal nerve supply that controls the reproductive system. Perhaps the same spinal misalignment that led to her low back pain also resulted in an impaired nerve supply to her ovaries, fallopian tubes, or uterus.

Helen, a 35-year-old factory worker, was a quiet person with severe low back pain and leg pain. She didn't say much as we successfully relieved and corrected her spinal problems. But after several months of care, she came in the treatment room and gave me a big hug. A bit set back, I asked what prompted her display of gratitude. "You stopped my period pains!" she gushed. "I'm a good Christian woman, but every month for the last 11 years, I've had to drink some whiskey to stop the pain of my periods. Then I go to sleep and stay in bed till they're over." I reviewed her record and noted she hadn't reported dysmenorrhea symptoms. She replied, "I didn't tell you because I didn't know you could help that kind of problem."

Betty, a 40-year-old emergency squad volunteer, had immediate and severe back pain and leg numbness after lifting an obese patient. Conservative chiropractic care helped her symptoms by only 40 percent after the first month of treatment; it was obvious there was disc damage or other pathology involved. An orthopedic consultation, CT scan, and myelogram showed a herniated disc; her symptoms were significant and unrelenting, and it appeared surgery would be necessary. Since her injury was work-related, there was a time delay for authorization of the tests and surgery. During this time, her symptoms steadily decreased with chiropractic treatment, and she improved without surgery. Years later, she has no symptoms, works full time, and enjoys a full range of activities of daily living.

Willard, a 50-year-old security guard, had suffered low back and leg pain for 30 years — ever since a truck fell on him during a military maneuver. Armed services doctors then did not include chiropractors; Willard's injuries were misdiagnosed as permanent, and he suffered until a friend told him about chiropractic. He obtained rapid and lasting improvement after corrective spinal adjustments. A bill commissioning chiropractors as officers in the armed services was just recently passed. This will allow appropriate treatment and prevent needless suffering like Willard experienced.

Dorothy was an active 12-year-old whose primary complaint was knee pain and occasional low back discomfort. Her biggest health problem, however, was severe ulcerative colitis or Crohn's disease. She had 15 bloody diarrhea stools per day and had been examined by doctors at the Mayo and Cleveland clinics. Her disease was so progressed that these specialists recommended an elective colostomy and removal of part of her intestines. Her knee pain was from Osgood-Schlatter's syndrome and responded well to adjustments, rest, and knee braces. More importantly, after several months of adjustments, her intestinal problems were gone. Her specialists called it a "spontaneous remission" and considered the timing after her chiropractic care "coincidental."

Jim, a husky 13-year-old, suffered from "enuresis" or bed wetting; medical and psychological treatment had not helped his case. Jim's low back and tailbone — one area where the nerve supply to the bladder can be altered — were misaligned. A short series of adjustments was followed by rapid improvement as Jim went from wetting the bed nearly every night to only once or twice per month. Eventually he obtained complete control of his bladder habits.

Pregnant females often experience low back pain during and after childbirth. Many older females have told me their chronic spinal and leg symptoms date back to the birth of their children. During the last three months of pregnancy, the hormone *relaxin* is produced to relax or loosen the bones that form the birth canal. Since hormones are delivered by the bloodstream, all ligaments (band-like soft tissues that hold bones together) are relaxed. Extra weight, altered gait, and straining during delivery can then more easily misalign low back and pelvic bones. This is why *all females should have a chiropractic checkup after giving birth.*

The *neck* or *cervical* spine is of primary importance for an optimally functioning nervous system since brain stem and spinal cord pressure can occur there. Recall that the upper neck sends nerve branches to the head and its organs while the lower neck supplies the shoulders, arms, hands, throat and chest organs.

Tom was a 33-year-old who had suffered from daily and severe migraines for 22 years after his sled hit a tree. Medical doctors treated him with various pain relievers but that didn't help. A long succession of psychiatric evaluations, drug treatments, and electro-shock therapy followed. After years of unrelenting pain and mind-befuddling medical treatments, Tom wanted relief at any price and tried to commit suicide. He was diagnosed as psychotic and certainly acted the part. He was dirty, tattooed, and looked mean; I was relieved that his mother came with him during his first visit to my office.

Tom got significant relief after just one adjustment of the first two vertebrae in the neck and his migraines went away quickly. Eventually he experienced only a mild and transient headache every couple of weeks. The most amazing part of this story, however, is the *transformation* that Tom underwent as he began living a pain-free life. First, cleaner clothes and a haircut; then the smell of Old Spice instead of marijuana. When he came in clean-shaven and wearing deck shoes, I didn't recognize him. He got a job after being "medically disabled" for years.

You see, inside Tom was still a person who wanted to live. The 11-year-old was ready to resume life again after a 22-year nightmare that could have been stopped anytime by a competent chiropractor! This true story is an all too frequent and needless tragedy. Why didn't one of his M.D.'s refer Tom to a chiropractor when medical treatment failed? Interprofessional cooperation is sorely overdue to help prevent tragedies like his.

I could fill a book with examples of patients who suffered with headaches for years, only to be quickly, inexpensively, and successfully treated with chiropractic care. Mary, age 49, had daily headaches ever since she could remember. Elsa, age 65, had headaches ever since her car wreck 45 years earlier. These patients often go through expensive medical testing and treatment without success. James, an active ten-year-old, had three CT scans and was put on Inderal after hitting his head and suffering severe headaches.

I'm not saying that D.C.'s can cure all cases of headaches. In a small percentage of cases, I cannot help the patient. In another small subgroup, I can only decrease the frequency and intensity of the headaches. The vast majority of headaches and migraines, however, respond quickly and completely to chiropractic adjustments and a healthy lifestyle.

Dan came in for neck pain with radiation of pain into the face. He had also progressively lost his sense of smell over the previous three years. After treatment, his ability to smell slowly returned; he reported this improvement with mixed emotions after he first smelled sweaty gym clothes, onions, and our local paper mill.

Connie's headaches and neck pain improved quickly, but she was especially grateful when her sense of hearing improved. She had excellent hearing until she had pneumonia at age 12; for 43 years afterwards, her hearing was muffled. Coughing may have misaligned neck vertebrae, and her hearing suffered until a normal nerve supply was restored. Parenthetically, hearing loss caused by loud noise is permanent; wise persons will avoid damaging their ears with loud music and other noises. Partial deafness is embarrassing and limiting.

Janice had neck discomfort with arm pain and numbness. After several months of chiropractic treatment, she went to her eye doctor for a routine check up and found that her vision had improved dramatically. Various visual symptoms sometimes improve after chiropractic adjustments; I recommend a concurrent consult with the patient's eye doctor to rule out medical problems.

Five-year-old Johnny was brought in by his mother for recurrent upper respiratory infections. He had been on antibiotics dozens of times and his pediatrician recommended ear and tonsil surgery. I put him on a program emphasizing good nutrition and proper waste elimination and began gentle spinal adjustments. I looked him in the eyes and told him that he didn't have to be sick all the time anymore. Four years later, Johnny gets a mild cold once or twice a year but hasn't needed antibiotics or surgical intervention. He understands, at this early age, that he can be healthy with a strong immune system, a normal nerve supply, and a positive mental attitude.

June's neck and headache symptoms brought her to my office, but we also hoped to improve her chronic and severe asthma. She was on high doses of so many medications that her skin would tear very easily from the slightest force. Her improvement has been slow but steady; after one year of adjustments, her breathing is 70 percent better. Her skin is much stronger now since she only requires a fraction of her previous drug dosages.

Lucille, age 50, had recurrent pains in the arms and chest as well as occasional irregular heart beats. All medical tests, including EKG and angiogram, showed no reason for these symptoms. She had viewed my educational video-tape on which I explain nerve pressure and related symptoms. "I wasn't sure if you could help me," she confided, "but your tape explained it all. When can we get started?"

Years of secretarial work had chronically subluxated the vertebrae in the lower neck and upper back — the area known as the "dowager's or secretaries' hump." She had become accustomed to the chronic tightness and soreness in this area but was alarmed when the arm and chest pains began. Chiropractic adjustments removed pressure on the nerves leading to the arms, chest, and heart. When a normal nerve supply was restored, the heart palpitations and other symptoms stopped.

Nerves from the middle back or *thoracic* spine radiate between the ribs to the front of the chest and to upper abdominal organs. A common misalignment in this area involves the joints between the spine and ribs. When misaligned, these joints on either side of the spine radiate pain and burning sensations to the shoulder, neck, and arm. These "costo-vertebral" subluxations (misalignments between the rib and vertebrae) are often misdiagnosed and improperly treated. Patients with fibromyalgia of the neck and shoulders (upper trapezius area) often have underlying subluxations of the spine and ribs. Patients are very grateful for precise and effective adjustments to these nagging areas.

Charlie came to our office for low back, neck, and midback pain of 15 years duration. These symptoms cleared up nicely, but Charlie was especially thankful for the improvement of his stomach condition. He had been diagnosed as having an ulcer and gastritis and took medications for flair-ups. Chiropractic treatments alleviated all gastric complaints, and I didn't even know he had this condition. Like our friend with dysmenorrhea, he didn't think chiropractors could help stomach problems so he didn't mention them in his history or Cornell Medical Index. Helping correct a condition that I don't know about is astonishing to patients and makes my day.

Other Chiropractic Cases

Patients often ask, "Can chiropractic help arthritis?" *Osteoarthritis*, also known as *degenerative joint disease* (DJD) or "everyman's disease," involves joint irritation and degeneration due to wear and tear. When skeletal structures are slightly out of position, undue stresses affect the bones and joints. Arthritic spurs may form as the body tries to fuse or stabilize the weakened and misaligned area. Chiropractic adjustments help restore normal joint alignment and flexibility to minimize arthritic aches and pains. Restoration of normal spinal curves and alignment can help arrest or minimize DJD progression. Rheumatoid arthritis is an autoimmune disorder, the exact cause of which is unknown. Proper diet, a healthy emotional state, and a proper nerve supply are factors in preventing and treating this disease.

Scolioses or spinal curvatures are another problem addressed by the Doctor of Chiropractic. From a chiropractic viewpoint, scolioses often develop due to nerve interference and unbalanced biomechanics. How can the spine grow straight if the brain isn't coordinating the body properly, the foundation of the spine is not level, and muscles are not balanced? The sooner spinal misalignment is detected, the better the chances of preventing, straightening, or minimizing a scoliosis. All children — especially girls — should receive chiropractic spinal exams, particularly if there is any history of scoliosis in the family.

Extremity problems of the ankles, knees, wrists, elbows, and shoulders are commonly treated by the Doctor of

Chiropractic. Any bone in the body can become subluxated; most chiropractors are adept at adjusting bones of the extremities. During a wellness care visit, Sandy mentioned going to a foot doctor: "I've been having burning pains at the base of my toes. The foot doctor put spacers between my toes; if that doesn't work, he wants to cut off part of the bones."

Dropped metatarsals, bones that end just before the toes begin, are the most common misalignment of the foot. These bones can drop down out of normal position, usually due to trauma in younger persons and chronic causes in older patients. Sandy's foot had been stepped on years earlier by a horse; this apparently misaligned the bones toward the ground. Adjusting these bones upward into the normal position is easily and quickly achieved.

A related disorder, *hammer toes*, often occurs after years of dropped metatarsals. The surgical treatment for hammer toes involves cutting the tight tendons; for dropped metatarsals, cutting off the end of the bones. In both cases, normal anatomy is destroyed and postsurgical problems (scar tissue complications and arthritis) can occur. The traditional approach in treating *callouses* or *corns* is to cut, freeze, or burn off this excess tissue.

But did you or your doctor ever wonder *why the body put them there in the first place*? Why on some toes and not on others? Remember that nature never does anything without a good reason. The body puts the callous there to protect or pad misaligned bones. Removing this extra padding goes *against* what the body is trying to do. I've seen callouses of 20 years duration go away as the misaligned bones are restored into their proper position.

Surgery is needed sometimes but, whenever possible, not as the first attempt at healing, please. *Try something conservative, natural, and noninvasive first; if absolutely necessary, take medication but use surgery as a last resort.* Once a body part has been cut or removed, the whole body is never the same. Unless an emergency exists, get opinions from different specialists — including a doctor who specializes in conservative treatment — before allowing any surgery. Health professionals, work together and communicate so your patients receive the least invasive and best health care possible. This teamwork will result in improved health and lower health costs.

Another common condition that often can be treated nonsurgically is *carpal tunnel syndrome* (CTS). There are eight small bones in the wrist and palm area that can become misaligned. The most common causes of this misalignment are using the palm of the hand like a hammer and "hyperextension" positions. Hyperextension positions are common with bike riders, waitresses, and laborers who push or lift weight with the wrist bent backwards. Falling with the hands outstretched to prevent the fall can also bend the wrist backward. A similar injury can occur during auto accidents as the person grips the wheel or puts their hands out to brace against the impact.

Whatever the cause, minor misalignment of these bones can exert slight pressure on nerves or blood vessels in the area. The most common symptoms that result are pain, burning, tingling, numbness, or weakness in the hand and forearm. Granted, there are other conditions, such as cysts or swelling in pregnant females, that cause carpal tunnel syndrome. However, I've conservatively and successfully treated hundreds of cases, often after surgery had been recommended.

Opal was a cheerful 80-year-old who had CTS surgery scheduled for both hands. A series of wrist adjustments completely alleviated her symptoms. Her muscle strength is good, sensation is normal, and she has been symptom free for two years. Shirley, a surgical nurse, sought chiropractic treatment for her CTS because she wanted to keep working and had seen surgical risks firsthand.

Some insurances will cover surgical but not chiropractic treatment of CTS. The insurance industry has traditionally been medically oriented; this encourages drug or surgical treatment of conditions that could be treated less invasively and at a lower cost.

Another common extremity problem is misalignment of bones in the elbow joint that can contribute to "tennis and golfer's elbow," also know as "lateral and medial epicondylitis." Ligaments that maintain the integrity of the elbow joint can't heal normally when these bones are slightly misaligned. Optimal healing of soft tissue strains and sprains occurs when there is normal structural alignment in the area. Similarly, bones of the knee, ankle, and shoulder can become slightly misaligned and should be checked for normal position and range of motion.

Mental, Spiritual, and Miraculous Changes

Some of the most gratifying results chiropractors see are the *inner* changes that follow treatment. After a program of corrective and wellness care, patients often feel younger, sleep better, and have more energy than they have had for years. This quantum leap in enhanced feeling and functioning serves as an impetus to improve other areas of life. For example, David *spontaneously* quit biting his fingernails after two months of chiropractic care despite trying to quit unsuccessfully for 15 years. Negative habits sometimes automatically fall away as nerve interference is removed and healthy lifestyle practices are implemented.

Nerve pressure, especially at the base of the brain, can

cause fatigue, insomnia, irritability, and other low grade but chronic symptoms. Removing this nerve pressure can help patients drop destructive habits that previously gave them temporary relief or euphoria. Some of my patients have automatically reduced or quit using cigarettes, drugs, or excess alcohol after starting chiropractic care. After chiropractic treatment, some patients feel sick or get headaches instead of getting a buzz or high from these substances. A healthy body and nervous system recognize these chemicals for the poisons they are and provide negative feedback (symptoms) about these unhealthy habits.

Improved functioning of the nervous system can serve as a *catalyst* for positive physical, mental, and spiritual changes. Structural integrity and optimal nervous system functioning are a missing link in the health care of many persons. Clear communication between the brain and all tissue cells is a vital ingredient for total health. In the future, routine evaluation of nerve supply and structural alignment after birth and all traumas may significantly decrease common individual and societal problems.

One factor contributing to an *inner transformation* after receiving chiropractic care may involve optimal cerebral spinal fluid flow. Another possible factor is the improved flow of the *life force* or more ethereal energies. Variously called ki, bioenergy, kundalini, chi, prana, and vital force, these energies are theorized to flow up and down the spinal area. Ideally, this flow is balanced and uninterrupted, vitalizing and *empowering* the individual via a connection with universal energies. For thousands of years, the science of yoga has taught *spinal alignment and flexibility* — very similar to chiropractic benefits — as a key to physical, mental, and spiritual harmony.

A healthy nervous system is a necessary component for a long and vital life. Most of my very active and healthy octogenarian patients have excellent spinal curves, flexibility, and alignment. Kelder's *Rites* or yoga postures emphasize movements of the neck and head, thereby aiding flexibility and normal alignment of the cervical vertebrae. Regular spinal stretching is probably one reason certain populations — like the Tibetan monks described in *Fountain of Youth* — live so long and healthfully. We each can learn from their example and likewise enjoy many benefits.

Early chiropractic philosophers saw the subluxation as a potential block between humans and Universal Intelligence or Divine energies. They theorized that healing occurs "above-down, inside-out" — from God to human and internally — when normal channels between the two are intact. R. W. Stephenson, D.C., described chiropractic's major premise: "Universal Intelligence is in all matter and continually gives to it all its properties and actions, thus maintaining it in existence."

Jim Sigafoose, D.C., says, "The chiropractic mission is to unite man the physical with man the spiritual." To increase scientific credibility, modern day chiropractic has downplayed its philosophy and focused on the anatomical and physiological aspects of the vertebral subluxation. The full import of chiropractic, however, includes recognition of a Life Force that flows into and through us.

Some chiropractors have experienced *miracle cures* that suggest exciting possibilities for future generations. Fred L. Hether, D.C., clinic director at Life Chiropractic College, relates a chiropractic miracle involving his grandson. Born prematurely, Mikey never moved and his lungs collapsed and his heart stopped several times. Medical specialists said he had no brain activity or reflexes and planned to "pull the plug" on his life support equipment. Dr. Hether adjusted Mikey and a specialist found immediate improvement in his reflexes. Mikey raised his little head and stretched as if awakening from a long, deep sleep. The neurologist said Mikey would be retarded, but he was walking at ten months and is a normal seven-year-old.

Joseph Flesia, Jr., D.C., tells of a six-year-old who was in a coma from birth and was given no hope of surviving because of his severe grand mal seizures. He awoke from his coma after one adjustment and is now a healthy young man. Flesia's granddaughter was born without frontal lobes of the brain. Even though no hope could be given, she received regular chiropractic adjustments and miraculously developed frontal lobes during her first few years of life. These events weren't supposed to happen but *did with chiropractic care.*

Granted, these miracle stories are fairly rare, but how often are chiropractic adjustments tried with such cases? Many persons only think of chiropractic as being useful for bad backs; how many premature deaths and how much needless suffering could be prevented with routine chiropractic adjustments? Let's find out. I'm not saying chiropractic is a cure-all; I am convinced, however, that correction of vertebral subluxation complexes — in conjunction with other healthy practices — can improve every aspect of life.

Chiropractors and Medical Doctors

Chiropractors and medical doctors are increasingly accepting each other and working together. In one study reported by the *American Journal of Public Health,* nearly three-fifths of medical family practitioners sometimes encourage patients to see a chiropractic physician. Only three percent of these doctors dismiss chiropractors as "quacks." New Mexico's leading HMO recently added chiropractic to its multispecialty services; an increasing number of hospitals have granted staff privileges to D.C.'s. Aubrey A. Swartz, M.D., executive director of the American Back Society, said, "We feel it is important to recognize that a great many people in this country receive chiropractic care and that there is a great level of patient satisfaction among them."

Herman Rubin, M.D., Fellow of the American Association for the Advancement of Science, stated, "It may never occur to them [his medical colleagues] that the headaches, stomach trouble, neuritis, or nervous irritability they are attempting to cure may be due to nothing more serious than a displaced vertebra which any competent chiropractor can restore in ten seconds." Carl A. Hoffman, M.D., an AMA past president, said, "I work very closely with the chiropractors in my area. They refer patients to me and I refer patients to them." James P. Warbasse, M.D., in *Surgical Treatment, Vol. 1*, wrote, "Subluxations of vertebrae occur in all parts of the spine and in all degrees. When the dislocation is so slight as not to affect the spinal cord, it will still produce disturbances in the spinal nerves, passing off through the spinal foramina [channels]. The value of [chiropractic] has not been fully appreciated."

Gary Gerard, M.D., Associate Professor of Neurology at the Medical College of Ohio, received remarkable improvement of his chronic headaches and neck pain after chiropractic adjustments. Of his experience, he wrote: "It was apparent that for all my years as a physician, as most medical physicians, I had not been open to nor had I taken the opportunity to consider the benefits of chiropractic care . . . I strongly recommend to my M.D. colleagues that we accept that health care is truly multidisciplinary and although medical physicians help many patients, so do chiropractic physicians."

Doctors who keep current with research literature and interdisciplinary conferences know there is a place in health care for both chiropractic and medical approaches. Unfortunately, some medical practitioners simply don't know what chiropractic is; hence, they don't know when or why to refer to D.C.'s. Most medical doctors are not sufficiently trained in spinal diagnosis and treatment. This is not a criticism, but a fact brought out in the AMA trials. No one person can learn and apply all facets of the healing arts. The AMA has recently ruled that it is ethical for M.D.'s to refer to D.C.'s and vice versa; this will help increase interprofessional communication and cooperation.

Consider just one example of a situation that occurs all too frequently. Tim was a healthy 35-year-old with a two-year history of low back pain after cutting firewood. His HMO health plan did not cover chiropractic care, so Tim sought medical treatment even though he knew about chiropractic's effectiveness. Medical diagnostic testing was extended over a six-month period; first an exam and X-rays, then a CT scan, MRI, and finally a bone scan. Tim saw a medical GP, a neurologist, an orthopedist, and a physical therapist. Various pain medications and physical therapy modalities did not help. Finally the diagnostic verdict arrived: "We don't know what the problem is; it looks like you'll have to live with it."

Exasperated, still in pain, and many dollars poorer — as was the HMO — Tim turned to chiropractic. With an exam and several X-rays (about $175), misaligned vertebrae were identified and treatment was begun. Tim felt better after the second treatment and soon experienced no pain for the first time in two years. His constipation and excess gas problems went away. In correcting the full spine, Tim's tension headaches, stomach pains, midback and chest pain disappeared. After 16 adjustments, Tim's treatments were extended to once per month. Total bill for corrections? About $800 — a fraction of the medical diagnostic and treatment costs that didn't help at all. If his M.D. had consulted me after viewing a normal CT scan, there would have been less pain, fewer lost work hours, less radiation from unnecessary tests, and less expense.

David Imrie, M.D., and Lu Barbuto, D.C., co-authored *The Back Power Program*, an approach for managing and reducing the risk of back pain. Dr. Imrie comments, "Currently, most patients go from one practitioner to another — until they find the one that is suitable for them. A chiropractor may be the last door they knock on and that's the needed treatment. It may have taken two or three years to reach that door." Inappropriate testing and treatment due to restrictive insurance and referral practices are all too common. Health care professionals of all types, we can do better than this.

A major factor that separated the professions and disrupted optimal patient care was an antichiropractic campaign by the American Medical Association. The AMA spearheaded a physician's boycott and *misinformation campaign* to "contain and eliminate the chiropractic profession." Several chiropractors successfully sued the AMA and other medical trade organizations for illegal monopolistic practices. A federal court ruled that the AMA was indeed guilty of trying to ruin chiropractic. A U.S. District judge described the effort as "systematic, longterm wrongdoing and the longterm intent to destroy a licensed profession."

Justice always prevails and many positive outcomes have already resulted from the extensive court data. Reams of documented court evidence have verified the clinical efficacy of chiropractic. Conversely, medical experts admitted the lack of M.D. training about the spine and musculoskeletal system. John Mennell, M.D., renowned orthopedist and medical author, testified that the average M.D. who is not an orthopedist receives only zero to four hours training on the spine and musculoskeletal system. Compare this with four years of spinal and musculoskeletal specialty training by chiropractors.

Again, I am not disparaging individual medical practitioners; they have so much to learn and remember that it's not humanly possible to cover all areas. This gap in medical expertise should, however, be recognized and chiropractic's contribution should be utilized.

Now is the time to spread *facts*, not misinformation and propaganda. There have been fewer than 200 reported cases of harm attributed to chiropractic adjustments in 30 years and over three billion adjustments. In comparison, recall the medical studies documenting 100,000 *deaths* and 1.5 million hospitalizations *yearly* due to medication reactions. And don't forget the 48,000 people who die in the U.S. *each year* from among the four million unnecessary surgeries annually. My malpractice insurance costs only $1600 per year for one million dollars coverage — a fraction of the cost for surgeons and medical doctors. The *safety and noninvasive nature of chiropractic* is reflected in these vastly lower malpractice insurance premiums.

Many studies — performed by medical or government researchers — have demonstrated the superiority of chiropractic treatment in musculoskeletal conditions. Chester Wilk, D.C., chief plaintiff in the successful court cases against the AMA, presented 7½ linear inches of documented research supporting the efficacy and validity of chiropractic. *The New Zealand Report* was an internationally conducted government study that began in New Zealand and covered Australia, Canada, Europe, and the United States. Utilizing leading medical, osteopathic, and chiropractic doctors, the study concluded: "Spinal adjusting is a vital, impressively safe and clinically effective form of health care. . . . Other health care professions should defer spinal

adjustments to chiropractors since they are the best qualified. . . . Chiropractic must be in all hospitals as part of the
health care team. . . . Modern chiropractic is a soundly-
based and valuable branch of health care in a specialized
area neglected by the medical profession."

David Imrie, M.D., has stated, ". . . 60-70 percent of
work-related injuries are due to the musculoskeletal system (spine, neck, back, arms, and legs). Many problems of
the extremities, like carpal tunnel, are related to the spine.
From my perspective, it is the least understood and most
poorly treated problem in medicine . . . I first realized that
my medical and surgical training was not sufficient to deal
with the problems that I was encountering in industry. . . . I
then started learning (chiropractic techniques). The techniques made sense and gave better results."

A California Worker's Compensation study conducted
in 1972 by Richard Wolf, M.D., showed that chiropractic
was twice as effective versus medical care in successfully
treating back ailments. An Oregon Worker's Compensation
Study by Rolland A. Martin, M.D., showed that persons
under chiropractic care were able to return to work in half
the time as those receiving medical care. Patient hospital
stays in Chicago's J. F. Kennedy Hospital orthopedic wards
were cut in half when incorporating chiropractic care versus a control hospital not offering chiropractic care. Kirkaldy
Willis, M.D., led a study in which chiropractor David Cassidy
treated patients with seven-year histories of chronic back
ailments. Dr. Cassidy obtained 87-percent successful results within two-three weeks, and these patients were without pain one year later.

The *Silverman Report* documented an 86-percent success rate for chiropractic adjustments of back ailments. AV
MED, the largest HMO in southeastern U.S., sent 100
patients to chiropractor David Silverman. Eighty of these

had been unresponsive to medical care and 17 were medically diagnosed with disc problems while 12 supposedly needed surgery. In addition to the 86-percent improvement rate, none required surgery and none were made worse. The HMO saved $250,000 and the M.D. conducting the study gave full credit to Dr. Silverman. A two-year study in Italy of 22 medical "backache" clinics using chiropractic found an 88-percent reduction in orthopedic hospitalizations and a 75-percent decrease in work-time loss. This study included 17,142 patients and was performed completely by medical doctors and university professors.

Daniel Cherkin, Ph.D., reported in 1989 that patients of chiropractors were three times as likely as patients of medical physicians to report that they were "very satisfied" with the care they received for low back pain. An independent study in Britain completed in 1990 concluded, "For patients with low back pain . . . chiropractic almost certainly confers worthwhile, longterm benefit in comparison with hospital outpatient management." Chiropractic patients suffered less pain and needed fewer days off work, thus saving the country millions of pounds in lost output and social security payments. As a result, the study recommended: "Introducing chiropractic into National Health Services should be considered . . ."

While the above studies clearly document successes with musculoskeletal cases (Type M), less research on organic or visceral problems (Type O) has been performed to date. *The New Zealand Report* concluded: "In a limited number of cases where there are organic and/or visceral symptoms, chiropractic treatment may provide relief, but this is unpredictable, and in such cases the patient should be under concurrent medical care . . ." That's a prudent recommendation; I detail this research to inform doctors and patients that there is another potential healing approach for organic as well as musculoskeletal problems. Any competent D.C. has had many clinical successes with various organic and visceral problems. Medical and chiropractic research should work together to clarify which Type O problems respond best so that conservative and noninvasive treatment can be used whenever possible.

The *Windsor Report*, a University of Pennsylvania medical study, concluded: "Spinal derangements affect spinal nerve function and can contribute to the development of organic disease, which ultimately causes death." Upon autopsy of 50 patients, 138 of 139 diseased organs had accompanying "spinal derangements (subluxations) at the level of the spine giving rise to the nerves to the diseased organs." Professor Werner Kunert, a West German cardiologist, has written the texts *The Vertebral Column, Autonomic Nervous System and Internal Organs* and *Functional Disorders of Internal Organs Due to Vertebral Lesions*. Both books deal with specific spinal manipulation and the effects on the thoracic spine and its associated nerve supply to the heart and other organs. Nilsson, D.C., M.D. et al reported a 94-percent success rate after two weeks of chiropractic treatment for infantile colic. The study involved 316 infants, one half of whom had prior unsuccessful medical treatment.

Manual Medicine — medical doctors adjusting the spine — has been researched more widely in Europe than in the U.S. Medical pediatric studies in 1987 by Dr. G. Gutmann evaluated 1000 cases of children with extensive symptoms including recurrent upper respiratory infections, restless sleep, disturbed mental and linguistic development, and abnormal posture and muscle development. Adjustments of upper cervical (neck) vertebral subluxations were the only treatment. Dr. Gutmann described the results: "All were treated successfully, almost without exception."

When doctors don't cooperate, patients of all ages suffer. Consider "Gladys," a 75-year-old with excruciating neck and arm pain who needed pain and anti-inflammatory medication as well as chiropractic adjustments. Despite my recommendations to see her M.D., Gladys refused and suffered. Why? Her medical doctor had yelled at her years before for going to a D.C. and she was afraid to tell him.

The case of Ann, a courageous 14-year-old with Marfan's Syndrome, makes the best case for interprofessional cooperation. This rare and little understood syndrome is usually accompanied by back pain, visual problems, heart disease, and loss of bladder control. Ann had significant spinal misalignment and instability — probably due to a hereditary predisposition — that could significantly pinch the vital nerve supply from the brain to all parts of the body. After a few months of adjustments, Ann's back and neck pain is gone; she has complete bladder control whereas she used to require diaper pads. We're working on the eyesight and heart symptoms. How many other "rare disorders" are — at least in part — due to nerve interference and could be helped with chiropractic adjustments *and* the best medical care?

Whatever the reasons for past discord, let's now focus on working together for the best of our patients. When asked whether better relations between M.D.'s and D.C.'s will be increasing, David Imrie, M.D., replied, "Because it's in the better interest of the patient, I think it will be. It is just a matter of time. Chiropractic has made tremendous progress in terms of credibility in the past twenty years."

Regarding his work and cooperation with chiropractors, Dr. Imrie says, "I thought that many of my medical colleagues would be very critical, but that hasn't been the case. Most of them said, 'Well done, it's about time . . .' We need increased discourse between the two professions. I think we can all benefit." All the health care approaches are important and vitally needed at different times. Communication and cooperation between professions will help clarify which approach is indicated and when.

Subluxation Revisited

Now you know about a crucial element for total health — proper alignment of skeletal bones, especially the vertebrae, and a normal nerve supply. Minor misalignments of any bone in the body can cause pain and other symptoms, joint problems, and exert pressure on the nerves and blood vessels. In short, it's important to keep the various parts of our bodies *in alignment.* The body is marvelously constructed, but its various parts can become slightly misaligned. Only a Doctor of Chiropractic is trained to detect and correct VSC and other skeletal misalignment.

If you were watering your flowers with a garden hose and the water stopped, what would you check? A ruptured water main, low water pressure, or other rare problems *could* be the cause. But what if you saw that a person had stepped on the hose, shutting off the water supply? Wouldn't that be a simpler problem to solve? Similarly, improper nerve supply and loss of normal function could be due to a brain tumor, a severed nerve, or nervous system disease. These causes are very rare, however, when compared with the much more common and easily treated *vertebral subluxation.* Taking the bony pressure off the nerve — like taking the foot off the hose — allows restoration of the normal nerve supply and a return to health.

In chiropractic and medical schools, students are taught another model about the causes of disease: "If you hear hoof beats in America, expect to see a horse, not a zebra." That is, doctors are trained to look for the most common causes first, then to rule out more exotic and rare disorders. Unfortunately, neuromusculoskeletal and spinal problems often receive "zebra" diagnostic tests and treatments before "horse" problems are ruled out. I often successfully treat patients who have spent thousands of dollars on medical tests or treatment, only to be told they have to live with the problem. *The vertebral subluxation complex is of epidemic proportions and should be considered as a common cause of health problems.*

Now that you understand much more about chiropractic, let's review the three most important reasons to have VSC detected and corrected:

(1) For *relief of symptoms* caused by nerve irritation, joint misalignment, disc pressure, muscle imbalance, and other bodily dysfunctions that are a direct result of the vertebral subluxation complex.

(2) For *correction and strengthening* of the spine while restoring normal structure as much as possible. Restoration of normal spinal curves can prevent and halt early spinal degeneration and arthritic changes.

(3) To ensure an optimal nerve supply from the brain to all parts of the body. Correction of VSC removes slight pressures on the spinal cord and nerve roots, thereby allowing full communication between the biocomputer brain and all tissue cells.

I'm convinced — and research is increasingly documenting this — that proper detection and correction of VSC can allow us to enjoy our full allotment of years in the most healthy and vital manner possible. In the future, it will be common knowledge that VSC causes or contributes to bodily dysfunction, needless symptoms and disease, low quality of life, and ultimately premature death.

Guy Riekeman, D.C., writes: "It has always seemed logical to be checked on a regular basis to maintain normal spinal function and health. But is there any proof of the longterm effects of chiropractic care?"

"A group of 97 chiropractic patients who had been under regular care for 18 years or more were recently tested by scientists at the Preventive Medicine Institute in New York. This nine-year study compared the chiropractic group to a control group of high-risk sick patients and well patients. In 18 of the 22 areas of health, the chiropractic group was as well as the well control group even though some of the chiropractic patients smoked, had poor nutrition, or were elderly. And in two areas related to resistance to virus and bacteria (Immune Response Index) and toxins like pollution (Oxidative Stress Response Index), the chiropractic group tested twice as healthy. Longterm chiropractic care can have a great effect on your health; an effect that far exceeds your initial symptomatic care."

The vertebral subluxation complex causes many common problems that can be treated easily, safely, and relatively inexpensively. *You haven't tried everything unless you've tried chiropractic.* Whenever possible, try a conservative approach first before using drugs and surgery. Ask your medical doctor about chiropractors; if you receive an angry warning about the dangers of chiropractic care, educate him or her. If your request for interprofessional cooperation is met with refusal, change doctors. That physician is simply not current with recent research and clinical findings. Doctors, of all types, form relationships so that discussion about mutual patients is only a phone call away. Our patients deserve the very best.

Recommendations for Optimal
Neuromusculoskeletal Health

Self-help measures can be employed to improve and maintain the health of the nerve, muscle, and skeletal systems. These include stretching, exercise, posture, proper occupational habits, and other preventive tips. Remember that the body has an innate intelligence that keeps all systems functioning optimally. This inner wisdom is greatly enhanced when we follow a few common sense health practices. Balance is the key word for these tips. Whatever you do, evaluate whether it feels right for your body. Strive for balance and moderation in all your activities of daily living.

Stretch the entire body, especially the spine, at least once per day. *Exercise* regularly for many whole body benefits. *Good posture* is one of the most important exercises to remember. Men, hold in those abdominal muscles so you don't develop a "Milwaukee goiter." Stand up straight with your shoulders back and look straight ahead. Remember the finishing school exercise of walking with a book balanced on the head. *Walk, sit, and stand tall.* Stand up straight with your back against a wall; with proper posture, your heels, shoulder blades, and buttocks should touch.

Proper occupational habits are important since each job has its own particular musculoskeletal stresses; examine your job and analyze which factors are problematic. What can be changed so that these stresses are reduced? Vary work positions so your head isn't bent or twisted consistently in the same direction. Elevate your desk or books *up* to you instead of your head *down* toward them. Take periodic stretch breaks to counteract repetitive abnormal postures. For example, if your job involves bending the head forward, periodically stretch your head backward. For a further discussion of proper occupational habits and postures, read *Sitting on the Job* by Scott Donkin, D.C.

Spinal "do's and don'ts" include a number of common sense practices that minimize spinal stresses. Avoid keeping a billfold in your rear pocket as this can twist and misalign the pelvis. Avoid "touch toe" exercises and conventional sit-ups; both of these straighten the lumbar curve and can contribute to back problems. Avoid cradling the telephone for prolonged periods of time between your ear and shoulder. This common cause of neck and shoulder problems can be minimized with a phone cradle or speaker phone.

Prolonged sitting strains and can misalign the low back. This is especially a concern for persons who must sit or drive a lot during their jobs. Take periodic breaks every hour or two to walk around and do your spinal stretches. A *lumbar support cushion* is a valuable aid for those who must sit a lot. From the side, the low back normally has a curve in it; excessive sitting tends to straighten this curve. Most chiropractors and department stores sell these cushions that support the lumbar curve and minimize low back stresses.

Proper lifting is important since many back injuries occur while lifting. Keep the back straight and squat down with the knees bent. Arrange the feet and hands in a *tripod* arrangement, the most stable configuration of three points. Avoid bending over at the waist, especially when twisting and lifting. When lifting or carrying weight, keep the object as close to your body as possible. Avoid reaching out in front of you and lifting simultaneously. Know the weight of the object to be moved and get appropriate help or mechanical devices if necessary. Avoid lifting heavy objects over your head or pulling them down from above. Have a clear route established before you pick up a heavy object. "Lift twice" — first in your mind as you plan ahead, then with your back.

Remember the key word *balance* in everything you do. When carrying wood or buckets of water, don't always carry the weight with the same hand. Change sides each trip or, better yet, carry some in each hand so you can stand up straight. The same advice holds true for mail carriers and persons carrying heavy shoulder bags. When crossing your legs while sitting, don't always cross the same leg over. Vary positions but primarily sit up straight with your feet flat on the floor.

I don't recommend the use of baby walkers and swings. These devices are designed for the convenience of parents, not the spinal health of babies. Parents think they're helping by providing early swinging and mobility, but both devices exert weight on the tailbone and pelvis. Young spines aren't designed to carry weight on the sacrum until the infant can consistently walk. Swings and walkers cause premature weight-bearing forces before the spine is prepared for this stress. F. H. Barge, D.C., an expert on scoliosis, states that these devices can cause infantile spinal instability. Such early misalignments and spinal stresses can cause or contribute to scoliosis formation in youngsters. Lendon H. Smith, M.D., says that the early use of walkers may lead to dyslexia, the reading difficulty, early in life.

In addition to range of motion stretching, several practices can help treat and prevent common ailments of the knees, shoulders, ankles, and wrists. If a moderate or severe strain or sprain of any joint has occurred — especially if significant swelling, bruising, or pain exists — consult your medical doctor or family chiropractor.

Mild injuries, however, can be helped with the "RICE" technique. The "R" stands for *rest,* "I" for *ice,* "C" for *compression,* and the "E" for *elevation.* Rest the involved area and avoid further stresses or weight bearing. Use ice for 20 minutes every one or two hours for the first 48 hours after the injury. Put a compression wrap around the area to reduce swelling and provide support. Elevate the area, especially with ankle injuries, to reduce swelling that can cause scar tissue formation. After the first 48 hours, start using heat for 20 minutes and begin gentle range of motion stretching. Then listen to your body; if a particular motion causes sharp pain, avoid that activity until the body heals.

Dropped metatarsals can be improved by rubbing the ball of the foot back and forth firmly over a golf ball for several minutes each day. This upward pressure on the foot helps restore alignment of the dropped bones. Wear properly fitting shoes with a good arch support, a firm heel counter, at least five eyelets per side, and sturdy "lasts" on the sides. Obtain a *ball fit* with the ball of your foot at the widest part of the shoe. Keep the heels of your shoes intact and even. Consult your podiatrist or chiropractor if significantly different wear patterns show on the heels or soles. Orthotics, arch supports, and shock resistant shoe inserts can help certain foot problems and persons who must stand on hard surfaces.

Minor wrist problems, such as carpal tunnel syndrome, can sometimes be self-treated. First, stop or minimize the actions that caused the problem in the first place. Wrist range of motion stretches and hand grip exercises strengthen associated muscles, tendons, and ligaments. *Door knob pulls* gently traction the wrist; grab a door knob or other immovable object with the symptomatic hand and stabilize this wrist with the other hand. Gently and slowly pull; this maneuver should not be painful and should be done only once or twice per day. Wrist braces provide extra stability until the area strengthens naturally.

Although I'm a proponent of self-help practices whenever possible, dangers exist when untrained persons try to manipulate their own bones or those of another person. "Cracking" your own back or neck could damage bones or stretch ligaments and cause bones to become more easily misaligned. When professional treatment is finally sought, the chiropractor's job is doubly difficult because of spinal instability and stretched ligaments.

ACTION STEPS

• Attend spinal care classes held by a local chiropractor.

• Get a spinal check-up for yourself and your family, especially if any of you have the symptoms discussed above.

• Remember that chiropractic adjustments are an essential part of vital health and proper body functioning. It's hard to appreciate the miracle of the creation when your back hurts or the mental impulses from the brain to tissue cells are blocked. Add chiropractic adjustments to your holistic health program and improve your total well-being.

• For additional information about chiropractic, read: *Chiropractic Speaks Out* and *Everything You Should Know About Chiropractic* by Chester Wilk, D.C.; *Chiropractors — Do They Help?* by Kelner, Hall, and Coulter; *The Confusion About Chiropractors* by Richard E. DeRoeck, D.C.; *So You're Thinking of Going to a Chiropractor* by Robert Dryburgh, D.C.

• See *Resources* for national chiropractic association addresses; call the state chiropractic examining board and associations for state and local information.

• Evaluate and select a D.C. based on the criteria discussed in the "Selecting A Good Chiropractor" section.

BALANCED NUTRITION

"Your choice of diet can influence your longterm health prospects more than any other action you might take."
— *U.S. Surgeon General*

"You are what you eat" is literally true since the body is constantly replacing itself. What we eat, breathe, and drink determines what kind of body we will have in the future. The human body is remarkably designed for long and vigorous life but requires proper nutrition to function optimally. *The Creator gave us everything we need for a long, vital, joyous, and productive life.* When we eat correctly — along with meeting other physical, mental, and spiritual needs — we can realize and act upon this truth. Maintain your bodily temple by giving it optimal nutrition.

Provide your body with healthy water, food, and air in appropriate amounts. Moderate your intake of fat, sugar, caffeine, alcohol, salt, processed, and junk foods. An old Shaker saying sums up the consequences of an unhealthy diet: "The whiter your bread, the sooner you're dead." Millions of years of evolution have shaped nutritional requirements; give your body what it needs. Until recently, there were no processed, artificial, or heavily sugared foods. The diet consisted of fruits, vegetables, beans, and whole grain foods with *occasional* sweets, meat, and dairy products.

The choice is yours. Do you *eat to live* or *live to eat*? Food *tastes* good for only a few seconds before swallowing. Once the food is swallowed, it directly improves or diminishes our health. Before eating, ask yourself: "Is this food going to increase or decrease my health?" Remember the key words *moderation, balance, and variety*; most of us can occasionally enjoy junk food, sweets, or fatty foods. The body can handle that when we eat a healthy diet most of the time. The body has an amazing ability to be healthy if we don't abuse it too much.

There is a direct connection between what you eat and the health status of your body. This is not a theory but a clearly established cause and effect relationship. *We literally become what we put into our bodies.* Do you want to be a strong, vital, and energetic person who eats healthy foods? Or do you want to be a sickly, tired, and depressed person who barely exists on a poor diet? The penalties for poor nutrition are serious, tragic, and preventable. Gary Todd, M.D., author of *Nutrition, Health, and Disease*, states that the average American diet is 45 percent fat, 30 percent white sugar, and much of the rest comes from white flour products. On this unhealthy fare, is it any wonder that body parts start collapsing around age 40 with a downhill route to the grave?

Is a healthy diet really that important? Surgeon General C. Everett Koop's report said Americans are eating their way to early graves with too much fat, salt, and alcohol. This report linked half of the top ten leading causes of death to diet, contributing to 1.5 million of the 2.1 million U.S. deaths last year. John McDougall, M.D., author of *The McDougall Plan* and *The McDougall Program*, states: "Research points clearly, consistently, and overwhelmingly to rich foods in the form of meats, dairy products, eggs, sugars, processed foods, and refined grains, and to lifestyle practices involving smoking, alcohol, caffeine, and physical inactivity as the major causes of death and disability."

Despite our high standard of living and the many billions of dollars spent each year on health care, most preventable diseases are still common. The 1988 National Research Council identified common dietary causes of heart disease, obesity, diabetes, cancer, and stroke. The culprits? Insufficient fiber, fruits, and vegetables with too much fat, red meat, salt, and sugar. The 1990 Dietary Guidelines for Americans recommend: Eat a variety of foods; maintain a healthy weight; choose a diet low in fat, saturated fat, and cholesterol; choose a diet with plenty of vegetables, fruits, and grain products; use sugars in moderation; use salt and sodium in moderation; if you drink alcoholic beverages, do so in moderation. The American Heart and Cancer Associations say virtually the same thing.

Yes, proper nutrition is vital for a long and healthy life. James Scala, Ph.D., author of *Making The Vitamin Connection*, decries: "The malnutrition of those who are just getting by, not quite sick enough to merit attention or relief, but caught in a self-perpetuating cycle of suboptimal mental and physical development that holds whole societies down for generation after generation. Even more scandalous — because it's totally unnecessary — is the malnutrition of those who are literally killing themselves with the diet of affluence. Like the malnutrition of poverty, the malnutrition of overprocessed food and overweight demands greater scrutiny from government, educational institutions, and industry."

This is not new information. In 1941, Surgeon General Dr. Thomas Parran said, "Many well-to-do Americans who can eat what they like are so badly fed as to be physically inferior and mentally dull."

Says Scala, "The average 'well-fed' man will die in his sixties or seventies (often earlier) *not* because it is the natural time for his body to fail him, but because he's been eating the wrong things all his life. With 60 percent of deaths related to what could be dietary management, it's obvious that life could be prolonged to achieve the full measure of an individual's lifespan, typically 90 to 100 years." Others cite the Biblical (Genesis 6:3) statement of 120 years as our birthright and normal lifespan. Humans should enjoy a long and vigorous life, then pass over quickly without prolonged suffering.

The Paleolithic Prescription: A Program of Diet and Exercise And A Design For Living by Eaton, Shostak, and Konner echoes these findings. Our early ancestors were robust and lived long unless they died of wounds or infection. Modern medicine has largely eliminated infectious diseases, but three-fourths of today's deaths are due to "diseases of civilization." Preagricultural humans ate less salt, less fat, less dairy products (only breast milk for infants), and less sugar and refined carbohydrates. They drank only water and used no tobacco or alcohol. Our current lifestyle habits, say the authors, are *mismatched* or discordant with our genetic inheritance. Poor health habits of excess salt, fat, sugar, cigarettes, alcohol, and inactivity *promote, foster,* and *accelerate* the diseases that prematurely kill most people today.

Many diseases and premature deaths are preventable largely through improved diet and other positive lifestyle changes. Don't wait until a serious, maybe fatal, disease occurs before thinking about your health. Start today by giving your body the healthy food it needs to reach and maintain optimal health. This is true prevention and an important part of 21st century health care.

Fortunately, it's getting easier to eat more healthfully thanks to salad bars, ethnic restaurants, food co-ops, health food stores and restaurants, and natural food sections in grocery stores. Remember that obtaining healthy food is a supply-and-demand situation; the more consumers buy healthy foods, the more available they will become. Demand accurate food labeling, minimal, and safe chemical use, and the healthiest products possible. *Read labels*, remembering that ingredients are listed in order of their quantity in the product. Don't be deceived by claims of "all natural" on the label. The FDA has no current guidelines for what constitutes "natural." Excessive fat, sugar, animal by-products, and salt are all "natural" but not necessarily desirable.

Educate yourself and start eating more healthfully and deliciously. Recommended cookbooks include those by the Diamonds and McDougalls; *American Wholefoods Cuisine* by the Golbecks; *The New Laurel's Kitchen* by Laurel Robertson et al; *Jane Brody's Good Food Book* and others by Jane Brody; *Whole Foods for the Whole Family, The La Leche League International Cookbook*; *The Moosewood Cookbook* by Mollie Katzen; and cookbooks by the American Heart and Cancer Associations.

Having discussed some general concepts about healthy eating, let's now explore specific recommendations.

Water

Water is an essential ingredient for life and makes up about 60 percent of our body. Being sufficiently *hydrated* or full of water is an important health practice. Drinking plenty of water helps the body stay healthy in many ways. Muscles, tendons, and ligaments are more flexible and less prone to injury when well-hydrated. Intervertebral discs, the cushions between vertebrae, are 90 percent water; sufficient hydration helps prevent premature disc degeneration.

Water is the best natural *laxative* and helps the bowels move more easily; persons who rely on chemical preparations would fare better with nature's laxative. Blood and other bodily fluids should be a certain viscosity or thickness. A well-hydrated person will have the correct blood viscosity, allowing circulation throughout the body with an *optimal blood pressure*. A higher blood pressure is required to pump thicker blood.

Gary Todd, M.D., maintains that water is "one of the best, and certainly the cheapest diuretic," aiding kidney removal of extra sodium. Drinking lots of water, especially 15 minutes or so before a meal, can help you lose weight; the water mass lends a feeling of fullness or satiety that helps you eat less. In general, the body functions best when well-hydrated and flushed with water. For all these reasons, drink plenty of water for optimal health.

How much is plenty? The standard recommendation is six to eight glasses daily. Another formula is two-thirds ounce of water per pound of body weight. For example, a 150-pound person should drink 100 ounces or about three quarts per day. Remember that urine should be odorless and have a light straw appearance; use these guidelines to monitor sufficient water intake.

If you eat and juice lots of raw, fresh fruits and vegetables each day, you are receiving the best source of organic water. Fruits and vegetables are about 90 percent water that has been filtered from the ground through the plant. Thus, persons who eat lots of fruits and vegetables may not need six to eight glasses of additional water.

If you feel thirsty, quench that need with water — not pop or other sugary drinks. Unfortunately, soda pop is the most common beverage consumed by Americans, and now this inferior product is being marketed worldwide. Can other liquids count toward total water intake? I agree with the viewpoint that there is no substitute for pure water. Only water is water. All other liquids — juice, coffee, tea, pop, and others — have dissolved particles in the water. To utilize water at the cellular level, these particles must be filtered by the liver, kidneys, and cells. Only pure water allows our cells to imbibe fluid easily for cellular functions.

Some persons don't drink water because of the taste and chemicals, but such water is better than no water at all. The body can filter some impurities out but can't healthfully exist over the years without sufficient water intake. Improved public water quality is needed, but there are several ways you can obtain healthier and more palatable water. Briefly boiling or leaving drinking water in an open container overnight decreases the chlorine content. Distilled water, certified spring water, and filtered water are other alternatives. Consult consumer surveys to evaluate the best distillation or filtration system for you.

Fat and Cholesterol

Excess dietary fat has been linked with suboptimal functioning and many diseases. Most health organizations recommend fat intakes of less than 30 percent of the total diet while some doctors recommend as little as ten percent. Excessive fat intake has been linked with increased heart disease, stroke, cancer, hypertension, diabetes, obesity, and other degenerative diseases. Excessive fat consumption prevents us from feeling and being vitally energetic and totally healthy. Obviously, there are many reasons for moderating your fat intake.

The American Dietetic Association (ADA) recommends decreasing fat intake while eating plenty of fruits, vegetables, and complex carbohydrates such as whole grain bread, pastas, cereals, grains and beans. The ADA also recommends: Eat moderate portions of lean meat, skinless poultry, fish, and nonfat or low-fat dairy products. Eat more unsaturated fats such as vegetable oils, nondairy spreads, and nuts. Avoid those foods high in saturated fat and cholesterol — fried and greasy foods containing or cooked in animal fat. Bake, broil, microwave, or poach meats instead of frying. Trim visible fat off meats and drain fat after browning. Use nonstick pans and vegetable sprays when sautéing.

Remember, *cholesterol is found only in animal products*. Referring to a group of vegetarians, William Castelli, M.D., director of the Framingham Heart Study states: "Their average blood cholesterol level is about 125, and we've never seen anyone at Framingham with a cholesterol level below 150 have a heart attack."

Excessive fats are primarily found in dairy products, meat, eggs, processed and fried foods. These are the foods you must monitor and moderate for a minimal fat intake. For example, a double cheeseburger, fries, and milkshake have *12 teaspoons of fat, five* in a fried chicken breast, and *seven* in a deep fried fish sandwich with fries.

Three simple tests will tell you and your doctor how closely you should watch your fat and cholesterol intake. The first is your *weight*, especially if you are more than 20 to 30 percent overweight for your height and body type. Your physician should have an updated height and desirable weight chart. *Percent body fat* can be easily measured with skin calipers. *The blood cholesterol level* should be less than 200 mg./dL. and certainly less than 240 mg./dL. HDL is the "good guy" component of the cholesterol complex that keeps our total cholesterol levels down. An HDL level above 35 and a LDL level below 130 mg./dL. is desirable. The American Heart Association encourages all persons over age 18 to have their cholesterol levels checked. The American Academy of Pediatrics recommends checking children if there is a family history of early heart attack or excess blood cholesterol.

Cholesterol is a necessary ingredient for every cell in the body; we couldn't survive without it. In fact, if we didn't eat any cholesterol at all, the body would manufacture it. In *Balanced Nutrition*, Stare, Olson, and Whelan discuss the "cholesterol scare" and how only 50 percent of the population can significantly change their cholesterol levels with the traditional "less than 30 percent" low-fat diet. Some persons have high blood cholesterol levels that require medication or very low-fat diets (less than ten percent) or both. R. James Barnard, UCLA Medical School professor and Pritikin Longevity Center consultant, found an average 23-percent cholesterol reduction among adults who ate no more than ten percent of daily calories in fat and who exercised regularly. The cholesterol level is only one risk factor and is most significant when other risk factors are present.

For more information on diet and cholesterol levels, read *The Pritikin Diet* by Nathan Pritikin, M.D., a pioneer in cholesterol and fat research. Having suffered coronary insufficiency in his early 40s, Pritikin followed his own advice with a high complex carbohydrate and low-fat diet. Decades later, his autopsy showed clear coronary arteries and a heart in remarkable condition.

I also recommend *The 8 Week Cholesterol Cure* by Robert Kowalski for a comprehensive coverage of this topic. Don't be misled by the title, however, since management of elevated cholesterol and other health risk factors is a lifetime concern.

Fiber

Fiber has been termed "the body's broom" because of its role in cleaning out the digestive system. Fiber or roughage is the nondigestible portion of food that aids regular bowel movements and absorbs substances like LDL cholesterol and bile salts. Fiber is abundant in fruits, vegetables, beans, whole grains and whole grain products. The old saying "an apple a day keeps the doctor away" is true primarily because of the fiber content of apples. Total fiber consumption has decreased 50 percent since 1910; not surprisingly, diseases associated with insufficient fiber have increased since then. *The Save Your Life Diet*, by David Reuben, M.D., provides an excellent overview on the role of fiber in health and disease.

Conditions associated with too *little* dietary fiber include heart disease, cancer, diverticular disease, obesity, appendicitis, adult onset diabetes, constipation, hemorrhoids, gall bladder disease, and varicose veins. More fiber, anyone? This is a literal example of "an ounce of prevention is worth a pound of cure." Dr. Reuben considers these common diseases to be *preventable* largely by obtaining sufficient fiber often removed during food processing.

Fiber helps prevent many diseases by removing body wastes quickly and eliminating the pressures of straining during a bowel movement. High-fiber foods help control weight because they take longer to chew and promote increased awareness of satiety. The sponge-like properties of fiber help moderate blood sugar levels. This is one reason why diabetes is rare in societies where fiber is a prominent part of the diet. In animal studies, fiber has also shown a neutralizing effect on dietary carcinogens. Clearly, there are many advantages of a high-fiber diet.

Ideally, we would obtain this fiber by eating lots of the

healthy foods listed above. The "fast-food approach" to obtaining sufficient fiber is to use wheat, oat, or rice *bran: two cents worth of bran* each day can literally save your life. Take the amount necessary for one or more daily bowel movements that are large in amount, low in odor, and passed easily without straining. For the average adult, this requires one teaspoon to one tablespoon three times per day. Half a teaspoon three times daily for children ages five-13 and half a teaspoon daily for those under five will usually suffice. Bran can be mixed with water, juice, dry or cooked cereal, yogurt, soups, applesauce, ground meat, and home-baked products. See Dr. Reuben's book for recipes with high fiber.

The Journal of the National Cancer Institute suggests that a diet rich in fiber reduces risk of colon cancer by 40 percent. Gary Todd, M.D., states: "It has been shown that breast cancer is forty times more likely to occur in women who are constipated, or are not regular." Furthermore, undeniable cardiovascular benefits have been found with a diet high (six servings per day) in fruits, vegetables, whole grain cereals and breads.

Caffeine

Caffeine — primarily found in coffee, tea, chocolate, and most soft drinks — stimulates or speeds up the nervous system. This temporarily increases alertness and energy, thus some person's preference for morning coffee. For those who enjoy caffeinated drinks, a moderate intake of two servings per day should present no physical problems for most individuals. However, you won't need a caffeine boost when you're healthy, rested, and eating fresh fruit for instant and natural energy in the morning.

Some persons crave and drink many cups of coffee or

soft drinks or both per day. This reliance on caffeine for an energy boost is like whipping a tired horse — eventually the body becomes exhausted and drops. Unless moderation and good health practices are followed, this artificial approach to increasing energy can ultimately be harmful.

A number of clinical correlations between caffeine intake and various disorders have been noted. Excess caffeine intake has been *associated* with fibrocystic breast lumps, increased bladder cancer, PMS, increased blood triglycerides, and urinary calcium loss that can contribute to calcium deficiency and osteoporosis. *The Wellness Encyclopedia* states: "Caffeine can produce trembling, nervousness, chronic muscle tension, irritability, throbbing headaches, disorientation, sluggishness, depression, and insomnia," but notes that such reactions are rare with *moderate* caffeine intake — about two cups per day. They state that no *conclusive* links exist between caffeine intake and heart disease, cancer, or fibrocystic breast disease.

Sugar

Moderating your intake of sugar and sweets is another key for total wellness. The National Research Council, USDA, American Heart and Cancer Associations, and 1990 Dietary Guidelines all agree: Eat less sugar and processed junk foods. Sugar is found in many products so read labels and choose those with little or no sugar. Look for words that indicate additional sugar content: *corn syrup, natural sweeteners, glucose, dextrose, corn sweeteners, barley malt, brown sugar, fructose, and grape sugar.* Some persons literally live on junk food and sweets, barely subsisting nutritionally on pop, pastries, and candy.

A ten-thousand-year-old Spanish painting shows a female getting honey from amidst a swarm of bees. Cravings for sweets may be age-old, but sugary products are much more easily obtainable now. Our taste buds sometimes overrule our common sense about good nutrition. Just a few generations ago, homemade sweets and baked goods were a rare and special treat. Today, machines and stores dispensing sugar-laden products abound. Our youngsters are bombarded with powerful advertisements that encourage them to eat more junk food and sugary products.

G. Harvey Anderson, Ph.D., states that major scientific reviews "have concluded that, other than for dental caries, there is no evidence that sugar intake at current consumption levels plays a role in the development of disease." The authors of *The Wellness Encyclopedia* state, "It [sugar] has been said to cause heart disease, obesity, cavities, hyperactivity in children, and diabetes . . . [but] it certainly isn't the dietary villain it has been portrayed as. At the same time, many of us consume more sugar than we really need because of its prevalence in many of the foods we eat, particularly processed foods and soft drinks."

Others take a more critical stance toward sugar and maintain that many physical and mental ills stem from an excessive intake. This viewpoint is described in *Body, Mind, and Sugar* by E. M. Abrahamson, M.D.; *Psycho-dietetics* by Cheraskin and Ringsdorf; *Sugar Blues* by William Dufty; *Low Blood Sugar and You* and *Psycho-Nutrition* by Carlton Fredericks, Ph.D.; and books by Dr. McDougall and the Diamonds.

We should minimize or moderate our intake of sugary junk foods for three basic reasons. First, sugar and excessively sweetened products are *empty calorie* foods; they have many calories but no or little inherent nutritional value.

A second reason for minimizing sugar consumption is the possible relationship with some disease states — for example, dental caries, behavior problems, obesity, and allergies. See *Nutrition and Physical Degeneration* by Dr. Weston Price; *Diet & Nutrition: A Holistic Approach* by Rudolph Ballentine, M.D.; or *Empty Harvest* by Dr. Bernard Jensen and Mark Anderson for photographic evidence of dental health before and after the introduction of sugar and refined products into different cultures. Before sugar was introduced, the teeth of native persons were white, straight, and cavity free. After a generation of sugar consumption, rotten and crooked teeth occurred routinely.

The Wellness Encyclopedia notes: "The jury is still out as to whether there's any consistent cause-and-effect relationship between sugar and behavior." Sugar is commonly listed as an allergy-producing food and thus may contribute to a myriad of physical and mental disorders. Lendon H. Smith, M.D., author of *Improving Your Child's Behavior Chemistry*, found that sugar and food sensitivities — notably dairy products but anything the child craves — were often responsible for hyperactive behavior.

The third problem with an excessive intake of sweets concerns *blood sugar levels* — the fuel our brain and body uses. Our brain is an amazing computer-like organ that controls and governs all the functions of the body. According to Denis Waitley, Ph.D., a computer the size of France and 100 stories high would be required to duplicate the capacities of the brain. The brain uses blood sugar (blood glucose) while conducting millions of functions simultaneously and coordinating many complex bodily interactions. Just as a race car requires a certain octane fuel for optimal performance, the brain works best at a certain blood glucose level.

Some persons experience an array of mental and physical symptoms that may be due to "subclinically" altered blood sugar levels. Dr. Abrahamson estimates that at least 20 percent of the population suffers from mild or borderline blood sugar handling problems. Others estimate true hypoglycemia to be rare. *Hypoglycemia* (too low blood sugar) and *hyperglycemia* (too high blood sugar) may cause many symptoms including: headache, depression, fatigue, anxiety, nervousness, inability to concentrate, loss of memory, dizziness, shakiness, and symptoms of neuroses or even psychoses. These symptoms may range from mild to severe; low blood sugar fluctuations may be especially apparent in between meals or if you skip a meal. The definitive test for blood sugar handling problems is the *six-hour glucose tolerance test.*

A healthy diet with a minimum of sweets aids optimal blood glucose levels and brain functioning. More frequent but smaller meals or healthy snacks may be needed to maintain a sufficient blood sugar level. Supplemental chromium at 200 mcg. per day has been found to help stabilize hypoglycemia. Sugary snacks are rapidly absorbed into the bloodstream and may quickly alter blood sugar levels, especially in sensitive individuals.

How many mental or physical problems are due, at least in part, to sugar-handling disorders? We don't yet know to what extent our well-being is affected by excess sugar. Julian Whitaker, M.D., says sugar can upset the immune system and white blood cell function. Can stable blood sugar levels and healthy living help reduce dependence on alcohol and drugs? Roger J. Williams, Ph.D., author of *Biochemical Individuality,* states, "It has been observed in many laboratories, including ours, that rats on high-quality diets voluntarily consume far less alcohol (also less sugar) than those on deficient diets."

For all these reasons, minimize sweets and refined sugar-containing junk foods. Allow yourself and your children a maximum of one sweet per day with two — like ice cream and cake — on special occasions. But be aware that a

12-ounce can of pop has nine teaspoons of sugar in it while a piece of chocolate cake with icing has 15. Don't routinely keep too many sweets in the home; this prevents temptation to kids and grown-ups alike. If you're a sugar-holic, go for a month without any sweets; then, once the habit of minimizing sweets is established, go back to an occasional sweet as a special treat. Cravings for sugary snacks will decrease as you retrain your body to enjoy healthy foods.

Reaching and Maintaining Proper Weight

Obese persons always suffer physically and sometimes emotionally for their weight imbalance. Less than five percent of obese persons suffer from a true glandular imbalance; the vast majority simply fail to maintain balance in three key areas. To maintain proper weight, one must eat *the right kinds of food, the correct amounts of food,* and have *sufficient exercise.* These behaviors must be practiced consistently as a lifestyle habit. Merely observing these practices for a short time will give just that — a short-term weight loss with rapid gains as soon as old habits are resumed.

Obesity increases the risk of cardiovascular disease, hypertension, diabetes, joint degeneration, gall bladder disease, stroke, and some cancers. Less disabling but much more common is the lack of energy, immobility, and excessive strain on all systems. Remember, we don't "pay the price" for poor health habits — like overeating — but enjoy the benefits of balanced and healthy living.

About 60 percent of adult Americans are overweight despite ample proof that excess fat intake and obesity are a threat to health and longevity. It has long been known that slightly underfed animals routinely outlive overfed counterparts. Benjamin Franklin said, "To lengthen thy life, lessen thy meals." Thinner animals also suffer fewer degenerative diseases, including autoimmune disorders. This relationship certainly holds true for the patients I've worked with; trimmer patients enjoy longer, healthier, and more energetic lives. How many healthy obese 80-year-olds have you met?

The rewards are great for those who successfully reach their proper weight. One of our staff members recently lost 100 pounds in one year. In addition to a physical transformation, she is like a new person in many other ways. She's more energetic, positive, and active. She has become more psychologically healthy with increased self-esteem and self-confidence. Imagine the relief in letting go of 100 pounds of excess baggage you've been carrying for years!

Again, the formula for maintaining proper weight is simple: *Eating moderate amounts of healthy and low-fat foods + sufficient exercise = healthy weight.* Your body has an optimal weight and following this formula consistently will help you reach and maintain that level. Why, then, do so many persons have trouble with excess weight? A comprehensive answer must address several factors: genetics, insufficient exercise, improper eating habits, and inner attitudes that contribute to overeating.

Research supports a *partial genetic basis* for obesity. Some learned behaviors are doubtless contributing to this correlation, but studies of adopted twins support genetic predisposition toward overweight. *Metabolic rates vary*; some persons have a "thrifty" metabolic rate that conserves energy and promotes obesity. The "setpoint theory" holds that each of us has a "set" body weight determined by genetic factors, the number of fat cells, and the metabolic rate. The setting isn't absolute and may vary ten to 20 pounds either way, but some persons have predispositions toward a heavier build. That's the bad news.

The *good news* is that within this preset genetic and metabolic range, change can occur with consistent effort. Your optimal weight can be reached and maintained by limiting dietary fat and increasing aerobic exercise. The authors of *Balanced Nutrition* state, "Diet and exercise can completely compensate for any genetic predisposition toward overweight and obesity, but it takes a considerable, constant effort over a lifetime."

Lack of exercise is a second factor in overweight. Recall that aerobic exercise increases the metabolic rate for 12 to 24 hours *after* exercise. Thus, exercise not only burns extra calories during the workout but continues to do so throughout the day. *Daily* exercise, then, serves to *effectively raise* the metabolic rate and helps offset slow metabolic tendencies.

Americans eat too much fat, meat, processed foods, salt, refined carbohydrates, sugar, and sugar-containing products. Since redundancy is the essence of learning, I'll repeat: fruits, vegetables, beans, whole grains and their products should predominate in our diets. Because of the low fat, high fiber, and water content in these healthy foods, it's difficult to eat enough to cause excess weight. John McDougall, M.D., points out, "Whole societies, past and present, have lived on starch-centered diets. Obesity is unknown in these people." If desired, eat minimal amounts of nuts, seeds, lean meats, eggs, and low or nonfat dairy products. Enjoy an occasional snack or sweet as a special treat. This is the dietary approach that will help you lose weight and reach optimal levels of health.

Inner attitudes can shape when, what, and how much we eat. Some claim they overeat when anxious, lonely, angry, or bored. But research suggests that most overeating is not due to psychological problems. The reasons "why" one overeats are secondary to the fact that we can change ourselves for the better. Obese persons may need to increase their willpower and select nonfood behavior alternatives. Visual imagery, goal setting, and support groups such as Overeaters Anonymous can also help.

You can't change your genetic inheritance, but you can change your diet, activity levels, and attitude. You can reach your proper weight if you truly desire to and consistently follow this approach. If you need a structured weight loss program, choose one that incorporates proper diet, exercise, and a behavior therapy support group. Develop healthy lifestyle changes versus going on a diet. Less than five percent of dieters lose 40 pounds and keep it off; nearly two-thirds of all dieters drop off their program within six weeks. Focus on improved eating and exercise habits that you can comfortably and consistently live with over the years.

The Diamonds, in *Fit for Life I and II*, make this point and provide information on lifestyle changes that work. *Balanced Nutrition* contains an excellent section on obesity and weight reduction strategies. Other resources for weight control information include the June, 1989, *Psychology Today* reprint "New Diet Mindset" and *The LEARN Program for Weight Control* by Kelly D. Brownell, Ph.D. The acronym "LEARN" stands for the various aspects of this program: Lifestyle, Exercise, Attitudes, Relationships, and Nutrition.

Weight loss is like climbing a mountain or training for a marathon — daily consistent and persistent efforts are eventually rewarded. Weight loss may temporarily *plateau*; stay at it and don't get discouraged. Quick weight losses usually come back quickly; think in terms of slow, steady, and lasting weight loss — one or two pounds per week. 3500 calories equal one pound; thus, reducing your intake by only 500 calories per day results in a pound lost each week. That's 52 pounds per year! The average recommendation for calorie intake to lose weight is 1500 per day for males and 1200 for females. Dr. Brownell doesn't recommend a less than 1000 calories per day unless under strict medical supervision.

Various *behavioral techniques* can also aid one's weight loss program. One simple way is to avoid overeating at any one time. The stomach is a muscular sac that stretches or shrinks over time depending on how much we put into it. Satiety or a feeling of fullness is reached when the stomach is full; make eating moderate portions easier by never stretching your stomach with excess food or drink.

Chew your food slowly and completely to allow the stomach to fully realize what has been eaten. If we rapidly wolf down our food, we bypass some of the mechanisms that monitor satiety and signal fullness. Satiety takes about 20 minutes after the meal to fully register, so if you still feel hungry or want a sweet after a healthy meal, wait and that feeling will often pass.

Other behavioral approaches involve plate and utensil loading techniques. *Don't overfill your plate*; load your fork and spoon with small bites. *Put your utensil down in between bites* to promote longer chewing and more awareness of how fast and how much you are eating. At home, eat your meals in the same place, thus limiting the number of locations associated with eating. Finally, you don't have to clean your plate. Try not to waste food, but it's better to feed the pets or compost pile than add extra calories when you're full.

Breastfeeding

Mother's breast milk is nature's perfect food for human babies. Breast milk was the *only* food fed babies throughout human history until quite recently. The last few generations have erred by overrelying on infant formulas and cow's milk. Fortunately, more grandparents are encouraging their grandchildren to get back to this natural approach. More and more doctors are encouraging breastfeeding again, having seen the health advantages firsthand. Even formula advertisements emphasize the superiority of breastfeeding, marketing formula as an alternative for mothers who can't or don't want to nurse.

Only a relatively few mothers must rely on formula feeding because they can't successfully breastfeed. Otherwise, there is no substitute for the real thing. Mother's breast milk is loaded with the right kinds of nutrients and antibodies for a growing baby's needs. Nutritionally, it is far superior to any product that any lab can concoct; some formulas contain excess fat and are deficient in important vitamins and minerals. Dr. Gary Todd comments on "how severely deficient the infant formulas" are and considers formula usage a contributing factor to our high infant mortality rate.

Psychologically, the comfort and closeness that result from breastfeeding are priceless. *Bonding* occurs between mother and child as they share intimate time together. When a mother nurses, her maternal hormones remain elevated, giving her the extra caring and empathy needed during trying times. Artificial, plant, or animal products cannot replace the superior nutritional and psychological advantages inherent in breastfeeding.

The "La Leche League" (LLL) is an international group of mothers and health professionals who promote breastfeeding; they provide support, information, and counseling during difficult times. My wife was a La Leche League leader and nursed our two daughters. I felt privileged to be part of a family where breastfeeding was natural and optimally health producing. Read *The Womanly Art of Breastfeeding*, the LLL manual. Most communities have a LLL group; ask your doctor or midwife for further information and see *Resources* for the national address.

There are a few basic problems that can occur for the mother who is not prepared beforehand. *Nipple confusion* occurs when the infant is given a bottle as well as breastfed. Bottles deliver liquid easily and require less sucking by the infant. Breastfeeding requires more suction; this may frustrate and confuse a baby who intermittently receives a bottle. Giving a nursing baby a pacifier meets needs for sucking that can interfere with breastfeeding. *Feed on demand*; advice about feeding on schedule to prevent spoiling the baby is outdated. Techniques exist to prevent and treat sore nipples. Finally, a mechanical "breast pump" allows working mothers to continue feeding only breast milk.

Breastfeeding is, in many ways, the *easiest* way to feed babies. The milk is always ready, fresh, and warm; with practice, a mother can discretely nurse anywhere. Nursing is especially a bargain for fathers: no heating formula, cleaning bottles, finding the nipples, or bottle feeding at 3:00 a.m. As for cost, breastfeeding is free. Calculate how much those cases of formula cost over the years and don't forget to figure in gas and time for trips to the grocery. Breast milk is the perfect and only food most babies will need until about six months of age.

Breastfed babies are less likely to become overweight children since the optimal nutrition causes less fat cell development. The amount and size of fat globules in mother's breast milk — not cow's milk — are designed for human babies. Leaving a child with a bottle of juice, formula, or cow's milk can cause early tooth decay; this isn't a concern with breastfeeding. The strenuous sucking that accompanies nursing also develops strong jaw muscles and beautiful facial structure. Orthodontic research shows that breastfeeding may prevent or decrease malocclusion and the need for braces later in life.

John McDougall, M.D., encourages breastfeeding and

warns against feeding cow's milk to babies. He states that cow's milk is suspected of contributing to adult food allergies, obesity, Hodgkin's disease, ulcerative colitis, coronary artery disease, and multiple sclerosis. Cow's milk fed to infants has also been associated with increased susceptibility to infection, decreased immune system competence, increased mortality, gastroenteritis, leukemia, and sudden infant death syndrome. He recommends breastfeeding exclusively until six to eight months and for 25 to 50 percent of the diet until two years of age. For those few mothers who can't breastfeed, he recommends surrogate mothers, a breast milk bank, soy-based formulas, commercial formulas made from denatured animal protein, or goat's milk with cow's milk as the least desirable alternative.

As we increasingly realize the miraculous design and intelligence of the human body, more persons will use this marvelous approach to infant care. The many advantages of breastfeeding by far outweigh the few conveniences of formula.

Nutrition for Youngsters

Introduce fresh fruits, vegetables, whole grains and their products when infants become ready for solid foods. *Baby food strainers* that prepare instant and healthy baby food are available at health food or department stores. Try bananas, apples, kiwi, pears, melon, and other fruits that your baby likes. Lightly steam fresh vegetables, run through the strainer, and watch your baby go after broccoli, carrots, cauliflower, potatoes, and other vegetables. You can be assured this food is fresh and relatively unadulterated.

Baby food manufacturers are obviously trying hard to improve their products. They've omitted much of the sugar, salt, fillers, and other additives that your baby does not need. Commercially produced baby foods will do in a pinch, but there is no substitute for fresh and whole foods. High-temperature cooking, freezing, canning, and storage cause fresh food to lose nutrients. Vitamins, enzymes, and other micronutrients necessary for vital health are often sensitive to temperature, light, and storage times. That's why we should eat at least 50 percent of our diet as fresh, raw, or lightly steamed or stir-fried. Don't our babies deserve the same excellent nutritional upbringing?

Ellyn Satter, R.D., A.C.S.W., author of *Child of Mine: Feeding with Love and Good Sense*, says to avoid forcing children to eat healthy foods; teach them by example and offer healthy alternatives. Keep only healthy food and nutritious snacks in the house so all family members aren't tempted by unhealthy junk foods. In time, children will come around and enjoy the taste of healthy and nutritious foods. Remember that their stomachs are small and their metabolisms high. Children usually function better with more frequent but smaller meals and snacks throughout the day.

As your children grow older, monitor their intake of sweets and junk food. At breakfast, start their day with fresh fruit as it contains fiber, water, vitamins, minerals, and quick energy. Then serve whole grain cereals with no or minimal sugar instead of overprocessed sugary brands. Oatmeal, hot wheat cereals, eggs, whole grain breads, and whole grain flour pancakes are other good ways to start the day nutritionally. Honey and maple syrup are natural sweeteners and okay for most persons when used sparingly and occasionally.

Satter emphasizes controlling children's exposure to TV programs that have commercials for unhealthy junk foods. By age 18, the average child has watched 15,000 hours of TV versus only 13,000 hours in school. Those TV hours include 350,000 commercials, 55 percent of which are about food, including 65 percent for heavily sugared products. James Scala, Ph.D., comments: "An analysis of advertising expenditures related to food shows that approximately 86 percent is devoted to foods that contain nothing more than empty calories. . . . Examples include soft drinks, candies, and cereals that provide little more than simple sugar. In fact, the advertising expenditures for two major soft drinks exceed the government budget (in USDA) devoted to nutrition education."

The American Academy of Pediatrics recently has said that food ads aimed at children should be banned from television because they promote profit-making rather than healthful eating. Excessive TV viewing has been linked with inactivity and consumption of unhealthy foods, contributing to childhood obesity and high cholesterol levels. Proper weight should be a concern for children as 70 percent of obese children ages ten to 14 will become obese adults. Obesity among American children appears to be increasing; the physical and psychological effects of childhood obesity could have serious future health implications.

Monitor your child's school lunches and send a nutritious home-packed lunch whenever necessary — which is most of the time. I recently joined my daughter for lunch at school and was appalled at the menu: salami and baloney on white bread, a pickle, potato chips, applesauce, milk, and a cookie. Any living or fresh foods in that meal? This is a typical SAD (Standard American Diet) meal with too much fat, sugar, and processed foods and no fresh fruits or vegetables. Parents, work with the PTA and food service manager to encourage healthier lunches with less fat, sugar, and salt while increasing fiber, fresh fruits, vegetables, and whole grain foods.

Dr. Scala states, "From the moment of conception,

every human being is endowed with a physiological potential as to physical growth, mental development, resistance to disease, and longevity. . . . More than any other influence, the quality of a person's diet, especially in the prenatal months and early childhood, determines whether his potential will be achieved — and perhaps extended beyond the limits we accept today — or permanently stifled."

Let's give our children the best possible nutritional start. Remember, lifelong exuberant health has much to do with what we eat. I know that busy schedules make it difficult to attend to nutritional details. In the short and longterm, however, the extra effort is well worth healthier, happier, and more well-behaved children. Make good nutrition for the entire family a high priority. Please take the time to educate yourself about this topic and start your children off on the right foot.

Vitamin and Mineral Supplementation

Nutritional experts vary greatly in their recommendations for vitamin supplements. Many feel that supplementation is unnecessary when a healthy and balanced diet is followed. Others recommend supplements because of soil deterioration, occasional inadequate diet, special needs, environmental pollution, food processing, and storage practices. But beware, vitamins are powerful substances in minute quantities, and hypervitaminosis can occur. Supplement distributors have a vested interest in selling these products; hence, be cautious about their claims and recommendations.

Vitamin use can lend a false sense of security if people think they can eat a poor diet as long as they take vitamins. One patient asked me about taking vitamin B-15 because "someone told me it helps you feel better." This patient smokes two packs of cigarettes per day, subsists on junk food, doesn't exercise, and is obese. She resists improving her health through lifestyle changes but hopes for a pill that will magically improve her well-being.

All experts agree: *There is no substitute for a consistently healthy diet.* There is further widespread agreement that *megadose* supplementation is not needed for healthy individuals. However, there are a number of experts who believe *minimal or moderate supplementation* is prudent. Drs. Kunin, Cheraskin, Ringsdorf, Scala, Mandell, Ballentine, Pauling, Whitaker, Smith, Hoffer, Passwater, Bland, Hawking, Cott, and others suggest there is a *therapeutic* and *preventive* role for supplementation. Eaton et al state: "Modest supplementation is unlikely to be harmful, and given our often imperfect nutritional diligence, may insure against lapses."

A very healthy person with a *consistently optimal* diet probably doesn't need supplementation, but how many of us fall into this category? Yes, the RDA's can be met via diet but how often are they? For example, folic acid is most abundant in liver, kale, asparagus, beet greens, wheat bran, endive, spinach, and turnips. When is the last time you ate any of these foods? The idea of *nutritional insurance* through *balanced and moderate* supplementation makes sense to me. Given conflicting opinions, I'll play it safe with a multivitamin plus minerals and 500 mg. of vitamin C.

If you have an existing illness, educate yourself about *therapeutic supplementation* and discuss these issues with your doctors. Read the books written by Gary Todd, M.D.; Julian Whitaker, M.D.; Kurt Donsbach, D.C.; and Lendon Smith, M.D. See *Resources* for programs with intensive nutritional supplementation approaches. Two-time Nobel Prize winner and nonagenarian Linus Pauling, Ph.D., author of *How to Live Longer and Feel Better,* advocates *optimal nutrition*, that is, using vitamin and mineral supplements to treat disease and aid vital health. Of vitamin C, Pauling says: "Every cancer patient ought to be taking high doses of vitamin C. And all other people should be taking vitamin C, too. . . . High-dose vitamin C potentiates the immune system in many different ways."

Nutritional prevention and treatment of disease holds great hope but is not widely understood or agreed upon. But remember, we have the most advanced nutritional balancing system *inside our bodies;* if you treat your body right, supplementation concerns are secondary.

"Orthodox" versus "Alternative" Nutritional Approaches

As we've discussed, nutritional experts vary greatly in their recommendations. Using the labels "orthodox" and "alternative" is an oversimplified but useful approach for characterizing these varying viewpoints. Alternative approaches include less widely accepted views that may gain orthodox approval in the future. However, how many persons suffer needlessly and die prematurely while alternative approaches wait for orthodox approval? How can we best use the advantages of alternative *and* more orthodox approaches while minimizing the disadvantages of both? Most treatment regimes have shortcomings but also real strengths; it is time for educational, research, and clinical emphases to consider the entire spectrum of health care approaches.

If a serious disease has already manifested, adherence to a very healthy diet is of the utmost importance. Becoming healthy requires lots of energy; healthy food provides the body with optimal energy while requiring minimal energy output for digestion and elimination of wastes. Alternative nutritional approaches for "incurable diseases" are discussed in: books already cited by Todd, McDougall, Smith, Whitaker, Pauling, and the Diamonds; *Rebuilding Health with High Enzyme Living Foods* by Ann Wigmore, N.D., founder of the Hippocrates Institutes; *Food Healing for Man* and others by Bernard Jensen, D.C., Ph.D.; *Wholistic Cancer Therapy* and other books by Kurt Donsbach, D.C., Ph.D.; *A Cancer Therapy — Results of 50 Cases* by Max Gerson, M.D., and *HEALING — The Gerson Journal; The Healthview Newsletter;* and books by N. W. Walker, D.Sc., John Christopher, N.D., M.H., and Dr. Herbert M. Shelton.

These approaches are not new, kooky, or radical. For example, Dr. Albert Schweitzer in 1959 said, "I see in Dr. Max Gerson one of the most eminent geniuses in medical history." Gerson testified before a U.S. Senate Subcommittee in 1946, providing proof of many nutritionally recovered "incurable" cases that included cancer, tuberculosis, multiple sclerosis, heart disease, diabetes, arthritis, allergies, and other autoimmune disorders.

Most of the techniques and centers used by the above practitioners have not been widely accepted by the orthodox medical community. However, the medical track record on most incurable conditions is often sorely lacking. Work with doctors who are willing to combine the best of conventional *and* alternative approaches.

The nutritional approaches we've discussed thus far are excellent and sufficient for many persons. Some alternative approaches, however, may benefit those with special sensitivities, health problems, or those striving to reach an optimal quantity and quality of life. These approaches include food combining, juicing, sprouting, increasing raw and living foods, occasional fasting, and using minimal animal products.

Vegetarianism

The advantages of a starch-centered (vegetarian) diet and the disadvantages of excessively rich foods (animal products) were known thousands of years ago. The vegetarian movement was founded in sixth century B.C. by Pythagoras to foster hygiene and increase kinship between humans and animals. Since then, much of the world's population has eaten a largely vegetarian diet. Read Genesis 1:29-30 and Daniel 1:8-16 for ancient descriptions of the benefits of a simpler vegetarian diet.

There is clear evidence that *excessive* consumption of animal products provides more fat and protein than we need. In the past few generations, many persons in western cultures have eaten meat two or three times per day; add to this a generous supply of high-fat dairy products, and it's no wonder so many adults are overweight and dying prematurely from coronary heart disease. Excessive animal product intake has been linked with an increased incidence of cancer, diabetes, obesity, kidney disease, autoimmune disorders, allergies, and gastro-intestinal disorders. John McDougall, M.D., states: "The abundance of medical and nutritional research carried out over the past eighty years . . . consistently endorses the use of a starch-centered diet and blames rich foods (meat, dairy products, eggs, and oils) for most of our ills."

Vegetarians show lower rates of all these diseases as evidenced, for example, in studies of Seventh Day Adventists. A University of Kentucky Medical School study investigated the effects of a low-fat, high-carbohydrate, and high-fiber diet on diabetes. Within a few weeks on this diet, 75 percent of adult onset diabetics on insulin and 75 to 90 percent on pills were freed of their need for medication. Even juvenile onset diabetics can reduce their insulin requirements by about 30 percent and stabilize their blood sugar levels on such a nutritional program.

Studies of Third World countries reveal that, despite a meager intake of meat and dairy products, *osteoporosis is scarce*. This appears to be due to four factors. Exposure to sunlight increases vitamin D stores that aid calcium utilization. Significant weight-bearing exercise and work increases bone density. Nondairy calcium sources from bone, clay, and minerals are used. Finally, excessive protein consumption increases calcium loss through the kidneys. Thus, those persons with minimal meat and dairy intake need only about 200 to 400 mg. of calcium to meet bodily requirements. Eating *less* meat and dairy products, then, is one way to prevent osteoporosis.

Says Dr. Castelli, "We tend to scoff at vegetarians . . . but the fact is, they're doing much better than we are." Adds Bonnie Liebman, M.S., R.D., "The meat industry may insist on denying the health benefits of vegetarian diets, but research on heart disease, cancer, high blood pressure, diabetes, and obesity argues otherwise. The research shows that vegetarians are lowering their risks of developing a host of the most serious diseases confronting our society."

Meat products can contain growth hormone, antibiotic, and other chemical residues. In 1981, 40 percent of all the antibiotics used in this country were put into livestock feed. In 1979, the Government Accounting Office reported that 14 percent of meat and poultry "contained illegal and potentially harmful residues of animal drugs, pesticides, or contaminants. Many of these substances are known to cause or are suspected of causing cancer, birth defects, or other toxic effects." An additional carcinogenic effect occurs when meats are cooked over high heat, especially when grilled over charcoal. A one-pound steak grilled over charcoal can contain as much carcinogenic benzopyrene as 600 cigarettes. Fried and broiled meats *initiate* and high-fat diets *promote* cancer of the breast, prostate, and colon.

Humans don't need nearly the protein intake we once believed to be necessary. Our daily needs are more than adequately met by 3½ ounces of meat per day or by meatless protein alternatives. Until a few generations ago, meat was more scarce and was used primarily as a condiment for flavoring. Meals revolved more around vegetables and grains with meat as a side dish. Recently this habit was reversed, with meat predominating in the meal while vegetables and grains became side dishes. This dietary reversal resulted in less fiber, more fat, and more difficult-to-digest protein.

The Physicians Committee for Responsible Medicine says Americans would be healthier if they avoided meat as the main course. It wants the Agriculture Department to change daily recommended food groups *from* meat, dairy, fruits and vegetables, and bread and cereals *to* whole grains, vegetables, fruits, and legumes. The committee says meat should be eaten more as a garnish or flavoring than the centerpiece of the meal. Gussow and Thomas, authors of *The Nutrition Debate*, state, "You don't have to eat meat to be healthy . . . most of the world's protein comes from plants, not animals, and many of the world's peoples live on diets with few, or no, animal products."

Francis Moore Lappe, in her books *Diet for a Small Planet* and *World Hunger, Twelve Myths*, discusses advantages of meatless meals and provides nonmeat recipes. Some grains, for example amaranth, contain more usable protein than meat and offer hope for feeding the world's starving persons. *Complimentary protein*, that is, two foods eaten together like beans and rice, can provide all the amino acids required for a healthy human existence. Other combinations include legumes and grains, for example, peanut butter sandwiches or lentils cooked with rice or millet. Recent studies suggest that eating these combination foods during the same *day* is sufficient for bodily amino acid needs.

ADA guidelines note that vegetarian diets are used "by any person who chooses to omit animal products for religious preferences, health concerns, environmental considerations, humanitarian issues, or economic or political reasons." Vegan diets that completely exclude animal products "can be healthy, but special care must be taken to ensure adequacy of vitamin D, iron, and vitamin B-12. If intake of these nutrients is not sufficient to meet the Recommended Daily Allowance, supplements may be necessary."

There is a *changing human awareness or consciousness* that is also contributing to less meat consumption. As Lappe describes, we could *feed the world* with the grains that we currently feed our livestock. One pound of beef production requires 16 pounds of grain and soybeans plus 2500 gallons of water. In Mexico, average beef yields are 22 pounds versus 13,000 pounds of shelled corn and 10,000 pounds of root and vegetable crops per hectare per year. The world's productive acreage could be used more efficiently to feed all the people of the world. A human being, usually a child, starves to death on our planet every 45 seconds! Meanwhile, many in Western cultures are dying from eating too much meat and fat.

Our awareness of *animal rights* — how we treat and use various animals — is growing. Animals can help us in many ways, but we should utilize their gifts without making them suffer in the process. We can treat them humanely as they assist us with food, by-products, labor, and research. An animal raised in an unhealthy and unnatural environment cannot be truly healthy. For example, veal raised in dark and narrow pens and chickens raised in wire cages are subjected to cruel and unhealthy practices. I'm not advocating cessation of meat eating or hunting; I am encouraging humane treatment, raising, and slaying of animals.

Our ancestors ate predominately plant foods. Anthropologist Marvin Harris, Ph.D., says that chimpanzees, our closest animal relative, eat meat about twice a month. Eaton, Shostak, and Konner state that hominoids (great apes) ate primarily fruit with vegetables second and meat a distant third. Plant foods were the mainstay of the hunting and gathering era diet while agricultural societies ate 90 percent plant foods with only secondary meat intakes. Their meat was much lower in saturated fat than today's beef.

There is additional biological evidence that humans are designed for meatless or minimal meat diets. Our teeth consist of incisors for biting and molars for grinding, a dentition pattern similar to other *herbivores* or plant eaters. Our hands are best suited for gathering and picking while our digestive enzymes are designed for *carbohydrate* breakdown. Our intestines are like that of nonmeat-eaters for processing plant foods that digest with relative ease. Meat-eating species can eliminate the by-products of meat quickly whereas our intestines may take days. This may account for the gas, foul-smelling bowel movements, and increased bowel cancer incidence in those who eat too much meat and too few plant foods.

Due to thousands of years of evolutionary habits, persons from Western cultures may require *minimal animal products* for normal metabolic functioning. The amount required, however, is much less than most of us usually eat. George Bernard Shaw recognized the need for occasional meat nutrients and ate liver once a month or so, calling it his "medicine." Dr. Bernard Jensen holds that vegetarianism is an *ideal* for which most persons are not ready. *Gradually* reduce the amount of meat you eat and use only healthy and low-fat meat sources. Eating meat only occasionally —

the way past generations did and many cultures still do —
may be the best solution for most persons.

Living Foods

Fresh and raw *living foods* contain the most nutritive
value and the optimal amounts of vitamins, minerals, proteins, carbohydrates, fat, chlorophyll, enzymes, and water.
The Creator and millions of years of evolution have pro-
vided optimal foods for our health and energy needs. In the
past few decades, humans have acquired the ability to perform some amazing technological feats with food. But we're
like kids with a new chemistry set; we don't quite yet know
how to or when to use our new powers. *"New, improved and
fortified" is not always better.* The nutritive value of food
decreases when we change, cook, freeze, process, store, or
otherwise tamper with it. In general, "If Nature made it,
eat it; if humans have made or fooled with it, beware."

I'm not advocating an all raw and fresh diet although
this provides vast healing advantages during certain illnesses. We all could benefit, however, by increasing the
amount of living foods in our diet. Dieticians have long
counseled: fresh is best, frozen next, and canned is the least
nutritious choice. Canned vegetables lose about 60 percent
of their original nutritional value whereas frozen foods lose
about 20 percent.

A recent Paul Harvey radio commentary best exempli-
fies what I mean by living and vital foods. A sunken ship
was recently examined after several hundred years of sub-
merged isolation. Among the ballast were various plant
seeds that actually sprouted and grew when given the right
conditions of soil, water, and sunlight. After hundreds of
years, those seeds still contained sufficient life-giving properties to grow healthy plants. There is a spark of life and

creative energy *in all living things*. This *life force* has long been recognized by other cultures — the Chinese called it chi, the people of India, prana. Whatever the name, there is a vital force or energy — part of God if you will — in all living things. These special properties are less abundant and may even be absent in dead and decaying matter.

Dr. John Christopher — naturopathic physician, master herbalist, and pioneer of natural health practices — suggested the following technique for determining whether a food is *living* or *dead*. Bury some of the food in the ground, water it, and give it sufficient sunlight. Living foods, containing seeds and nuts that can sprout will bear fruit and provide more living food. Food that has been destroyed or devitalized will be a putrid pile of garbage after some time in the ground. Try planting fruits, vegetables, *raw* nuts, whole grains, or seeds and watch the *miracle of new growth and life*. Conversely, plant a hamburger, doughnut, candy, or any processed item — but don't hold your breath while waiting for something to grow.

As my wife bought our usual ton of fruits and vegetables, the supermarket clerk hesitantly asked, "You always buy so much produce; do you own some monkeys?" I take this as a compliment; our closest animal relatives are much healthier than we — mostly due to better diet and exercise habits. The gorilla has legendary strength, lives over 100 years, keeps its teeth and hair, and maintains an active sex life — all on a diet consisting primarily of fruits, vegetables, nuts, and plants.

Make *living foods* at least 50 percent of your diet each day in the form of fresh and raw fruits, vegetables, sprouted grains, nuts, and seeds. This requires more time than picking up "junk food" from a drive-through, but the extra effort is well worth it now and over the years. *The healthiest way of living is not always the quickest or most convenient.* If we don't obtain essential nutrients in healthy and natural foods, the body may resort to cravings or overeating in an attempt to meet its needs. Remember, eat lots of fresh and raw foods as close to the natural state as possible and you'll enjoy many benefits.

Food-Combining Principles

Proper food-combining principles have long been endorsed by health care practitioners and natural hygiene experts. Read *Fit for Life* by the Diamonds for a complete discussion of this topic. Some skepticism regarding alternative approaches can be healthy but not if important information is discarded just because it's different. Improper food combining can contribute to fatigue, gas, obesity, constipation, diarrhea, indigestion, ulcers, hemorrhoids, bowel cancer, diverticular disease, irritable bowel syndrome, and suboptimal nutrition. Americans spend three billion dollars annually on antacids and other indigestion relief preparations. It's time for openness to some different — although not really new at all — approaches to what, how, and when we eat.

Certain foods don't digest well together. Proteins and starches require different types of digestive juices for optimal breakdown. For simplicity of explanation, let's discuss foods in four basic groups: proteins, starches, vegetables, and fruits. Proteins, requiring an *acidic* pH, include all flesh foods, dairy products, eggs, nuts, and seeds. Vegetables can digest equally well with either an acidic or *alkaline* pH. Fruits are very easily and quickly digested, but should be eaten alone. Starches, requiring an alkaline pH, include everything else: breads, grains, cooked potatoes, beans, legumes, pasta, baked goods and pastries.

Digestive juices cannot be both acidic and alkaline

simultaneously; mixing these two extremes of pH levels results in a neutral pH that isn't useful for either protein or starch digestion. This is why *starches and proteins should, for the most part, be eaten during separate meals.* Eating starch and protein — like meat and potatoes — together makes efficient digestion impossible. The result is incomplete digestion with partial *putrefaction* of proteins and *fermentation* of starches.

Again, moderation is the key. I'm not suggesting that you never mix proteins and starches again. That would preclude such common fare as pizza, any meat sandwich, grilled cheese, and peanut butter sandwiches. I do recommend that you apply these approaches *most* of the time, especially when eating meat.

A properly combined meal should leave the stomach completely within three hours. An improperly combined meal may remain in the stomach for six or more hours; that's why we feel bloated after an improperly combined meal. Thus, it is better to designate your meals either *protein* or *starch* and combine one of those categories with vegetables. For example, eat a large salad and steamed vegetables with your meat for a protein meal. At a starch meal, eat anything except protein or fruit; for example, spaghetti with meatless sauce, bread, and vegetables.

How much disease and premature aging is due to a chronically poor diet? Peter Kelder, in *Fountain of Youth,* discusses the importance of properly combining foods. Mixing starches and proteins, he writes, ". . . not only can cause gas and immediate physical distress. Over time, it also contributes to a shortened life span, and a lesser quality of life." Trying to digest and dispose of an improperly combined meal requires extra energy output by the body, thus the after meal fatigue and general low energy levels of the average person. Remember that our amazing body can slog along and make the best of a bad situation for many years before succumbing to suboptimal and negative lifestyle factors. Or you can be trim, vital, and energetic now and for many years to come. How important is it to eat the way you've always eaten?

Natural Hygiene theory describes the digestive tract as having three main cycles: *food intake, assimilation, and elimination.* The time for eating most of our food is noon to 8:00 p.m. From 8:00 p.m. to 4:00 a.m., the digestive energies of our body are focused on assimilation; that is, digestion and utilization of foods. From 4:00 a.m. to 12:00 noon is a time for relative rest of the digestive system as the body eliminates wastes. Coordinating these cycles with appropriate eating habits allows optimal digestion, nutrient utilization, and waste removal.

Eating fruit properly is another important factor in food combining. Simply put: "Eat fruit alone or leave it alone." Fruit is predigested and, when eaten alone, exits from the stomach into the small intestine within 20 minutes. If we eat fruit with or immediately after other foods, the fruit is blocked from its normal and rapid course of digestion. Fruit sugars then begin fermenting and increase bacterial growth, gas production, and other improper digestion by-products. This is why some persons think they can't eat fruit; indigestion symptoms after improper combining are nature's way of complaining. Fruit is a perfect food when eaten alone or 20 minutes before other food. Since properly combined meals take about three hours to leave the stomach, wait that long after lunch or dinner before eating fruit again.

Whenever possible, I recommend eating nothing but fruit until noon. At the least, start your morning with fruit and wait 20 minutes before eating other breakfast foods. The relatively rapid absorption of fruit sugars can be a special boost for persons with hypoglycemia or low energy in the morning. Fruit is full of nutrients, organic water, and fiber and thus nourishes, hydrates, and cleanses the digestive system. Eating only fruit until noon allows the body to focus on elimination processes. Eat a piece of fruit every hour or so as needed; you'll be amazed at the energy and lightness you'll feel.

If — after a properly combined lunch — you are hungry by late afternoon, eat a snack of fruit that digests and raises your energy level quickly. Eat dinner before 8:00 p.m. so the body can then focus on digestion, absorption, and delivery of nutrients. A fruit snack three hours or more after dinner won't interfere with the optimal functioning of the digestive system and will satisfy those late night cravings. Habitual night-time eating should be avoided except for an occasional treat of popcorn or other healthy snack.

The last food-combining recommendation is: *Avoid drinking fluids with your meals*. Gastric juices of a specific pH and strength aid optimal digestion times and efficiency. If we drink fluids during our meal, we *dilute* or weaken the digestive juices. Thus, it is better to drink something about ten minutes before a meal to wet your whistle; after a meal, wait 30 to 60 minutes before drinking. This allows proper digestive juice action on the food and starts the digestive process off on the right foot.

To *recap*, food-combining, recognized as an integral part of a healthy lifestyle for many centuries, includes:

• Eat fruit alone and wait about 20 minutes afterwards before eating other foods. Wait about three hours after a properly combined meal before eating fruit again.
• Don't drink fluids *during* your meal.
• Stop eating (except for fruit) after 8:00 p.m.
• Follow, most of the time and especially with meat,

food-combining principles of eating protein and starch at different meals.

The degree to which you will want to follow these principles depends on your particular state of health and desire to be vitally healthy. Following these guidelines is also an easy way to lose pounds and reach your optimal weight. Try this approach for a month or two and see how much better you feel and count the pounds you've lost. You can always go back to your "regular" way of eating, but chances are good you won't after implementing these naturally right approaches.

Juicing and Sprouting

Juicing and sprouting are simple and delicious ways to obtain lots of living, fresh, and raw foods. Fruit and vegetable juicers cost $75 to $200; citrus juicers about $25. A juicer separates the liquids from fruits and vegetables while depositing the pulp separately. Most juices purchased in grocery stores are *made from concentrate*, are acidic, and have gone through processing that kills many nutrients. Juicing at home provides a truly fresh product that provides many vitamins, minerals, enzymes, and other health-producing nutrients. Drink within 15 minutes after juicing for optimal enzyme activity. Regular intake of these nutrients helps your body reach full and vibrant functioning.

Experiment and make your own vegetable juice combinations. I like a mixture of four carrots, six stalks of celery, 1/2 green pepper, 1/2 cucumber, a small tomato, and 1/8 section of a small beet. It tastes great and is surprisingly sweet. Melons, apples, oranges, grapefruit, pineapple, and grapes are my favorite fruits to juice. *Sip* juices to prevent too rapid a fluctuation of blood sugar levels. "Chew" or *flush* in the mouth for a few seconds before swallowing to mix the juice with saliva for optimal digestion. A mild yellow-orange coloration on the hands and feet is due to beta-carotene storage and is *not* a sign of vitamin A hypervitaminosis.

Sprouting is also an excellent way to obtain living foods and only a widemouthed jar, nylon net or cheesecloth, and a rubber band are needed. Obtain *raw* nuts, seeds, and grains from your health food or grocery store. If they have been cooked, roasted, or otherwise exposed to high temperatures, they will not sprout; this is the acid test of whether something is living or dead. Sprouts are an excellent source of vitamins, minerals, enzymes, and chlorophyll.

Put two tablespoons of seeds or grains in a jar and wash them well with water. Drain and thoroughly shake out the water through the screen over the jar's opening. Put the jar on its side after shaking the seeds around so they are distributed on the lower side. Cover the jar with a handtowel to speed sprout growth. Rinse and drain the seeds at least twice each day, draining off all the water and not letting them dry out.

When the sprouts reach the size you like best, put them in full sunlight until tiny green leaves appear. Tightly cover and store in the refrigerator, eating while fresh — within three to four days. Use these tasty sprouts in your salads, stir-fry vegetables, Mexican, oriental, and other dishes. Alfalfa, mung bean, lentil sprouts, and wheat berries are most commonly used, but you can sprout any living nut, seed, or grain.

Juicing and sprouting will become common practices as more of us realize the importance of raw and fresh *living foods. You can't make something out of nothing*; we can't support a living system optimally for long on dead and devitalized foods. For additional information about sprouting and juicing, read Dr. N. W. Walker's *Guide to Diet and Salad* and the Diamonds' *Fit for Life.*

Chemicals and Foods

Many persons are concerned about the cumulative effects of chemicals in our food, air, water, and various products. Do we have the technology or sufficient test of time to assess the longterm effects of herbicide, pesticide, antibiotic, and growth hormone use? The EPA says pesticide residues are the third highest cause of environmentally induced cancers, behind cigarettes and radon. The USDA states, "Crop loss due to insect damage has doubled since WW II, from seven percent to 14 percent. Insecticide use is up over ten times in that same period." Insecticide-resistant insects thrive while these chemicals may cumulatively harm animals and humans. Consumer and legislative pressure should be exerted to ensure that we receive the safest possible foods.

From another perspective, there is a certain amount of "chemical phobia" today, especially among health enthusiasts. That is, some persons view *any level of all chemicals* to be harmful; this is going too far the other way. Some well-meaning consumers get upset about minuscule amounts of chemicals expressed in "parts per billion" or "parts per trillion." One part per trillion is equivalent to one drop of water in 36 Olympic-size swimming pools.

The authors of *Balanced Nutrition* state that 500 pounds of Alar-treated apples *consumed in one meal* would be necessary to cause significant chemical contamination. They conclude that our food does not contain "levels of harmful residues of pesticides, hormones, and other toxic or carcinogenic chemicals sufficient to cause illness."

Bruce Ames, a biochemist who devised carcinogenic

testing, maintains that many foods contain natural carcinogens in concentrations 1000 times greater than those sprayed with Alar. FDA toxicologist Robert Scheuplein reported that 99 percent of cancer deaths caused by carcinogens in food are due to *naturally occurring carcinogens* — food molds, well-cooked protein, and items with fermentation by-products. So let's avoid knee-jerk reactions that involve more fear than facts. It would be great if we could feed the world without using any chemicals, but it's just not currently feasible. So we must balance the real with the ideal.

Certainly, improvements should be made in present agricultural practices with goals for increased organic farming and reduced chemical amounts and strengths. "Ecologically-sound" agricultural practices that aid the farmer, consumer, and environment should be increasingly implemented. Nonpetroleum-based alternative fertilizers are available now; these include seaweed fertilizer, rock dust or stone meal, colloidal soft rock phosphate, and composted organic matter.

Let's not create an "us versus them" scenario with the farmers or agribusiness as the bad guys who secretly pile on toxic chemicals without a thought toward the consumer. D. Mark Hegsted, Ph.D., states: "Some of the activist-consumer representatives have not been very helpful. By overemphasizing and overstating the risks associated with the American diet, demanding excessive controls, suggesting that we are all being deliberately poisoned, and such, they have often polarized the situation to the point that the voices of moderation become lost in the argument." Let's all work together from as many angles as possible to decrease chemical exposures while keeping these issues in proper perspective.

Free Radical Pathology

Free radical pathology, first described by Dr. Denham Harman over 30 years ago, is theorized to be a significant cause of several *degenerative diseases and premature aging.* Highly reactive molecules called "free radicals" can damage cells by altering genetic material, enzymes, or cellular structures. This can result in blood vessel disease, clot formation, development of malignancies, early aging changes, and a host of other common ailments. Free radical production is *increased* by cigarette smoke, pollution, lack of oxygen, radiation, toxic metals, chlorinated water, food additives, alcohol, and fats and oils — especially the unsaturated varieties.

Read *Nutrition, Health, and Disease* by Gary Todd, M.D., for a more thorough discussion of the significance and treatment of free radical pathology. Basically, we can *minimize free radical formation* with exercise, a healthy diet, and avoiding offending substances. More specifically:

• Increase your intake of anti-oxidants: vitamins C and E, beta-carotene, niacin, riboflavin, zinc, selenium, chromium, manganese and other nutrients primarily found in fresh fruits and vegetables.

• Avoid cigarette smoke, dusts, pollutants, and fumes.

• Minimize radiation from all sources including diagnostic X-rays.

• Exercise and practice deep breathing to increase oxygen in the body.

• Minimize aluminum toxicity by avoiding antacids, antiperspirants, cosmetics, and food additives that contain aluminum.

• Moderate or avoid alcohol.

• Minimize use of all oils and fats including unsatur-

ated fats from plant sources.
- Maintain a trim body weight.
- Slow cook, boil, or stew meat versus frying or grilling.
- Minimize foods fried in any type of fat, especially those cooked in reused oils.

Food Allergies

This is another important topic that I briefly bring to your attention for further study. We each vary in our sensitivities or tolerances to the outer environment. Robert Forman, Ph.D., author of *How To Control Your Allergies* reports some 20 million allergy sufferers who need serious attention. C. Everett Koop's *1988 Surgeon General Report on Nutrition and Health* stated: "Qualified health professionals should advise persons with food allergies and intolerances on the diagnosis of these conditions and on diets that exclude foods and food substances that induce symptoms."

Allergies can be an appropriate and normal response by the body. Runny sinuses, coughing, draining ears, and diarrhea are attempts to flush out the offending substances. For example, it's normal for the sinuses to drain for awhile after inhaling fumes, smoke, grass particles, or other irritants. Thus, some "allergy" symptoms make sense and are *adaptive* for the body; these reactions remove unwanted substances and give us feedback. The body is rejecting these substances, creating symptoms that tell you to use them less or not at all. Allergies, then, may not be a disease so much as a signal from the body that *something needs to be changed.*

Dr. Forman recommends the *clinical ecologist* specialty of allergists as these doctors consider the potential role of food allergies in physical and mental afflictions. See *Resources* for the national address of clinical ecologists in the U.S. "Clinical ecology," says Dr. Forman, "emphasizes identifying and minimizing the effect of environmental exposures that can be harmful to a person rather than just using drugs to alter the body processes or to cover up symptoms . . . using drugs to trick the body into an absence of symptoms creates more serious problems in the long run."

Genetic factors may predispose one toward experiencing food reactions but these can be minimized by consistent adherence to the factors that can be changed. *Modifiable factors* include:

* Improving general health, immune system strength, and acid-base balance of the body.
* Chiropractic adjustments can help correct allergies by restoring proper nerve supply and assisting normal body and immune system functioning.
* Change *how* you eat. Chew food thoroughly and eat slowly; eat a wide variety of foods; create a *pleasant meal environment*; and *don't overeat*. Incomplete digestion can result in *foreign-appearing substances* in the body and bloodstream; the body may then treat certain foods as recurring foreign invaders and develop allergic responses.
* Change *what* you eat. The most common allergy-producing foods are milk and dairy products, sugar, eggs, yeast, wheat, corn, and soy beans. Start with these first, using the food rotation and elimination techniques recommended by Dr. Forman, Dr. McDougall in *The McDougall Plan*, and *Is This Your Child?* by Doris Rapp, M.D. Marshall Mandell, M.D., author of *Allergy, The Unrecognized Cause of Physical, Mental, and Psycho-somatic Illness* says that overprocessed foods containing sugar and white flour are also common triggers. Canned foods offend more often than

fresh sources.

    • If home evaluation and treatment doesn't help, consult a clinical ecologist or physician who works with dietary changes — not just drugs to mask symptoms.

One common cause of allergies, *overconsumption* of dairy products, can be easily remedied by reducing one's intake. Some persons, however, cannot tolerate even moderate amounts of milk and milk products. About 70 percent of the world's population are lactose intolerant, that is, they do not have sufficient *lactase*, an enzyme that helps break down milk sugar. Incomplete digestion of dairy products may result in foreign substances that elicit an autoimmune response. And why shouldn't humans be deficient in the enzyme needed to digest cow's milk? Humans are the only animals that drink a different animal's milk and drink any milk past infancy. *Even cows* — except for baby calves — don't drink cow's milk.

Doctors have long known to suspect dairy products as a common cause of allergic symptoms. Dr. Walker states, "Milk is the most mucus forming food . . . and from infancy to senility it is the most insidious cause of colds, flu, bronchial troubles, asthma, hay fever, pneumonia, tuberculosis, and sinus trouble." Dr. McDougall cites many cases in the medical literature that suggest excessive dairy product consumption contributes to the development of cancer, heart disease, arthritis, allergies, autoimmune diseases, kidney stones, ulcerative colitis, and multiple sclerosis.

Child care expert Dr. Benjamin Spock and other medical doctors are questioning the nutritional value of milk and warn of possible harm to some children. The Johns Hopkins University director of pediatrics said that milk is often contaminated with traces of antibiotics, can cause allergies and digestive problems, and has been linked to juvenile diabetes. He stated that other foods — such as kale, broccoli, or fish — provide more calcium without the fat in milk.

I don't advocate abstaining from all dairy products although that wouldn't be a bad idea for anyone suffering from the diseases listed above. I do recommend — as do the National Research Council and the American Heart and Cancer Associations — a reduced intake of dairy foods with an emphasis on low or nonfat products. This approach supplies all the calcium needed. Gary Todd, M.D., states that eating a high complex carbohydrate diet with a 500 mg. calcium supplement is sufficient for pregnant, lactating, and postmenopausal females.

Fasting

A modified fast — drinking only fruit and vegetable juices for one or more days — has several useful applications. Fasting can help a person lose weight, cleanse the body, rest the digestive system, and assist health restorative mechanisms. During an impending or existing illness, fasting aids healing processes by allowing the body to cleanse itself of accumulated wastes and mucous. Children, especially, will listen to innate messages when ill and not eat or eat less.

For those with arthritic conditions, cancers, and other autoimmune disorders, I recommend consuming only fresh and raw fruit and vegetable juices at least one day per week. This modified fast can also aid weight loss by curbing the overeating cycle and helping the stomach shrink. For those who "don't like the taste of healthy foods," go without any solid food for a day or two and see how good steamed vegetables and whole grain rice tastes. Prolonged and total fasting — drinking only water — is not something I recommend for most persons because of blood sugar problems, low electrolytes, and other potentially serious reactions. I have fasted totally and didn't feel good during or afterwards.

The most important lesson I gained from total fasting was a profound appreciation for the food that we take for granted. Hunger is an intense physical and mental experience; some of our fellow human beings have no choice as they starve to death. Go without a few meals and better realize the horror of starvation. Let's eat more healthfully, simply, and in smaller amounts for total health and wellness. You may want to fast for preventive, weight loss, therapeutic, or other reasons. And let's do all we can to stop world hunger *now*.

Why Eat Healthfully?

Many of us have been living in a dingy basement, thinking that is all life holds in store for us. Adopt an optimal lifestyle and realize that you own a glorious mansion above that basement. We were born to experience life abundantly while enjoying, helping, and loving one another. In so doing, we remember and serve God. When we work on ourselves and become the very best we can be, the world's problems will solve themselves. Jesus taught us the Lord's Prayer, saying, "Thy kingdom come, on earth as it is in heaven." He wouldn't have told us to pray or reach for that ideal if it weren't possible.

I mention all this in a chapter on nutrition because I am so convinced that our total wellness is significantly affected by what we put into our bodies. Too many of us drudge through the day, virtual slaves to the poor lifestyle we live. It's hard to appreciate the miracle of life within and all around when we're ill or only marginally existing. Apply healthy habits of good nutrition, exercise, a healthy nervous system, rest, self-actualization, and spiritual growth. Then enjoy the total health and happiness that naturally flow from being a balanced human being. Please eat and live more healthfully so you can unleash the special person you really are.

Giving Thanks

Blessing the food before eating is an age-old and transcultural custom. A word of prayer "honors" the food and gives thanks for the life in it. All parts of the creation are alive, endowed with a part of the Creator within. When we realize this, eating becomes a sacred process of alchemy just as Teddy in J. D. Salinger's *Nine Stories* realized that his sister's drinking milk was like pouring God into God. The animal or plant that we consume gives its life force or energy for our sustenance. That life form becomes incorporated into our being and thus lives on. Give thanks for the food that sustains life and allows you to become the best possible you more and more each day.

Nutritional Summary

This is admittedly a lot of information; don't try to change everything at once or too quickly. Change habits at your own pace so your positive changes become permanent, not an overnight fad. Be patient as your body starts changing within; you may experience a cleansing crisis — like a cold — as your body "cleans house." You may temporarily feel a need for more rest as your body uses its new energy to heal.

If you eat the way I've described *most* of the time, your diet will be excellent. Allow yourself occasional treats and digressions while, for the most part, eating healthy foods. Your body will thank you for it with an increased quantity and quality of life.

ACTION STEPS

Follow the recommendations that nearly all nutritional authorities agree upon: eat predominately fresh fruits, vegetables, beans, legumes, nuts, seeds, whole grains and their products. Use moderate lean meats and low or nonfat dairy products, if desired. Limit fat, salt, sugar, caffeine, and alcohol.

- Drink six to eight glasses of water per day.
- Follow proper food-combining principles most of the time.
- Eat lots of raw and fresh foods. Only *living foods* can support high levels of energy and health over the years. Juice, sprout, and eat salads, steamed vegetables, and stir-fry vegetable dishes.
- Maintain your proper weight.
- Breastfeed babies and remember that good nutrition is especially important during the childhood years.

Remember, "you are what you eat." A number of common and fatal diseases are the direct result of a chronically poor diet. Prevent disease and experience a "heaven on earth" state of well-being by giving your body the food it needs. Satchel Paige said, "If I knew I would need this body so long, I would have taken better care of it much sooner." Over the last 20 years, I have worked with many dying and seriously ill patients. Every one of them wished they could do it over again — they would eat more healthfully, exercise, and take better care of themselves.

For most of you, *it's not too late.* I urge you to take the time and energy to educate yourself and change your lifestyle habits. Please don't wait until it's too late; *start today* to transform yourself into the vital, healthy, and energetic person you can be.

SELF-ACTUALIZATION AND STRESS MANAGEMENT

"As a man thinketh in his heart, so shall he be . . ."
— Jesus
"Our life is what our thoughts make it."
— Marcus Aurelius

We each have the potential to become self-actualized and to successfully manage stress. What happens *to* us isn't nearly so important as what happens *inside* us. Abraham Maslow, Ph.D., in *Motivation and Personality*, described the hierarchy of needs; these include survival, safety, acceptance by others, self-esteem, and self-actualization. All are important and ideally lead to loftier pursuits like service to others and meaningful relationships. Without higher goals to strive for, we find ourselves wondering with Peggy Lee, "Is that all there is?"

How we perceive and react to stresses we encounter is crucial for our well-being. We don't have to become burnt-out or overly stressed by the events around us. A certain amount of stress is good and desirable; "eustress" is that amount that challenges us and makes life interesting. The only people who have no stress are six foot under. Since we each have various stresses in life, the key is to effectively *manage* it. Changes, problems, challenges, and other "stressors" all contribute to the fascinating fabric of life. We grow most when we must reach within and discover the depths of our potentials.

One key to handling the stresses of life is to maintain an *enlightened perspective*. The word perspective has a root meaning "to look through" and is defined as "the relationship of the parts of a whole, regarded from a particular standpoint or point in time." As you journey down life's path, focus on the *big picture* and try to see past trivial or temporary obstacles. Winston Churchill had inscribed on his tomb "And this too shall pass." A hopeful perspective and strong faith help us keep going when unexpected turns develop along the road of life.

Ancient Chinese and Egyptian symbols depict *crisis* and *opportunity* as two sides of the same coin. Developing a positive and faith-filled perspective allows us to grow and learn from crises or "bad" events in life. *Our challenge is to find the opportunity in each crisis.* Napoleon Hill stated, "Every adversity, every failure and every heartache carries with it the Seed of an equivalent or a greater Benefit." Some of life's most important lessons *seem* scary because they are different or require inner growth and adaptation; they are important because they teach us who we are and what we can be. An *inner* optimistic outlook helps us thrive and reach our goals despite *outer* events.

A story from India reminds us to keep a hopeful perspective and *live in the present moment*. A wise man was walking through the jungle, enjoying the sights and sounds of nature when suddenly a fierce Bengal tiger began chasing him. The yogi ran until he came to the edge of a cliff; with no other options available, he climbed down a thin grapevine. Looking down, he noticed sharp rocks and certain death below. Looking up, he saw the tiger waiting patiently and the grapevine starting to unravel. But just a moment before the vine broke, he noticed some wild strawberries growing on the cliff wall. He gently plucked one and ate it, thinking it was perhaps the best strawberry he had ever tasted . . .

Earl Nightengale taught that we become what we most fervently think about; *our life reflects our most dominant inner thoughts.* The wise man from India had reached an inner perspective from which he enjoyed each present moment. He knew that fully living each present moment is the key to true happiness and inner peace. He knew that there is no sense in worrying about events over which we have no control. He knew that life is eternal and that we are One with the Creator. He maintained an inner calm and enlightened perspective — the perfect way to enjoy passing over to the other side.

We have much more control over our life, health, and happiness than most of us realize. At least 50 percent of physical illnesses are psychogenic — that is, involve the mind and thus are amenable to mental and spiritual healing. Bernie Siegel, M.D., writes, "The extent to which we love ourselves determines whether we eat right, get enough sleep, smoke, wear seat belts, exercise, and so on. Each of these choices is a statement of how much we care about living. These decisions control about 90 percent of the factors that determine our state of health."

When Jesus asked the man who had been lame for 38 years, "Wilt thou be made whole?", He was asking, "Do you really want to be healed?" An old saying gets to the heart of the matter: "One of the minor pleasures in life is to be slightly ill." Eric Butterworth, in *Discover The Power Within You*, says, "Man does not always have the courage to face up to the challenges of life. He escapes in many directions, one of which may be into sickness." Dr. Leslie Weatherhead, minister and psychologist, states, "Disease is often — if unconsciously — an escape mechanism." Dr. Hutschnecker, in *The Will to Live,* points out that sickness often comes from a will to be sick, and that health must be preceded by a will to be well, a will to live, and a will to overcome. He says that sickness is often a subconscious attempt to escape from life.

I know life seems hard at times. The chapters of *Balanced Living* on psychological and spiritual wellness will plant seeds that will aid your optimal *inner growth.* Remember that you always have the *power to choose* your outlook and perspective. It's like the partial glass of water question; it's half full to the optimist and half empty to the pessimist. You can perceive life differently — more optimistically — than you might have in the past. Your inner peace, health, and personal success depend, to a large extent, on your positive outlook and will to thrive.

Consider the story of identical twins who were interviewed by psychologists; one twin was an optimist and the other was a pessimist. The pessimist was put in a large room full of the latest toys and games. The optimist was put in a room full of horse manure. Hours later, the two were interviewed.

The pessimist was depressed; "I'm bored," he bemoaned, "and what about all the children in the world who don't have any toys when I have so many." To their surprise, the optimist was whistling and singing as he energetically shoveled through the manure. "With all the horse crap in here," he shouted enthusiastically, "there has to be a pony somewhere!"

Which way do you look at life? John Milton said, "The mind is its own place, and in itself, can make a Heaven of Hell, a Hell of Heav'n." *How we think literally creates the world we live in.* For example, research has documented the powers of optimism in preventing and treating disease. Cancer, heart disease, diabetes, multiple sclerosis, autoimmune disorders, and immunity levels have responded favorably to laughter, group therapy, positive thinking, visual imagery, and a zest for life. Improving your mental outlook can add years to your life and, more importantly, make those years more like heaven on earth.

Yes, our attitudes, beliefs, and expectations can drastically shape our lives and accomplishments. An amazing example is Roger Bannister's four-minute mile, a feat long considered impossible until he achieved it. Within the next year, 37 others reached this milestone as did 300 more in the following years. What changed? Not the bone structure, biomechanics, or cardiovascular conditioning. Human beliefs and expectations changed — *runners believed it could be done* and thus, it could. What other records in all areas of life will be broken as we increasingly realize the limitless nature of our potentials?

The way you view and react to the world can be *reprogramed* more positively. We have the power to choose right thoughts and actions so we can enjoy success in every realm of life. William James, Ph.D., M.D., LL.D., Litt.D., and author of *The Varieties of Religious Experience*, stated, "The greatest discovery of my generation is that human beings can alter their lives by altering their attitudes of mind." Emerson said, "Great men are they who see that spiritual is stronger than any material force, that thoughts rule the world." Since we utilize only one to ten percent of our brain's capacities, the sky's the limit.

Aldous Huxley, in *Doors of Perception*, said that the brain is like a powerful receiver/transmitter that is capable of picking up and sending many more and distant signals than we previously imagined. All the solutions to the world's problems are stored inside, just waiting to be discovered and unleashed. With all of us working together and utilizing our true potentials, life will be vastly better. That's the up side. The bad news is we have a lot of work to do. One need only read the papers and watch the news to be reminded that we haven't reached utopia yet.

I'm aware of all the blatant problems on Earth. But I believe *more strongly* in our individual and collective potentials for change and improvement. *The vast majority of human beings are good people*; a few rotten apples get most the headlines and skew our perception of humanity. Most people are trying hard and doing their best. Persons who have walked around the world or across the country consistently report: less than one percent of people are bad; the rest are very loving and caring.

I see positive changes slowly but surely shaping things for the better. This *psychology of optimism* allows me to work faithfully and expectantly each day. I believe that, with God's help, we are capable of surmounting life's challenges. Look at the amazing changes in the world recently: the fall of communism, arms reductions, and increasing environmental awareness.

As enough of us improve ourselves, the world will similarly be transformed. A young boy kept interrupting his father who was trying to read the Sunday paper. Thinking he would keep his son occupied, the father tore a large picture of the world from the paper. He tore it into many pieces and told his son to reassemble them. He was surprised at how quickly his son correctly completed the task. "It was easy, Dad!" the youngster shared, "You see, there was a picture of a person on the other side. When I put the person together, the world came together!"

Don't worry so much about all the problems of the world. Trust in God to take care of the big picture. Start today by improving yourself and becoming the best you possibly can. Then brighten the corner where you are. Your changes will affect others and the domino effect will carry it from there.

Ken Keyes, in *The Hundredth Monkey*, described an inspiring phenomena of change. Scientists had observed the eating habits of monkeys for decades; when a sweet potato fell in the sand, it would not be eaten because of its gritty covering. One monkey, however, discovered that the sand-covered food could be washed off, rendering it edible again. Learning occurred and an increasing number of monkeys began washing their potatoes. When a *sufficient number* of monkeys formed this habit, all the monkeys on the island soon began washing their potatoes. The most amazing part of the story is that, *simultaneously*, monkeys *on other islands* began washing their food.

This phenomena of *synchronicity* has been observed with inventions such as the wireless transmitter and airplane. The time was ripe for these ideas, and they were received at the same time through receptive individuals. *Similarly, the time is ripe for positive and optimal changes on Earth.* Our survival as a species depends on our ability to learn from past mistakes and start working together. Beyond survival issues, the time has come for all persons to realize their full potentials and enjoy utopia living.

Alexander Graham Bell spoke of the *conquering force* within each of us: "What this power is, I cannot say. All I know is that it exists . . . and it becomes available only when you are in that state of mind in which you know exactly what you want . . . and are fully determined not to quit until you get it." Get in touch with that part of you, identify your dreams and goals, and get to work.

The movie *Awakenings* showed patients with severe parkinsonism who enjoyed a miraculous release from their frozen postures. For the first time in decades, patients could talk, walk, dance, and really live. One person spoke of feeling "resurrected" and said, "If people felt as good as I did, nobody would make wars." Our hearts were touched by the new life they experienced and saddened when they returned to their prior catatonic existences. But how much more exciting that *most of us have now and every day to enjoy life fully.* And how sad that so many take life for granted and don't take advantage of the splendor around us. *Let's all awaken* and appreciate the many blessings we have.

Psychological balance includes realizing and using our inner potentials for the betterment of ourselves and our world. Common stresses of life become relatively trivial when we realize our higher purpose and potentials. We become *empowered* when we have a lofty goal and work toward it. Victor Frankl, M.D., psychiatrist and survivor of Nazi death camps, illustrates this in his book *Man's Search for Meaning.* He observed persons who survived — and even thrived and grew — despite oppressive conditions that killed others. These survivors had a higher goal, *a reason to live,* that motivated and energized them.

Imagine how wonderful life will be as more and more persons become enlightened and express their full physical, mental, and spiritual powers. Centering on higher goals helps us better cope with the ups and downs of life. Carlos Castenada, in *The Teachings of Don Juan* and other books, encourages us to be *impeccable warriors* as we go through life. The Apostle Paul spoke of his daily battles and fighting "the good fight." These analogies speak to the challenge of doing our best as we pursue our calling in life.

Make improving your state of mind a high priority. You've heard it said that when you pass on, "you can't take it with you." Your state of mind or level of consciousness is one exception to this rule. Your inner vibratory state or level of "the kingdom within" is what's left when the body dies; thus, wise persons tend to their inner mental and spiritual growth. We each have enjoyed positive and harmonious states of mind, moments or hours when we felt one with God and the universe. We've all had those peak experiences when we felt we could soar like eagles.

You can eventually have this good feeling and higher consciousness *all* of the time; for now, try for *most* of the time. It takes practice and dedication to reach this goal; don't get discouraged if the process seems confusing or difficult. Trust your inner wisdom, take one day at a time, and make your changes slowly and naturally. Positive efforts performed consistently eventually achieve powerful changes for the better. Consider the alternate outcomes depicted in *Back to the Future* after Michael J. Fox made just a few positive suggestions and changes in his future parent's lives. As a result, there were remarkable differences in his parents and the entire family.

None of us are too old to change; the saying about "old dogs and new tricks" is a myth. Let's discuss changes we can make to become more self-actualized and successfully manage the stresses of life.

Techniques For Stress Management and Self-Actualization

• A *daily "to do"* list is a simple but effective way of being more organized and productive. Keep a piece of paper on or near you throughout the day. Write daily tasks that need doing and cross them off when the job is completed; this keeps you on task and gives you immediate positive reinforcement. On the other side of your paper, jot down new insights as they arise spontaneously throughout the day. Don't entrust million-dollar ideas to memory. At the end of the day, copy these ideas over to a notebook for future reference and utilization. Transfer incompleted tasks and new information to your home calendar or future "to do" lists.

   • Have *two calendars* to aid planning and follow-up. Use a home calendar with sufficiently large spaces to schedule events. Also keep a small calendar with you through the day for scheduling when you're away from home.

   • Use a *pro and con list* whenever faced with a difficult decision. List the pros and cons — advantages and disadvantages — of each decision and notice which list is longer. Prioritize the items and see which ones are really most important to you. Viewing your options in black and white often clarifies decision making.

   • *Manage your time effectively.* Prevent procrastination; prioritize tasks and reward yourself at regular intervals for accomplishments. Break down large jobs into smaller tasks; Lucy Hedrick, author of *Five Days to an Organized Life*, describes this approach as "eating an elephant one bite at a time." Avoid excessive daydreaming, indecision, and impulsiveness — the classic time wasters. Schedule time for work and play — including exercise, family, and leisure periods. "Creative laziness" recharges your battery and allows the unconscious to produce constructive ideas.

   Learn to say "no." Start early in the day and get a jump on the day's activities. Do the hard jobs first and reduce nonessential activities. Whenever possible, delegate jobs that others can do just as well. With a little effort, self-discipline, and organization, time management can greatly enhance your efficiency and free up valuable time.

   • Proper *legal preparation* decreases personal stress by reducing the number of worries about "what if . . ." Keep your *will* updated and make a *living will* to ensure your wishes are followed should you enter a hopelessly vegetative coma. Married couples may want a *durable power of attorney* agreement to minimize legal and financial hardships should one spouse become incapable of managing his or her own affairs. Consult your attorney about these simple but important documents.

• *Reduce financial stresses* by living within your means; don't try to "keep up with the Jones'." Develop a budget and follow it. Invest in a longterm savings plan — a small but regular monthly savings adds up to surprisingly large amounts over the years. Brian Tracy, author of *Getting Rich in America*, points out that saving $100 per month from age 21 to 65 at ten percent interest yields more than one million dollars.

Read *The Richest Man in Babylon* by George S. Clason, then start saving ten percent and giving ten percent to your favorite causes or charities. Learn to live on 80 percent of your income and watch the other 20 percent come back to you with interest. Make an extra house payment once per year or take a 15-year home mortgage to substantially reduce total home interest payments. Use credit cards for emergencies only and avoid those high interest payments. For cars and other major purchases, consider buying good and used versus new. The fleeting ego boost from having new is not worth the accompanying depreciation.

• Remember the stress reduction benefits of daily *stretching* and regular *exercise*. Even ten minutes of brisk walking can significantly reduce anxiety and muscular tension.

• A *hot bath* is another effective way to combat cumulative stress and muscular tension. Hot showers may feel good but don't allow sufficient time for the heat to reach deep muscles. Soak the neck, upper traps and shoulders where tension often accumulates. Allow yourself the luxury of soaking a couple times per week for 30 minutes. While soaking, you can read, listen to music, or just relax. When available, hot tubs or whirlpools are even better.

• Both therapeutic *massage and reflexology treatments* have tremendous relaxing benefits. German doctors prescribe a series of ten massage treatments as readily as a bottle of tranquilizers. Massage breaks the muscle tension-anxiety cycle quickly, effectively, and without side effects.

• Practice *thought reprograming*, also known as "pattern interruption," with the help of a rubber band around your wrist. Snap the rubber band whenever you think of something you want to change and then visualize or state what the preferred behavior is. For example, a person quitting smoking can snap the band when the urge to smoke occurs. Or if you catch yourself thinking you can't reach your goals, snap the rubber band and see yourself succeeding.

• Remember to *pace yourself* as you run the race of life. Rome wasn't built in a day. Longterm studies show that calmer Type B personalities are just as or even more productive than their faster-paced Type A counterparts. But we already knew that from the story of the tortoise and the hare. Life is a marathon race, not a sprint, so "easy does it." Charge up your batteries with regular vacations, long weekends, naps, extra sleep, and lazy weekends. It's okay to be lazy sometimes. My patients who live healthfully into their 80s and 90s are usually easy going and don't get too worked up about every little thing.

• Find at least *a little time for yourself each day*. This seems impossible for some persons, but if we don't, we pay a heavy price in poor health and lost potentials. We all deserve some fun and relaxation out of life every day. The puritan work ethic needs to be balanced with play and time out. "All work and no play makes Jack and Jane dull people." You'll actually get more done and be able to help others more when you lead a life of balance.

• A simple technique called *future tripping* can help you through tough times. Think or imagine ahead one, five, ten, or more years and see yourself being successful and happy. Visualize reaching your goals in spite of or *even because of* the difficulties you presently face. Remind yourself that most major stressors are time limited and will change in nature as time passes. *Time is a great healer of all wounds*. Trust yourself and the universe and enjoy your visions of a brighter tomorrow.

• *Remember the 80/10/10 rule*; 100 percent success all the time is impossible. Unrealistically high expectations can set us up for failure and self-criticism. In most settings, things will go smoothly 80 percent of the time and fairly well another ten percent; the other ten percent are the events governed by Murphy's Law. So if you're reaching your goals 80 percent of the time with gusts of 90 percent, that's great.

Whenever things get rough, mentally remind yourself "80/10/10." John Sculley, CEO of Apple Computers, says he has learned more from mistakes than from successes and states, "If you aren't making some mistakes, you aren't taking enough chances." Perfection is a lofty ideal but one we'll seldom attain; strive to do your best but don't be afraid to risk failure.

• *Minimize exposure to persons who are energy drainers*. Have you ever talked with someone and felt depressed or fatigued afterwards? If such a person is a family member or unavoidable for other reasons, try these approaches:

1. Whenever they start harping on the negative, divert the conversation to the positive.
2. Instead of sitting around rehashing "ain't it awful" stories, get them out for a walk or other activity.
3. Be assertive and tell them that you don't

want to hear negative complaining. If they
persist, leave.

Similarly, limit other sources of negative mental input. If any group, church, music, or television show focuses too much on negative or depressing views, change your input.

We can become de-energized by too much focus on unfortunate events; taking just small *action steps* fills us with hope and contributes toward the solution. This advice is nothing new; Abraham Lincoln said, "Most people are about as happy as they make their minds up to be." Nearly 2000 years ago, St. Paul said, "Whatever is true, whatever is noble, whatever is right, whatever is pure, whatever is lovely, whatever is admirable, if anything is excellent or praiseworthy, think about such things."

• *Hugging* is a healthy habit; it's been said that we need ten hugs each day to thrive, four per day just to survive. Hugs are a warm way of expressing that we are all interconnected. Look for and take advantage of opportunities to hug someone — it's good for both of you. Charles "Tremendous" Jones, one of the world's best and most frequent huggers, tells about receiving a letter after one of his talks: "Thank you for your inspiring talk and hug you gave me, Mr. Jones. I'm sure you remember me — I'm the elderly man who was sitting in a wheelchair by the door. That hug sure meant a lot to me. You see, my wife died ten years ago and you're the first person who has hugged me since then."

Our YMCA group recently caroled at a local nursing home where one of my patients, 88-year-old Maude, greeted me with a big hug. Later, one of our group asked, "Was that your mother in the wheelchair?" The implications of his question indicate how we have lost touch with hugging. Listen to and read Dr. Leo Buscaglia; some persons are *literally* dying for love and affection.

If each of us would reach out to *just one other person,*

this problem would be solved. Take care of your family members and remember your elders; visit shut-ins; organize church or group visitations to nursing homes and hospitals. *Hug each other*. AIDs can't be spread with a hug. Holding each other for a moment renews the hope and faith that reside within each of us. We remember that we're not alone, that there is hope and a reason to keep striving.

• *Appreciating what we have and giving thanks for it* is another key to self-actualization. *Happiness is being content with what we have, not always wanting what we don't have.* Yes, set your goals and never stop growing and achieving. But remember that happiness lies in the journey, not just reaching the destination. The "grass always seems greener" on the other side of the fence. Some persons waste their lives always chasing the carrot dangling in front of them — a newer car, bigger home, more attractive partner, and so on. They don't realize that true happiness comes from the little joys in life, not ego boosts and material objects.

• *Count your blessings*; we all have so many things to be thankful for. I was taught this lesson at college when I was starting to go bald. I envied a thick-haired student who was walking on the other side of a short concrete wall. As he passed the wall, however, I saw that he had only one leg. It's like the saying, "I complained about having no shoes until I met a man with no feet."

• *Accentuate the positive.* As the minister in the movie *Pollyanna* pointed out, why not be happy and positive — there are at least 826 Biblical references to rejoicing and happiness. A patient who had undergone one mastectomy discovered a lump in the other breast and was scheduled for a mammogram. I mentioned that she was holding up well under the stress. Sue replied, "Well, there are some bad things in life but there are so many more good things. I try to focus on the good." Her mammogram was normal, probably in part due to her super attitude.

Another constantly positive patient, Jim, had recently lost a wife to cancer and a son to AIDs while his daughter barely survived a brain tumor. When I asked how he dealt with all the tragedy so well, he replied, "My motto is: If you can't fix it, don't sweat it." He had learned to accept the things he couldn't change and to make the most of life.

• *Fully enjoying the present moment* is another key to psychological balance. *Present time consciousness* means living one day and one moment at a time. An old Sanskrit maxim says: "Look well to this day, for yesterday is but a dream; and tomorrow is only a vision. But today well-lived makes every yesterday a dream of happiness, and every tomorrow a vision of hope." The word "happiness" comes from the root word meaning "to happen." Happiness comes from a life of action — fully living the present moment and being in harmony with the Tao, the middle road of life.

Afterword: If I Could Live It Over . . . by Nadine Stair is a delightful perspective of life written at age 85: "If I had to live my life over again, I'd dare to make more mistakes next time. I'd relax. I would limber up. I would be sillier than I have been this trip. I would take fewer things seriously. I would take more chances. I would take more trips, I would climb more mountains, swim more rivers. I would eat more ice cream and less beans. I would perhaps have more actual troubles, but I'd have fewer imaginary ones. You see, I'm one of those people who live seriously and sanely hour after hour, day after day. Oh, I've had my moments. And if I had it to do over again, I'd have more of them. In fact, I'd try to have nothing else, just moments, one after another, instead of living so many years ahead of each day. I've been one of those persons who never goes anywhere without a thermometer, a hot water bottle, a raincoat, and a parachute. If

I had it to do again, I would travel lighter than I have. If I had to live my life over, I would start barefoot earlier in the spring and stay that way later in fall. I would go to more dances. I would ride more merry-go-rounds. I would pick more daisies."

The Station by Robert J. Hastings has a similar message about *enjoying the journey of life*. A partial quote reminds us, "Sooner or later we must realize there is no station, no one place to arrive at once and for all. The true joy of life is the trip. The station is only a dream. It constantly outdistances us. 'Relish the moment' is a good motto . . . It isn't the burdens of today that drive men mad. It is the regrets over yesterday and the fear of tomorrow. Regret and fear are twin thieves who rob us of today . . . Life must be lived as we go along."

Experiencing life as a series of "eternal now" moments leads to that wonderful state of consciousness known as *enlightenment*. We've all experienced those golden times when we become completely absorbed in the moment and forget about time and space. You've perhaps experienced these moments when playing with children or pets, walking in nature, reading a good book, or enjoying a hobby. In these moments *when we turn off our worrying and thinking, we enjoy an inner peace and quiet*. This is the goal of meditation and other "centering" practices: to develop a "one pointedness of mind" from which we appreciate the splendor within and all around us.

Living in the present moment recognizes that each action takes us down the fork of a crossroads. *Don't look back*! An occasional analysis of the past can show us trends and errors; for the most part, however, don't relive past decisions and second guess yourself. Life is full of choices and each moment is replete with new opportunities for growth. Live in the present moment and remember you have everything needed for heaven on earth.

• *Believing in your own abilities* is another key to stress management and self-actualization. Remember the children's story of the little train that said, "I think I can, I think I can." One key to tapping our potentials lies in believing you can do it. Napoleon Hill said, "Whatever the mind can conceive and believe, the mind can achieve." Remember the scene in *The Empire Strikes Back* in which Luke Skywalker lost his space craft? Yoda used mental powers to levitate the sunken craft from the mire when Luke couldn't. Luke gasped, "I don't believe it!" To this, Yoda replied, "That is why you failed."

Believe in yourself and don't give up until you reach your goals. Calvin Coolidge wrote: "Nothing in the world can take the place of persistence. Talent will not. Nothing is more common than unsuccessful men with talent. Genius will not. Unrewarded genius is almost a proverb. Education will not. The world is full of educated derelicts." Shakespeare said, "Our doubts are traitors, and make us lose the good we oft might win, by fearing to attempt."

Charles M. Dannheim was an artist, went to college, kept a 60-acre ranch, worked as a ranchhand for others, and had a wife and children. A busy schedule for anyone but especially impressive since Charles is a quadruple amputee. Nearly killed by 7800 volts from a power line, Charles had four artificial limbs, but his determination and enthusiasm helped him excel in all areas of life. "I can't figure out why I'm here today," said Dannheim. "God just had some purpose for me, I guess." His is a beautiful example of mind over matter, of mental fortitude over physical limitations.

Earl Nightengale told about a friend who was an excellent golfer despite having only one arm. It's been my experience, says his friend, that the right attitude and one arm will beat a person with a poor attitude and two arms most of the time. Consider the 1990 winner of the World Cycling Championship for the Disabled. John Rinehart bicycles 400 miles per week before a big race. He has no right leg or arm below the elbow yet bikes with no artificial limbs. Says Rinehart, "I never thought of myself as being different. I just had to be more creative. . . . I never put any strikes against me." Examples like these inspire and motivate us to become all that we can.

• *Pursue your peace of mind.* The Duke University Sociology Department identified factors contributing to peace of mind. These included:

1. "The absence of suspicion and resentment — not holding grudges."
2. "Not living in the past; avoid an unwholesome preoccupation with old mistakes and failures. "
3. "Not wasting time and energy fighting conditions you cannot change."
4. "Refuse to indulge in self-pity; accept the fact that nobody gets through life without some sorrow and misfortune."
5. "Cultivate the old-fashioned virtues — love, honor, compassion, and loyalty."
6. "Don't expect too much of yourself; unrealistically high self-expectations inevitably lead to feelings of inadequacy."
7. "Find something bigger than yourself to believe in. Self-centered people score lowest in any test for measuring happiness."

The Bhagavad-Gita teaches, Do what you do but don't be attached to being the actor or to the fruits of your actions. This approach helps free us from the trap of attachments and desires. Like Johnny Appleseed, plant good seeds, then move on. He didn't wait around and worry whether each seed would grow. He trusted in his actions and the power of Nature to do the job. Trusting yourself and God cultivates peace of mind and prevents burn-out.

• *Follow your calling.* "Go confidently in the direction of your dreams, live the life you have imagined." Follow your heart and do what you feel called to do. We each have a wise inner voice that guides us toward our mission in life. Bernie Siegel, M.D., says, "It's doing what feels right to you that brings your life to fruition." Each of us has a special calling — an inner dream; the pieces of this earthly puzzle will fall into place when we each pursue our bliss. Goethe said, "Whatever you can do, or dream you can do, begin it. Boldness has genius, power and magic in it."

• *Humor and laughter* are important for psychological balance. Josh Billings summed it up: "There ain't much fun in medicine, but there's a heck of a lot of medicine in fun." Norman Cousins, in *Anatomy of an Illness,* described his recovery from a crippling arthritic condition with the aid of rest, vitamin C, a positive outlook, and lots of good belly laughs. Laughter *is* one of the best medicines. Research shows an increased immune response, decreased anxiety, and reduced muscular tension with hearty laughter. Since prevention is the best approach to health care, *take the time to enjoy* humorous shows, books, and comedians. Enjoy hearty laughter that Cousins termed "internal jogging."

• *Have faith in the power of good and God.* An unknown author, in *Footprints In The Sand,* reminds us that we're not alone and we're in good hands: "One night a man had a dream. He dreamed he was walking along the beach with the Lord. Across the sky flashed scenes from his life. In each scene he noticed two sets of footprints in the sand — one belonging to him and the other to the Lord. When the last scene flashed before him, he looked back at the footprints and noticed along the path there was only one set of footprints in the sand. He also noticed that this happened during the lowest and saddest times in his life."

"This really bothered him, so he questioned the Lord: 'Lord, you said that once I decided to follow you, you would walk with me all the way, but I noticed that during the most troublesome times of my life there was only one set of footprints. I don't understand why, when I needed you the most, you deserted me.' The Lord replied, 'My precious child. I would never desert you. During your times of trial and suffering, when you saw only one set of footprints, it was then that *I carried you.*'"

I mention faith in God during a psychology chapter because *spiritual solace is a potent stress management and self-actualizing aid.* Remembering spiritual truths may be the only comfort if death is imminent, a loved one is suffering, or all seems lost. These events are difficult to understand from an emotional perspective, thus the importance of a bed rock foundation of spiritual faith and belief.

Listen to Norman Vincent Peale's words of wisdom: "Fear knocked on my door; Faith answered; No one was there." Trust the Cosmic Designer that all things will make sense someday. Buckminster Fuller, author of *Critical Path* and other erudite works, when asked about the most important message he could share, answered "that the Universe is friendly." Acknowledging this truth empowers us to do our best each day. We're not alone and it's worth the effort no matter what our outward circumstances may be.

• Remember the Alcoholics Anonymous *Serenity Prayer:* "*God, grant me the Serenity to accept the things I cannot* change, the Courage to change the things I can, and the Wisdom to know the difference." *Internalize this truth* and make it part of your philosophy of life.

• Post *positive sayings* where you'll see them often. Some of my favorites are:

- When life gives you lemons, make lemonade.
- Winners make stepping stones out of life's stumbling blocks.
- Instead of saying "Why me, Lord?", say "Try me, Lord."
- An obstacle is not the end, it is a new beginning.
- The race is not always to the swift but to those who keep on running.
- Those who say it can't be done are usually interrupted by others doing it.
- The harder you work, the luckier you get.

- Our minds become more positive on a diet of *inspirational and motivational tapes and books*. With a steady stream of higher thought, we can more consistently look at the bright side. Remember that we become what we most often and fervently think about. Enrich your heart and mind with the works of positive and *enthusiastic* individuals. By the way, the word "enthusiasm" comes from two root words meaning "filled with God."

Ram Dass, a psychological and spiritual teacher who has done much exploring for and sharing with the rest of us, writes, "You will be wise, a simplicity out of which comes the wisdom of your being. A human birth is a very precious matter. You have all the ingredients necessary to know God fully in this lifetime." He quotes from varied sources, for example, Shinso, "Does one really have to fret about enlightenment? No matter what road I travel, I'm going home." and Thomas Merton, "We have what we seek. It is there all the time, and if we give it time it will make itself known to us." His books include: *Be Here Now, The Only Dance There Is, Grist For The Mill, A Miracle of Love,* and others.

Bernie Siegel, M.D., gives first hand accounts of the mind's critical role in healing and preventing "incurable" diseases such as cancer, diabetes, AIDs, arthritis, obesity, asthma, neurologic disorders, and multiple sclerosis. Bernie says, "If you want to get to heaven without dying, live in the present moment. . . . The past is over. It is time to ask what we can do right, not what we did wrong. Forgive yourself and move on." He is the author of *Love, Medicine, and Miracles* and *Peace, Love, and Healing*.

Richard Bach says, "Argue for your limitations and you get to keep them. . . . You are never given a wish without also being given the power to make it true. You may have to work for it however . . . Here is a test to find whether your mission on earth is finished: If you're alive, it isn't." Bach has authored *Illusions, Jonathan Livingston Seagull, One, The Bridge Across Forever*, and others.

Wayne Dyer, Ed.D., writes, "Each person on this planet is inherently, intrinsically capable of attaining dizzying heights of happiness and fulfillment. . . . It is my belief that anyone can reach a high level of human development, can in fact become self-actualized, a No-Limit person, if he or she works at it. It boils down to the choices you are willing to make . . . you can motivate yourself and choose greatness even if you've never done it before." Read *Your Erroneous Zones, Pulling Your Own Strings, The Sky's The Limit, Gifts from Eykis*, and *You'll See It When You Believe It.*

Says Denis Waitley, Ph.D., "You are born with infinite value and you only have to use what your Creator has given you . . . Success is working harder or smarter — usually both — at what you enjoy and are good at . . . What you see is who you'll be . . . Poverty is untested potential, resulting from self-imposed limitations . . . If it's to be it's up to me." His works include *The Psychology of Winning, 10 Seeds of Greatness, Being The Best,* and *The Subliminal Winner.*

I could go on and on. Wally "Famous" Amos; John H. Johnson, author of *Succeeding Against the Odds*; Og

Mandino; David J. Schwartz, Ph.D. and author of *The Magic of Thinking Big;* Jess Lair, Ph.D., author of *I Ain't Much, Baby — But I'm All I've Got*; and others I've mentioned. There are many wise and loving individuals who have shared their insights and inspirational views in multimedia formats. Surround yourself with these positive voices and reprogram your computer tapes.

• *Hope always exists* no matter what happens in life. Sometimes that's hard to believe and feel, but looking at life with a universal or enlightened perspective helps. The sun is always shining even when, from the ground, it appears cloudy and dreary. Fly high enough above the clouds and see for yourself. Similarly, there is always reason for hope and faith, but sometimes we just can't see it. We have to rise above the clouds of despair and doubt so we can experience the truth that "hope springs eternal." What is there to fear when we remember that life is eternal, that we are children of God and part of the Creation? Franklin D. Roosevelt put it aptly when he reassured the wartime population, "There is nothing to fear but fear itself."

• *Developing an enlightened "right seeing"* is one of the most important lessons we can achieve. Right attitudes and a lofty vision help us transcend whatever challenges we may encounter. *The ground of psychological health is knowing who we really are.* Many personal and societal problems are due to misunderstanding our true nature. Thousands of years ago, Socrates said, "Know thyself." These two words speak volumes to those who would better their lot in life. When we remember that we are eternal souls and an integral part of God, what is there to fear? Knowing who we are allows us to participate in life more fully. We can better handle the temporary trials and tribulations of life when we remember our Source.

Use these techniques as needed to find *your* way and path. Let your changes unfold naturally, don't rush or force them. We each have different lessons to learn and "uncooked seeds" to deal with. Life is like a smorgasbord in that everything we need is available for our optimal growth. In time and with a little effort, you will learn to manage stress more effectively and to become more self-actualized.

Ventilation

"Ventilation" means to bring in the fresh and put out the stale or foul; psychological ventilation is important for true wellness. We need to "get things off our chest" and let go of negative emotions from past events. All of us have experienced sadness, anger, guilt, resentment, embarrassment, and hurt. If kept inside over the years, these negative emotions contribute to significant physical and emotional ailments. They can effectively keep us from *opening to life.*

Don't allow yourself to dwell too much on past failures and hurts; excessive preoccupation with the past can cause depression and keep us from fully enjoying the present. Let's discuss several ways to let go of negative emotional baggage.

• Regular *prayer* — talking to God — is a great form of ventilation. The Creator knows our problems and needs before we do and intimately cares for each one of us. God understands, loves, forgives, and accepts you no matter what your station in life. Not a bad deal. Take advantage of this supreme love and share your burdens with the Source of all life.

• Most of us can benefit from *self-help techniques.* Native Americans had a unique method of *catharsis* or releasing negative inner emotions. They would dig a hole in the ground, then yell all their problems into the hole. Then they would fill the hole back up — emotions released, no one hurt, no expense. *Primal scream* techniques have a similar effect in releasing negative feelings. Hold a pillow over your mouth and scream out pent-up emotions. Use your hands or a whiffle ball bat and beat up a pillow or cushion.

• *Psychological counseling* is another way to rid oneself of old negative emotions. I recommend professional help if your situation is severe or if self-improvement techniques don't help. Don't be embarrassed to seek guidance from mental health professionals or ministers. Knowing when to get outside help is a sign of strength and wisdom. You won't "go crazy" from admitting or talking about your problems. You'll discover that nearly all persons have periodic crises that require some outside help. Each county has a mental health center with counselors, psychologists, and psychiatrists. A "sliding scale" fee structure makes their services affordable for everyone.

• *Writing out your concerns* also helps; seeing your problems on paper makes them seem more manageable. Write out all your feelings and negative emotions, then tear up or burn the paper to complete the release. Or list your problems and your blessings and see which list is longer. When faced with a difficult decision, remember the "pro and con" list so you can better assess which path to take.

• *Self-talk* is another technique that is easy and effective. Take a walk and talk to yourself: "Okay, I have this problem. What are my options? What shall I do next?" Utilize a Dale Carnegie tip and consider: "What is the very worst that could happen in this situation? If the very worst did happen, what could I do then?" Looking at the worst case scenario — which rarely happens — helps you put things into perspective and deal with it.

• Remind yourself that *worrying doesn't help anything*. On the contrary, excessive worrying can cause physical and emotional problems. *In Being The Best*, Dr. Denis Waitley points out that of all our worries, 60 percent are unwarranted, 20 percent are in the past, and ten percent are petty. Of the remaining ten percent, only five percent are real and justifiable, and we can't do anything about half of them. Thus, only about two percent of all our worries are real, significant, and under our control. Focus on those things you can change and improve. Don't let the other 98 percent drain your energy or cloud your mind. Mark Twain said his life had been filled with many worries and anticipated problems, most of which never happened.

• *Let family and friends help* during times of emotional stress; ventilate and share your deep dark secrets with someone you trust. There is tremendous curative value in "letting the cat out of the bag." We all have "skeletons in our closet" from the past; *self-disclosure* helps us release these and forgive ourselves or others. I'm not recommending excessive complaining or forming mutual pity parties; however, sharing concerns with a caring person often helps immensely. Sidney Jourard, Ph.D., in *The Transparent Self*, recommended self-disclosure as a primary technique for releasing inner negative content.

As part of my training in clinical psychology, I went through two years of group and individual psychotherapy. Like most of us, I had some actions, thoughts, and feelings that I wasn't proud of or comfortable with. As I shared these in counseling, I experienced a profound relief and release. From the group and therapists, I received *consensual validation*; that is, *most persons had experienced similar thoughts, feelings, and actions*. Opening up to others is a tremendous way of reaching self-love, self-forgiveness, and self-acceptance.

You see, we all are pretty much in the same boat. It's like the old saying, "There's a whole lot of good in the worst of us and a little bit of bad in the best of us." Life is for learning. A baby learns to walk by first crawling, then falling repeatedly. Similarly, we all make mistakes and learn by trial and error. Ideally, we learn from our mistakes quickly and don't hurt others along the way. But sometimes we don't know which road to take and later wish we had chosen differently. *Realize you're not the only one who has "sinned" or made mistakes.* This is not a rationalization for continuing inappropriate living but the basis for *self-forgiveness* that can transform us into better persons.

Our brains process millions of thoughts and feelings daily. Is it any wonder, then, that we all have occasional and transient bizarre, conflicting, or confusing thoughts? Some persons don't realize this and punish themselves because of past inappropriate thoughts or feelings. They carry a burden around with them and feel second class and different. The Bible speaks of avoiding sin by thought, word, and deed; this is an ideal we each should work toward.

But which one of us is perfect? So don't flagellate yourself for a lifetime because of past inappropriate thoughts, words, or deeds — especially the minor and transient variety. Oliver Wendell Holmes said, "The greatest thing in the world is not so much where we stand, as in what direction we are moving."

Death wishes, angry words, sexual experimentation, periodic discontent and re-evaluation of one's life — are all common and normal in the course of a lifetime. Do you have poor self-image, sexual concerns, sibling rivalry, or a perceived lack of parental attention? So do many others. How many persons have experienced guilt, anxiety, and low self-esteem because of immature life choices? We can strive for saintly living, but most of us will fall short of the mark.

Don't let past thoughts, words, or deeds keep you from loving, forgiving, and accepting yourself and others. Maturation often involves trial and error learning. Make a distinction between the doer and the deed; you may have made mistakes but that doesn't make you bad.

Accept your uniqueness and recognize that everyone marches to a different drummer. A wide spectrum exists regarding age, color, sexual orientation, religious beliefs, and other areas. The strength and beauty of humanity lies, in part, in the tremendous variation among individuals. We each have unique talents and gifts to contribute as we journey through life. Don't spend your life trying to emulate some artificially contrived "normal" pattern. Accept yourself as you are while always striving to improve.

Meditation and Relaxation: Quieting the Rational Mind

The ancient philosopher Cicero said, "Only the person who is relaxed can create, and to that mind ideas flow like lightning." Psalms 46:10, "Be still and know I am God," reminds us to calm down and center on the truth of God's sovereignty. Quieting the mind helps us remember we're part of God, life is eternal, we're not alone, and we should live each moment fully. And remembering these truths helps quiet the mind.

Alan Watts, in his book *Meditation*, states: "Most of us think compulsively all the time . . . if I think all the time . . . I'm living entirely in the world of symbols and I'm never in relationship with reality . . . the difference between myself and all the rest of the universe is nothing more than an idea — it is not a real difference. Meditation is a way in which we come to feel our basic inseparability from the whole universe . . . By going out of your mind you come to your senses."

Our cerebral cortexes are fairly new innovations in the evolutionary scheme of things. These twin computers have amazing abilities but many of us haven't learned how to control them. Thus the saying, "The mind makes a wonderful servant but a horrible master." Some persons suffer from incessant thinking, worrying, wondering, remembering, and double-checking. These functions are important when balanced but in excess can block achievement of self-actualization and inner peace.

The brain has been compared to a drunken monkey that thinks it is the master of the house. The monkey runs all around, chattering constantly and acting a fool. This creates a lot of noise and may even be entertaining for a time. In the long run, though, the house becomes a mess and uninhabitable. Another analogy compares the brain with a wild elephant, charging around at will and destroying everything in its path. The elephant needs to become more tame and available for doing calmer and clearer work. How then, can we begin to calm the mind and increasingly become the master of our life?

The good news is that it's relatively easy and is free. We simply must take some time each day to get quiet within; this can be done in any number of ways. *The key is to really experience life in the present moment.* Enjoy life for a few moments without worrying, analyzing, thinking, or otherwise dissecting the experience. Most of us perceive life one or more thoughts away from the real experience: "I'm eating now; I'm playing with the kids now; I'm working now;" and so on. The anxious mind constantly labels and categorizes our experiences so that we never quite enjoy or know the real event.

Watch children digging in the sand or playing make believe and observe their total involvement in the moment.

Some common activities that help us turn off our minds' computer and relax are: gardening, walking in nature, playing with pets or children, reading, watching a good movie or play, exercise, meditation, yoga, caring for others, spiritual study, prayer, cooking, sewing, and games.

Regular enjoyment of these activities and timeless moments are crucial for total health. We need to relax and let ourselves get into the flow of life; this helps remind us the world is a beautiful place. Simple and small pleasures help recharge us and counteract the negative sides of life. The movie *Awakenings* summarized the lessons learned, "that the human spirit is what needs to be nourished. Work, play, friendship, family. These are the things that matter. This is what we've forgotten. The simplest things."

Take time to enjoy various activities and let yourself become immersed in them; notice how good it feels to stop thinking and worrying incessantly. You deserve to enjoy life so take the time to be good to yourself. Try to carry over a timeless and joyful involvement into as many life activities as possible. Store up these moments that remind us of the Kingdom within and all around. This helps refute the illusion that life is a tragic rat race.

There is much overlap among relaxation, meditation, autogenic training, biofeedback, and self-hypnosis techniques. Meditation and yoga classes are taught in many colleges, health facilities, and church groups. More specifically, there are a few techniques and resources I can recommend. *Transcendental Meditation* (TM), taught by Maharishi Mahesh Yogi, is a long-established and well-organized meditation program. The Self-Realization Fellowship, started by Paramahansa Yogananda, has centers and a home study program for learning *Kriya Yoga*. I have used these techniques for nearly 20 years and am thankful to the founders and teachers. For additional information about meditation and relaxation techniques, read *Journey of Awakening: A Meditator's Guidebook* by Ram Dass; *The Varieties of the Meditative Experience* by Daniel Goleman, Ph.D.; *Beyond Biofeedback* by Elmer and Alyce Green; and *The Relaxation Response* by Herbert Benson, M.D.

One meditation technique involves *working with the breath* while you sit quietly with eyes closed. Focus your awareness at the tip of your nose as you breathe slowly and deeply at a rate that is comfortable for you. You may want to silently repeat the word "one" with each inhalation and exhalation. Pause for a moment after each breath and let the exhalations last slightly longer than the inhalations. If you become aware of stray thoughts or the mind wandering, quietly return your focus to your breathing and the word "one." Don't chastise yourself for letting the mind drift; meditation should be an effortless and gentle process.

Do this for 15 minutes, then sit quietly for a few moments before arising. Don't set an alarm but simply open one eye to check a clock when you feel the time has elapsed. A daily practice like this helps to quiet and discipline the mind. While meditating, the mind may generate many reasons why you should be doing something else. This is like the wild elephant temporarily becoming even more frenzied after initially being chained. In time, you'll become calmer and will enjoy a quieter and deeper state of mind. *With practice, this level of consciousness generalizes into your normative state.*

Relaxation techniques such as *Jacobsen's progressive contraction-relaxation* can be mastered with a little repetition. Lie down or sit comfortably in a quiet place while breathing slowly and deeply. Progressively tighten, then relax the major muscle groups. First, contract the muscles of the feet and legs. Hold that tightness for a few seconds before letting all the tension go. Let your muscles feel completely relaxed, warm, and heavy. Then tighten the muscles of the buttocks, abdomen, back, shoulders and neck, arms and hands, and the face.

With each muscle group, contract and hold before relaxing. For the face, do three parts:

1. Raise the eyebrows high for the forehead muscles.
2. Close your eyes tightly for cheek and eye muscles.
3. Clench the jaw tightly for jaw muscles.

When you have contracted, then relaxed each muscle group, take a few moments to enjoy how good relaxation feels. Notice the difference between tension and relaxation; with practice, you can quickly and easily attain total relaxation. If any body area still feels tense, repeat the technique for that area until your entire body feels deeply and pleasantly relaxed. The benefits of this technique are numerous and will carry over into your daily life. You will be more aware of when you tense up and why. You then can take a few deep breaths, silently saying, "All muscles feeling completely relaxed, warm, and heavy," and release the tension.

Another technique involves *touching forehead reflex points* that help us deal with stress and reach a deep relaxation. These reflex points can be felt as bumps or knobs a few inches directly above the eyebrows. Touch these points lightly with the three middle fingers of each hand twice a day for five minutes; the middle of the day and just before bedtime are good for most persons. While touching the points, you have a number of options. First, you can just let the mind go blank, watching thoughts go by but not being attached to them. You can pray or think of happy times in your life. While touching the points, it's even okay to think about all your worries.

In general, I don't recommend dwelling on fears or concerns; you can, however, worry productively while touching the forehead points. These reflexes theoretically activate deep centers in the brain that allow us to reach acceptance or generate alternative solutions. That is, using these reflex points helps us clarify whether it is a problem we must accept or one that we can change. If the situation can be changed, what are your options or alternatives?

A third relaxation technique involves working with the breath while focusing on *exhaling the negative and inhaling the positive*. Sit or lie down in a quiet setting with the eyes closed. Say a prayer or affirmation that you are going to release the negative while filling yourself with positive energies. Release and exhale darkness, sadness, guilt, anger, envy, hopelessness, hurt, and any other negative emotions. With each out breath, visualize or imagine a dark cloud leaving your body. *Breathe in* good and positive aspects — light, hope, faith, love, joy, peace, and energy. As you inhale, visualize your entire body filling with a warm and glowing white light. Then give thanks for help from above as you *accentuate the positive and eliminate the negative.*

Visual imagery is another way to reach a deep state of relaxation and inner harmony. Visualize, picture, or imagine yourself at a favorite nature setting — perhaps the ocean, mountains, or by a stream or lake. With your eyes closed and while breathing slowly and deeply, imagine the details of this setting as vividly as possible. For example, *feel* the warmth of the sun and the sand or grass under your toes, *hear* the waves crashing or water gurgling, *see* the blue sky and water, *smell* the pine trees or flowers. Paint a sensory picture in your mind and enjoy the beauty and peace of this setting. You can recreate such beatific scenes for as long or as often as you like. Remember that, quite similarly, we create beauty — or the lack thereof — in our inner and outer worlds. Affirm that you deserve to enjoy and utilize life's best.

Note any spontaneous thoughts or possible solutions that your quiet mind generates during any of these techniques. Be sure to write them down afterwards and re-evaluate them at a later time. These calm, clear insights are "diamonds in the rough" that can transform your life for the better. TM literature describes inner or cosmic ideas as arising like bubbles from an ocean floor. If the mind is turbulent — like choppy waves — the bubbles get popped and don't receive full mental awareness and recognition. Meditation allows us to gracefully spring off a diving board, reach the calm ocean floor, and enjoy heightened awareness.

Love, Acceptance, and
Forgiveness Technique

The *Love, Acceptance, and Forgiveness* technique (LAF) is designed to speed the release of internalized negative emotions. These emotions are usually caused by trauma or are associated with some significant person in our life. Death, divorce, physical or mental abuse, sexual abuse, broken relationships, and other psychological traumas can create significant negative emotions. Time is one of the best healers of these scars, and one to two years is sometimes needed to totally get back on your feet. Even with a positive mental attitude and a balanced life, it takes time to heal after such traumas.

Some persons, however, don't let go of the past and find themselves thinking or dreaming a lot about past events: "If only that hadn't happened, if only I could turn back time" and other irrational thoughts may occur. Even worse, some persons may block out an event and spend consider-able emotional energy to suppress offending feelings. This approach may be okay for awhile as temporary denial pro-tects us from shock. Continued repression of significant negative feelings, however, is ultimately a futile and self-limiting strategy.

The LAF technique assists in sweeping these old cobwebs from the attic of the mind. Using this technique for a few weeks is usually sufficient for each problem area. Only rarely will an individual uncover emotional material that requires professional help. If you experience significant and persistent depression, crying, anxiety, or suicidal ideation, consult a mental health professional. The vast majority of us, however, can safely and advantageously use this approach. You will feel more free and energetic after letting go of ghosts from the past.

"Janet" had gone through an incredible amount of trauma in the previous year: she had been raped, her apartment was burglarized, her best friend "went insane," and her family lost their business and home. Janet was severely depressed, anxious, and suicidal; she could not hold down a job or do housework. Her recent marriage was in an upheaval because of her inability to function normally.

I taught her the LAF technique and followed her progress with weekly counseling sessions. Within several weeks, she experienced improvement of her symptoms and daily functioning. She reached acceptance of past events much more quickly than usual and said, "I wish all those things hadn't happened, but there is no way I can change them. It's time to get on with my life and pick up the pieces." Follow-up sessions at six months, one and two years showed functioning and ideation to be within normal limits.

The goal of this technique is to reach an inner state of love, acceptance, and forgiveness toward yourself and the other person(s) involved. One key to this approach is realizing, *"We're all doing the best we can with what we have to work with."* No one was born destined to be bad or evil, but a child who has been abused or mistreated sometimes treats others that way. Gary Greer, Ph.D., said, "Remember that all persons want to be loved and want to give their love to others."

Consider that "There but for the grace of God go I." The best of us might be much like the worst of us if we had been mistreated and unloved. I'm not condoning mistreatment of others or advocating letting criminals off scot-free. Once a misdeed has occurred, however, there is no benefit in carrying around the negative aftermath. Continued negative feelings and thoughts help no one; on the contrary, they exert powerful harmful effects on the person who harbors the negativity.

With this background and philosophy in mind, you're ready for the LAF technique. Become comfortably and deeply relaxed. Pray or affirm that you will let go of past events that are holding you back. Ask for help from above and within as you prepare to literally become a new person. Visualize yourself and the other person involved and imagine yourself saying, "I *love* you as another child of God." This isn't sexual love or even the love you may feel for close friends and family. This love comes from recognizing we're all One spiritually and should "love one another" as Jesus taught. You may not feel any love in your heart or want to say this. Simply saying "I love you" in your imagination is sufficient to get the ball rolling.

Next, picture yourself saying, "I *accept* what happened back then. It's over and I'm going to let it go. I can't change it and will accept that it's over." On different days, you can vary your message. You may want to make a general statement like the one above. Or you may want to be more specific: "I accept that my parent died when I was young," or "I accept that I was physically abused as a child." Remember the Serenity Prayer and ask for the "serenity to

accept the things I cannot change."

Finally, visualize yourself saying, "I *forgive* you for what you did (or didn't do). I know you were doing the best you could with what you had to work with." Again, you may not feel forgiveness in your heart yet but you are planting seeds for the process to occur.

"It takes two to tangle," let go of your end of the rope in this emotional tug-of-war. Letting go of old negative emotions starts a chain reaction of inner healing and growth. You may also vary the general or specific nature of your forgiveness statement: "I forgive you for leaving me, for dying so young, for not being there when I needed you."

Next, *reverse the roles*. Imagine the offending or significant other person expressing love, acceptance, and forgiveness *toward you*. Make their message general or specific as various aspects of the old problem come to mind. After visualizing mutual expressions of love, acceptance, and forgiveness, picture hugging each other. This may seem repulsive and the last thing you would want to do, but hugs are healing and symbolize "burying the hatchet." This is just your imagination so there is no harm in visualizing it.

After finishing the visualization, take a few moments to relax and breathe slowly and deeply. Exhale negative and inhale positive emotions and energies. Thank God for guidance and help in finally letting go of these old skeletons. Affirm that you will feel more calm, energetic, and peaceful afterwards. Leave all old tensions and negativity behind; you don't have to keep it inside anymore.

You may experience a temporary increase in nightmares, depression, and crying as you uncover old emotions and let down your defenses. A "retracing" phenomena may occur temporarily as old negative emotions are released. That is, you may feel angry, guilty, sad, or whatever emotion has been blocked over time. This is a transient stage and well worth weathering to get rid of the *underlying problem*. Remember, this heart-and-soul work is done in the privacy and security of your home. No one has to know your deep, dark secrets although you may want to share them with others some day. Use the various ventilation techniques to deal with any emotions that resurface.

You don't have to change anything in the outer world unless you want to. You don't have to contact the other person or say anything to them. After using the technique, however, you may want to make reparations or communicate with the other person. Follow your heart about this and take your time. Make sure you can *comfortably* visualize love, acceptance, and forgiveness before you actually recontact the person. This technique works equally well if the other person is alive or dead. In either case, there is a tremendous sense of well-being and peace to be gained by loving, accepting, and forgiving all from the past.

"Tom" experienced low self-esteem and confidence and felt the relationship with his father was a contributing factor. His father was usually too busy and never called unless there was a death or problem in the family. Tom couldn't remember his dad ever hugging him or saying "I love you." I taught Tom the LAF technique on Wednesday afternoon and he practiced it that evening.

In our next session, Tom excitedly told me about a miraculous turn of events. On Thursday, *the day after* Tom started the technique, his dad called. "I've been thinking about you all day," his dad started. "I realized that I never call to just talk. How are things going?" After a good conversation, Tom's dad grew quiet. "I also realized it's been a long time since I told you I love you but I do."

Is it a coincidence that Tom's dad called the day after this heart-and-soul work began? As an unknown writer said, "Coincidence is God's way of performing a miracle anonymously." Tom's dad lived two thousand miles away, but he felt the *energy changes* that occurred with the LAF technique; psychological and spiritual healing that transcended boundaries of time and space occurred. When we truly desire to grow and let go of the past, we receive help from above, inside, and all around.

Reprogramming the Biocomputer

Since we become what we think about, one approach to self-improvement involves *positively reprogramming our brains*. First century philosopher Epictetus said, "Men are disturbed not by things, but by the views which they take of them." It's not the outside event that causes our feelings but rather what we tell ourselves about the event. Our thoughts and statements program our brains; these programs can be optimistic and positive if we consistently think and speak that way. "To become, act as if." Changing how you talk, think, and act eventually carries over and literally helps change who you are. Whenever you feel depressed or upset, think back to what you just thought or said. What did you tell yourself?

If your date stands you up, you could think, "We must not have been suited for each other," versus "No one will ever love me." If you spill a glass of water, you could think, "Accidents happen," versus "I'm such a klutz; I always spill things!" Do you see and hear the difference?

We create our own realities so be aware of what you say and think about yourself. My patients often must be educated about this crucial fact. They say things like: "It's killing me; I feel like I'm on fire; it's crippling me up; I thought I would die," and other disease-enhancing statements. Remember, "As you think, so shall you be," so think and speak with nurturing and loving content.

Watch for "put down" thoughts or statements and ask others to help you be more aware of negative self talk. Whenever you catch a negative expression, refute it, and replace it with a more appropriate positive one. If asked to perform a difficult task, you might automatically think, "I know I'll blow it. I'm all thumbs." If so, immediately reprogram a more positive tape such as, "I can improve on past performances. I know I can do it right this time."

Sobel and Ornstein, in *Healthy Pleasures*, list common erroneous ways of thinking that you'll want to avoid:

- Am I thinking in all-or-none terms?
- Am I assuming every situation is the same?
- Am I confusing a rare occurrence with a high probability?
- Am I assuming the worst possible outcome?
- Am I overlooking my strengths?
- Am I blaming myself for something that was beyond my control?
- Am I expecting perfection in myself and others?
- How could I have handled this situation differently?
- What difference will this make in a week, a year, or ten years?

Consider these questions and start now to reprogram your mind more positively. Remember, your brain follows the instructions you put into the biocomputer. With practice of these techniques, you can feel better about yourself and improve your performance in every area of life. Since we're each the author of our life stories, why not write positive, successful, and happy ones? Recommended readings include: *A Guide to Rational Living* by Ellis and Harper; *Reframing: Neuro-Linguistic Programming and the Transformation of Meaning* by Grinder and Bandler; *Unlimited Power* by Tony Robbins; *A Handbook for Higher Conscious-

ness by Ken Keyes; and *Woulda, Coulda, Shoulda: Overcoming Regrets, Mistakes, and Missed Opportunities* by Freeman and DeWolf.

Healing with the Mind

Visual imagery and other mental healing techniques can help overcome a variety of ailments. Read *Getting Well Again* by the Simontons for a discussion of these approaches. . Dr. Simonton's "terminal cancer" patients who used these techniques lived 2½ times as long as the control group. Other excellent resources include *The Power Within* by Wendy Williams and books by Norman Cousins and Bernie Siegel, M.D. Says Siegel, "The resolution of conflicts, the realization of the authentic self, spiritual awareness, and love release incredible energy that promotes the biochemistry of healing."

For advanced cases, "mind over matter" techniques alone may not be sufficient but can be useful in conjunction with more orthodox treatments. Remember that the human body is the most magnificent healing center imaginable; within each of us resides the best pharmacy, surgical suite, and rehab program available. Our miraculous biocomputer — when properly communicating with the entire body — is the key to self-healing. Don't underestimate it. Appreciate the many miracles within you and *believe in health more than disease.* Believe in the ability of your body to heal itself from any ailment.

Don't talk or think excessively about what's wrong with you; rather, focus on positive topics of hope and healing. We were created to be healthy, active, and vigoro·· Remember this truth and use your mental powers to p vent and minimize illness.

Goal Setting and Affirmations

Goal setting aids achievement of our potentials in all areas. A person without goals is like a ship without a rudder; most of us spend more time planning our vacations than our lives. If you fail to plan, you plan to fail. A few hours spent on goal setting can bring huge increases in success and growth. What are your goals in life? What do you want to achieve? The 1953 Yale graduating class contained only three percent who had clear and specific goals written down. Twenty years later, those three percent were worth more financially than the other 97 percent combined. Those three percent also scored superior on ratings of happiness in life.

Many high achievers, for example, Notre Dame football coach Lou Holtz, use goal setting. At age 28, he was unemployed and with their third child on the way, he said, "I don't think I've ever been any lower in my entire life. But my wife was supportive and she bought me a book about goal setting." Says Holtz, "The only reason I'm the head coach at Notre Dame is that I've had goals and I've had dreams. Deep down inside, you'd better have a dream and you'd better have a goal or things don't happen. I'm a firm believer in goals."

Talk show host Arsenio Hall said he has planned his success since a child. "I'm very special. I'm gifted. I was sent here to do this. Now that sounds weird but the bottom line is . . . I planned this since I was 12." As an orphaned teen, Dr. Wayne Dyer told his brothers that someday he would be on the *Tonight Show* with Steve Allen. Many years later, with Johnny Carson hosting the show, Wayne was invited a night when Steve Allen was a guest. This was not a ncidence but rather the predictable result of strongly consistently held goals.

Write down your goals in the following areas: spiritual, physical, family, occupational, psycho-social, and financial. List every goal that comes to mind, no matter how large or small, practical or seemingly impossible. *The sky's the limit* so let yourself express all your inner dreams and goals. Next, rewrite each goal using the following guidelines:

• *Use present tense statements* as if it is already happening, for example, "I *am* making ___ dollars per year," "I am a patient and loving parent," versus "I can or will . . ."

• *Be specific* with all dates, numbers, and wording. "I weigh a trim 150 pounds by June 1, 1993," versus "I am losing weight." "I run 15 miles per week," versus "I'm in good shape."

• *State what you want, not what you don't want.* Focus on the desired goal, not past undesirable habits. For example, "I enjoy the health and vitality of being a non-smoker," versus "I must stop smoking so many cigarettes."

• *Use the 50/50 Rule of Belief;* that is, make your goals high enough to challenge you but sufficiently within reach so you'll believe you can do it.

• *Remember the KISS Rule:* "Keep It Short and Simple." Don't combine two or more goals in the same sentence.

Next, review the list and prioritize each goal as to its importance. Which goals do you want to pursue first? Start with a few relatively easy ones that can be achieved within a few weeks or months. This gives you rapid positive reinforcement and confidence in the power of this technique to affect change. Read your goals the first thing in the morning and the last thing at night before sleeping. Pray or affirm that you will be able to change for the better and fulfill your talents. You can become a different person, *reborn* to discover and harvest the vast potentials within.

Henry David Thoreau said, "If one advances confidently, in the direction of his own dreams and endeavors, to lead the life which he has imagined, he will meet with a success unexpected in common hours."

Over time, you will want to change, reprioritize, and delete some goals. One college president stated that the college wasn't doing its job unless students changed their course of study at least three times. Similarly, it's okay to change your priorities; as you start to work on a goal, you may discover it wasn't that important to you.

Go as far as you can see; when you get there, look around and see where you want to go next. Read books and listen to tapes that further discuss the miracle of goal setting. These include *It Works* by R. H. J., *Unlimited Power* by Anthony Robbins, *New Age Thinking* by Louis Tice, *The Psychology of Winning* by Denis Waitley, *Think And Grow Rich* by Napoleon Hill, *Dare To Win* by Mark Victor Hansen, and *See You At The Top* by Zig Ziglar.

Affirmations are first cousins to goal setting and the principles are the same. Write out positive affirmations and post them where you'll read them often — on your bathroom mirror or refrigerator door. Repeated exposure to lofty ideals changes the way we view life and our possibilities. Goals and affirmations are powerful techniques for identifying and achieving your dreams. Suggested affirmations include:

- Today is going to be a great day!
- I think only good thoughts and I feel good!
- Every day I feel better and better!
- I am happy and enjoy life!
- I choose health and happiness!

Don't forget Emil Coue's classic, "Everyday in every way I am getting better and better." Generate your own affirmations and fill your heart and mind with positive expectancy.

Raising Children Consciously

"Children are not things to be molded but people to be unfolded." Kahil Gibran in *The Prophet* said: "Your children are not your children. They are the sons and daughters of life's longing for itself. They come through you but not from you. And though they are with you yet they belong not to you . . . You are the bows from which your children as living arrows are sent forth. The archer sees the mark upon the path of the infinite, and He bends you with His might that His arrows may go swift and far."

Zig Ziglar tells about growing Chinese bamboo trees; after planting the seed, one must water and fertilize it for four years *while nothing grows*. But in the fifth year, the tree grows 90 feet tall in six weeks. He asks: "Did it grow 90 feet in six weeks or five years?" This is a good analogy for the patience and persistence required for optimal parenting. Real growth and success in any endeavor require dedication and effort. You may not see the results of your work for many years to come but keep loving and working with them.

Raising children optimally is a difficult task; no wonder mothers aren't paid a salary — the job is worth a million dollars a day when done well. As one poet said, "God couldn't be everywhere so He created mothers." I would also include fathers as more men discover their nurturing and parenting strengths. *Being a good parent is one of the most important jobs in the world.*

Our society has taken a step backward by relegating child raising to day care centers and baby sitters. Whenever possible, have one parent care for the child, at least for the first few years of life. Optimal parenting early in life can set up lasting positive relationships and prevent future problems. Healthy, happy, and loving children are more important than nice cars, homes, and other material goods.

We started our family while I was in graduate school and borrowed money to live on after my wife quit her job to be a full-time mother. We've never regretted that decision. Raising children well is a priority of the utmost importance. A working mother's earnings are often meager after the expenses of babysitters, a second car, wardrobe, office gifts, increased taxes, and meals out. The greatest cost, however, is that few persons will raise a child like only a mother can.

Remember the three L's when having a baby: *Lamaze, Leboyer, and La Leche*. These three approaches to childbirth and care provide an optimal start. Lamaze stresses a drug-free (whenever possible), gentle, and teamwork approach to birthing. French obstetrician Dr. Frederick Leboyer describes the Leboyer technique in *Birth Without Violence*. Dim lights, peaceful music, a warm bath, and skin on skin contact provide the most reassuring environment after birth. As discussed, breastfeeding — as taught by the La Leche League — gives a newborn ideal nutritional and psychological support.

Some adults must undergo psychological treatment in an attempt to overcome traumas associated with the birth process. Consider the shock after nine months of quiet, dark, warm, and fluid surroundings — then suddenly thrust into a bright, noisy, mechanical, and scary world. All this after being pushed through a pressurized tunnel that could crush your skull. Then needle sticks, plastic nipples, and lying by yourself without that heartbeat you've grown so accustomed to. Using Lamaze, Leboyer, and La Leche can minimize birth trauma and prevent psychological stresses that may adversely affect one throughout life.

Children go through a variety of stages, so don't get too upset by minor and temporary changes in behavior. When a child becomes unruly or unhappy, consider common causes first: "Are they hungry and perhaps experiencing low blood sugar? Are they tired? Are they upset about a specific event or fear? Are they ill or in pain?"

Children sometimes aren't aware of or can't communicate discomfort or needs. Ask them what is wrong and check the above categories before judging their behavior as "just being bad." Childhood and adolescent growth spurts can be physically or mentally exhausting and engender temporary bratty behavior.

Children are sensitive so treat them gently. Watch what you say and do around them since children learn by example. Dorothy Law Nolte, in *Children Learn What They Live*, notes: "If children live with criticism, they learn to condemn. If children live with hostility, they learn to fight. If children live with ridicule, they learn to be shy. If children live with shame, they learn to feel guilty. If children live with tolerance, they learn to be patient. If children live with encouragement, they learn confidence. If children live with praise, they learn to appreciate. If children live with fairness, they learn justice. If children live with security, they learn to have faith. If children live with approval, they learn to like themselves. If children live with acceptance and friendship, they learn to find love in the world."

Since children are so sensitive and perceptive, closely monitor their incoming stimuli. For the most part, limit TV viewing to entertaining but educational public television programs. Allow cartoons with commercials as a special treat but monitor the content; negativity, violence, and senseless pranks are often accompanied by sugary and junk food advertisements. Don't let young children watch music video stations, news, and other more adult programming.

Dr. Denis Waitley says, "Most of what is available on TV is junk food that leads to mental malnutrition and poor emotional and spiritual health."

Scenes and messages of sex, violence, and turmoil can be powerful and upsetting for children *and* adults. By the time children finish high school, they have seen 15,000 hours of television and 30,000 incidents of violence and aggression. A Michigan State University study showed that the average 14-year-old watches 1400 sexual acts or references to sexual acts on TV each year. In addition, the same teen watches at least 21 R-rated movies per year. "There's little indication that parents exercise any control, positive or negative, over TV viewing by teens." This study was aptly funded by the Office of Adolescent Pregnancy Programs.

Simple *behavior modification programs* can reshape problematic behaviors. Identify two or three specific behaviors that need to be changed, for example, going to sleep quickly or acting appropriately. Give a "happy-gram" or gold star (the tokens) for each successful behavior each day. When the child earns a certain number of tokens, they get a small reward — frozen yogurt, a family outing, or small toy. Keep a chart of the behaviors and successful accomplishments. Gradually increase the number of tokens that must be earned before a reward is given. Start with two days worth (four-six tokens) and gradually increase to a weeks worth (14-21).

A similar approach uses quarters to reward or punish behaviors. The child gets a certain number of quarters each week if they behave appropriately. However, if a parent must ask the child to do something *more than twice,* the child loses a quarter. At the week's end, the child gets to keep all the quarters they haven't lost. Use lots of praise and calm firmness with both techniques. These techniques help parents retrain appropriate behaviors without repeatedly reminding the child what to do. In general, praise and reward good behaviors, don't give too much attention to inappropriate ones, and firmly but lovingly punish when necessary.

Elders remark that hard work throughout life was important for developing maturity, integrity, and self-responsibility. They caution today's parents who make it too easy for their children, thereby denying lessons taught by chores and family teamwork. The plant world provides an excellent analogy. If a plant is watered too often, a *shallow* root system results, preventing stable growth. The healthiest plants *have to struggle* a little and thus put down a deep root system. This firm foundation keeps it rooted during windy days and makes tall growth possible. In the same way, graduated levels of work and responsibility help a youngster learn important lessons that serve him or her throughout a lifetime. Some adults have worked hard to reach success but then deprive their children of the same opportunity.

Create an optimal environment for your child's physical, mental, and spiritual growth. Children are one of our greatest hopes for the future. They are a lot of work but also a lot of joy. Elders also encourage us to enjoy our children while they are young because in a blink of an eye they'll be grown; don't end up like Harry Chapin's character in his song "Cats In The Cradle." Model stable and balanced behavior; expose them to positive art, music, literature, and religious influences. Children are like sponges, ready to soak up incoming information. Let's make those messages positive, hopeful, inspirational, and motivational.

One game I made up when our children were little was, "I've got a secret." I told them, "I've got a secret for you," and whispered a positive message in their ears such as

"You're smart." I alternated "secrets" such as "beautiful, creative, talented, lovable, special, God loves you, healthy, strong," and so on. They had already heard these messages many times before so their response to my "secret" was "I already know that." Then I went to great lengths to think of another positive "secret" and the game continued. The net result was a lot of fun — especially around age three — and the establishment of a positive self-image. They *already knew* they are all those positive attributes and I hope they never forget.

Consider the poem, "Heaven's Special Child," by Edna Massimilla:

A meeting was held quite far from Earth.
'It's time again for another birth.'
Said the Angels to the Lord above,
This Special Child will need much love.
His progress may seem very slow,
Accomplishment he may not show;
And he'll require extra care
From folks he meets down there.
He may not run or laugh or play,
His thoughts may seem quite far away.
In many ways he won't adapt,
And he'll be known as Handicapped.
So let's be careful where he's sent,
We want his life to be content.
Please, Lord, find the parents who will do
A special job for you.
They will not realize right away,
The leading role they're asked to play,
But with this child sent from above,
Comes stronger faith and richer love.
And soon they'll know the privilege given
In caring for this gift from heaven.

Their precious charge, so meek and mild,
Is Heaven's Very Special Child.

While the physically and mentally handicapped present
the most challenging cases, in a very real sense, each child
is a special challenge. Every child has his or her own particular set of needs and idiosyncrasies. Try to maintain the
perspective that *every child is "heaven's special child"* given
to our care for a short time to cherish, nurture, help, and
learn from.

Recommended reading for raising children includes:
Toddlers And Parents by T. Barry Brazelton, M.D.; *How To
Raise A Healthy Child* by Robert Mendelsohn, M.D.; *Dare
To Discipline* and other books by James Dobson, Ph.D.; *The
Early Childhood Years* by Theresa and Frank Caplan; *What
Do You Really Want For Your Children?* by Wayne Dyer,
Ed.D.; and *Raising Positive Kids In A Negative World* by
Zig Ziglar.

Appreciating Aging and Our Elders

Thinking young, taking care of oneself, and staying
active are the keys to enjoying a long and full life. How old
would you be if you had no idea how old you were? Improved
health care, hygiene practices, occupational habits, and
education have helped our senior citizens enjoy active and
productive lives into their eighth and ninth decades. George
Burns has already booked an engagement at the Palladium
in London on his 100th birthday! Ida, a trim and energetic
octogenarian who walks four miles daily and hikes up small
mountains, said, "Having the health I'm blessed with is
because of hard work, eating healthy food, exercise, prayers,
good friends, and a Heavenly Father who watches over me."
Our culture has an imbalanced and narcissistic over-

emphasis on youth and beauty. All of us grow old, and the physical body eventually slows down, starts decaying, and changes. It's not bad; it's just different. Remember the importance of perspective and see the beauty in each stage of life. Work to keep the physical body as healthy and functional as possible for as long as you can. As time wears down this vehicle, however, don't fret; each stage of life has its own importance and purpose.

Older age is exquisitely designed to impart lessons that often elude younger and more active persons. As the body slows down and the five senses lose their clarity, seniors naturally experience frequent meditation like reveries. Older and bedridden persons can learn lessons that make bodily changes eminently worthwhile. These zen-like states teach us the *truth;* the only thing that happens when we die is we "drop our body" much like a snake sheds its skin.

Our eternal self or soul is one with the Creator and thus is indestructible; our body is merely an encasement that serves us for awhile and then becomes unnecessary. Take refuge in the faith and hope inherent in your spiritual beliefs. Since we each can have eternal life with God for the asking, why all the fuss about aging and dying? Growing older is a gradual preparation for letting go of everything and taking the next step in life.

A Paradise plant transplanted from Florida slowly lost all but one leaf; that last survivor was torn, brown, and drooped. I started to use the pot for a different plant but decided to give it another chance. That withered leaf enabled the survival of the entire plant as first one new shoot broke through the soil, then others. Now it's a huge and beautiful plant. The withered leaf finally died completely; cut up and returned to the soil, it has re-entered the cycle of "life and death."

Similarly, our elders have helped us get where we are now and are preparing to depart to the other side. They deserve our love, best treatment, and respect. Rather than sedating them in nursing homes, let's provide environments for optimal living. Grown children, care for your parents *at home* whenever possible when they need extra care. Remember the Golden Rule. Your parents spent years raising you while you were a helpless baby. Being a helpless elder is the flip side of the coin so return the favor. Honoring our elders and mutually growing from that experience is part of the grand design. Rather than bemoaning growing older, our society will increasingly explore the *adventures* and *benefits* of aging and dying consciously. Read books on aging, death, and dying by Elisabeth Kübler-Ross, M.D., Herman Feifel, Ph.D., and other gerontology/ thanatology authors.

Loving Relationships

Dr. Karl Menninger said, "Love cures people. Both the ones who give it and the ones who receive it." Healthy relationships help us grow toward balance and enlightenment. A relationship with another person is a sacred privilege to be appreciated and enjoyed. Like a garden, relationships need to be cultivated; those who nourish and respect significant others gain flowering relationships as a result. Of marriage, Kahil Gibran says, "Let there be spaces in your togetherness . . . Love one another, but make not a bond of love: Let it rather be a moving sea between the shores of your souls . . . And stand together yet not too near together: For the pillars of the temple stand apart, And the oak tree and the cypress grow not in each other's shadows."

Commitment is one of the most important aspects of a good relationship. W. H. Murray stated, "Until one is committed there is hesitancy, the chance to draw back, always ineffectiveness . . . the moment one definitely commits oneself, then Providence moves too. All sorts of things occur to help one that would never otherwise have occurred." A real sense of freedom and openness to growth occurs when we know another person really loves and accepts us. Marriage can be the highest form of relationship as two persons commit themselves for better or worse.

I'm not, however, recommending marriage for all persons and in all situations. One elderly lady, contemplating suicide, confessed, "I haven't loved my husband for 40 years, but we stayed together because that's what we were taught." The "we'll-make-it-work-if-it-kills-us" attitude aptly describes the stress-related illnesses that predominate in a longterm negative relationship. For example, breast cancer is higher in women who have a tough marriage with lack of autonomy.

Continuing an empty shell of a marriage for the sake of following religious, social, or moral convention benefits no one. Obtain marital or pastoral counseling during troubled times. But if a marriage or relationship is truly unhappy after years of trying, let it go and find a better partner. Life is too short to continually live in an unhappy and destructive relationship.

Most relationships go through tough times. Those who weather these temporary storms often come through them stronger and wiser. Strong winds that bend but don't break a tree make it stronger, more flexible, and more prepared for the next gusts. *None of us are perfect*; focus on the *good* in each other instead of amplifying the less desirable points.

One of the building blocks of a healthy relationship is realizing the divinity within each other. In *Life Is For Loving*, Butterworth writes, "Love is not to be found. It consists not in finding the right person but in becoming the right person . . . True marriage comes about as two people sense and see in each other something of the divine potential that is always present beyond appearances. This leads to a mutual commitment to help each other mate with one's God-self."

When a relationship does end — by death or separation — let the other person go and, when you're ready, find another good relationship. There's more than one fish in the sea and more than one "perfect person" for each of us. Some people remain in self-imposed isolation because of a deceased loved one's memory. Let go of the departed one and keep living. A 75-year-old whose second wife had died said, "She was a good woman but death is part of life. And people weren't meant to live alone. I've already got my next one picked out; only thing is, she's a Catholic nun so I've got my work cut out for me." (P. S. They recently married.)

Recommended books for nourishing healthy relationships include: *Life Is For Loving* by Eric Butterworth; *The Art Of Loving* by Erich Fromm; *Courtship After Marriage* by Zig Ziglar; *Living, Loving And Learning* by Leo Buscaglia; *Notes On Love And Courage* and *Notes To Myself* by Hugh Prather; and books by Wayne Dyer, Denis Waitley, and other self-improvement authors. A chain is only as strong as its weakest link; likewise, a relationship is strongest when people are at their physical, mental, and spiritual best.

Becoming A Fully Functioning Human Being

Buckminster Fuller, when asked what each person could do about all the problems facing humanity, answered, "Live life with as much integrity as you can." *Integrity.* Being honest, doing your best, going the extra mile, giving it your best shot, being sincere, and doing the right thing. Can you imagine how great life will be as each person lives with integrity? Remember, brighten the corner where you are. Change yourself and watch the world change. Each of us is an *integral* part of the solution to the problems of life.

Neurotic persons frequently complain about the way things are. Average persons put up with it. Self-actualizing persons do something about it. Dr. Wayne Dyer, in *The Sky's The Limit*, describes how we can become "no limit persons." The neurotic wastes a lot of energy stewing over what might have, could have, or should have been. Fully functioning persons see a job to do and pitch in. Becoming mobilized and addressing the problem is the highest functioning reaction to the anger and stress that we all experience. As we each use our God-given talents, we can solve life's problems and experience abundance and peace. Donate your money, labor, time, or prayers — all input is important.

Establish a balance between work, play, rest, and service to God and others; all are important for the fully functioning human being. As mentioned, Maslow called these levels of involvement the *hierarchy of self-actualization*. Esoteric Judaism has a model called *spheras of Kabbalah* where as the Hindu system of energy or life emphases is termed *chakras*.

There are seven chakras or energy centers, each with a different life-emphasis and correlated anatomical area. These correspond with the endocrine gland noted in parentheses. The first chakra (associated with the reproductive organs) is located around the genitals and is concerned with *survival issues*. Energies and needs about death concerns, food, water, and shelter are associated with this area. Death anxiety is a concern for most persons. The other concerns are obviously important but are met for most of us in the western culture. Some persons, however, even though their basic needs are met, worry excessively about survival needs.

The second chakra (pancreas) is located just below the

navel. Energy levels here are associated with *pleasure* of all types — sex, eating, drugs, alcohol, and other sensual pleasures. While we all enjoy pleasure, excessive hedonism can lead to a life of imbalance. A classic example would be a "Don Juan" personality who always seeks another sexual conquest in a life devoid of love and commitment. An imbalance involving oral gratification can contribute to obesity, smoking, and substance abuse.

The third chakra (adrenals) is located just below the breastbone, over the "solar plexus" region. These energies are associated with *power*, mastery, money, and winning. Again, a certain amount of these are fine in a balanced life. The person who overdoes it, however, is like the executive who scratches his or her way to the top, only to find it's lonely and empty there. We all like to win, but those who die with the most toys often aren't balanced.

The fourth or "heart" chakra (thymus gland) is located over the center of the sternum. These energies of *love* correlate with our emotional heart, the one that aches with extreme heartbreak. Most of us have noticed a heavy pressure over the chest when moved by sad or touching emotions. The fourth chakra is the bridge between earthly and transcendent energies — between the upper and lower energy centers. These energies include passionate, platonic, and — the most important kind — *unconditional love.*

The fifth chakra (thyroid) is located over the throat and is associated with *planetary consciousness.* These are higher levels of love, recognizing we are *all* brothers and sisters. These energies help us act upon the words of Jesus: "Inasmuch as ye have done it (clothed, fed, took in, visited) unto one of the least of these my brethren, ye have done it unto me." (Matthew 25:40) When touched by concern for planetary issues, you may feel "choked up" and notice throat constriction.

The sixth chakra (pineal gland) is located between and just above our two eyes. This is the "third eye" or center of higher powers of *wisdom*, insight, and abilities that some term supernatural or extrasensory. As we grow in love and a desire to serve others, we are given or can cultivate higher powers and abilities.

The seventh or "crown chakra" (pituitary gland) is located over the crown of the head. These energies are correlated with *cosmic consciousness* — a consistent realization that God is All. Many of us have glimpsed this level of enlightenment and felt accompanying peace, hope, energy, and unity with the Creator. From this level we remember there is nothing to worry about, that life is an eternal and everchanging dance of energy. Life is ultimately just and good; there is a Divine intelligence and order in the universe.

With each chakra, the key is to be balanced and upgrade our energies as much as possible. Some people spend most of their energy at levels one through three and then wonder why life seems empty. Ideally, our energies flow up and down these levels as appropriate. The natural progression of life is to experience the higher levels while maintaining a balance in the lower ones. Some persons have *energy blocks* or fixations that keep them inordinately concerned with lower level pursuits.

Get your priorities straight. Chakras four through seven lead to the inner peace, joy, and harmony that all persons seek. Keep the lower chakra pursuits in balance and enjoy the entire spectrum of life. Use this information for self-analysis and make life changes as needed; if your life isn't balanced, what is missing? The purpose of life is to reach a *balance* between these seven energy levels and associated potentials. A simple technique can aid this process. After using standard relaxation preparations, visualize pure white light infusing each chakra and gently flowing upward. Pray or affirm that your energies at each level are becoming more upgraded and balanced. For additional information about chakras and energy balancing, read: *Joy's Way: A Map For The Transformational Journey* by W. Brugh Joy, M.D.; *Human Energy Systems* by Jack Schwartz; and *The Only Dance There Is* by Ram Dass.

Surviving Tough Times

An Egyptian surgeon imprisoned during war had to treat the wounded with the barest necessities of equipment. As a result, he discovered a new healing technique and later was instrumental in introducing chiropractic into Egypt. His inspiring message was, *"That which seems bad at the time often results in an eventual greater good."* Hope always exists. Every cloud has a silver lining. Remember these truths when you are going through tough times. Read Rev. Robert Schuller's books *Tough Times Never Last, But Tough People Do!* and *Success Is Never Ending, Failure Is Never Final* and remember the truth of these titles.

A Detroit hospital volunteer, Fanniedell Peeples, comforts babies dying of drug withdrawal, AID's, and other diseases. She was born with disabling scoliosis and was orphaned at age seven, spending much of her childhood in foster homes. "I cried for years," she says. Her tough times aided inner heart and soul growth that prepared her for working with dying infants. "I stroke and I care and I rock as they're on their way out . . . I tell them, 'I love you and I'll miss you.'" They've missed so many things. We owe them the dignity to leave as human beings at least." She continues, "If you look at them real good the moment it's over, they never looked better. The struggle and the pain is gone. They look like cherubs."

Tough times can — in the long run — be a blessing in disguise. Her early sorrows and misfortunes have allowed her to serve others in a way that might not have been possible with an easier life. In the same *People* magazine article, other stories of courage and hope in the face of adversity were told: a 61-year-old antidrug activist who, despite being shot by drug dealers, still refused to back down; a 29-year-old automobile accident victim whose organs were donated so that others could live; triplets orphaned by their alcoholic mother and drug-addict father but adopted by a family despite medical and financial hardships.

These are just a few real life examples of people helping each other and making the best of a tough situation. The great God who designed, created, and sustains the entire universe helps us make victories out of grief. Our hardships will make sense someday and can have a greater meaning now if we just try and ask God's help.

Problems or failures are part of life. Thomas Edison "failed" in 25,000 experiments as he tried to perfect the electric storage battery. It took him nearly 9000 attempts to complete the electric light bulb. Michelangelo said, "Much does he gain, who, when he loses, learns." Remember: "When the going gets tough, the tough get going." When tough times come — and they occasionally will — surround yourself with positive and inspirational friends, books, and tapes. Be good to yourself and charge up while planning your next move. Then continue onward.

During a serious crisis, it's common to have fleeting thoughts of giving up or even suicide. These are usually warning signals that you need a break and some outside help. Thoughts of "ending it all" are signals you are hurting and want to ease the pain. Don't think you're crazy or immoral for having suicidal thoughts. Nearly everyone has briefly entertained the idea when burdens of life seem too heavy to bear. Contact your local mental health center, crisis line, minister, or other resource for the help and hope you need.

Hope

Now you have many new ideas and techniques for achieving self-actualization and managing stress. Put this information to use and be ready for profound inner changes. As you face decisions and obstacles in life, remember — *you always have the power to choose.* Even in the face of tragedy and misfortune, you can always control your attitude. Focus on your strengths; with determination and ingenuity, there are always creative solutions. Remember the Simontons' motto: "In the face of uncertainty, there is nothing wrong with hope."

James Allen, regarding the power of thoughts, said, "You are today where your thoughts have brought you; you will be tomorrow where your thoughts take you . . . you will always gravitate towards that which you, secretly, most love." The Dhammapada states, "We are what we think. All that we are arises with our thought. With our thoughts we make the world. Speak and act with an impure mind and trouble will follow you as the wheel follows the ox that draws the cart . . . speak or act with a pure mind and happiness will follow you as your shadow, unshakable."

Life is for learning so enjoy your curriculum. Difficult lessons are often the most important ones so keep your hope and faith strong when the going gets tough. W. Clement Stone encourages, "With every adversity, there's a seed of equivalent or greater benefit for those who have positive mental attitude and apply it and if they will ask for help from the One who can give them help."

Help, love, accept, and forgive one another and especially yourself. Don't be too hard on yourself when you make mistakes. Look at failure as a learning experience; tomorrow is a new day. We each are a lot alike in many ways. We all have various insecurities, fears, worries, and idiosyncrasies. So what's the big deal? The first step toward growth and improvement is accepting where you are today. Let the past go and don't hold yourself back another moment. Take life one day at a time and begin expressing your full potentials and talents. This is the path toward psychological balance and true stress management.

Within each of us — no matter what our station in life at this moment — is an infinite array of potentials and talents. We each have a dream inside — a special goal or purpose in life. Follow it, nurture it, and never give up. With our vast inner potentials, a loving God, and a friendly Universe, we are sure to eventually succeed and prosper.

ACTION STEPS

• List five priority items *for you* from this chapter and begin to change those areas. After you change those, pick five more.

• Review the goal setting information and write your goals.

• Read and listen to the authors listed.

• Fill your life with positive and growth-producing habits on a consistent basis and watch the real you unfold.

• Take the time each day to become relaxed and centered, using technique(s) that work best for you.

• Seek inputs that reinforce your growing belief that we each are important and can improve ourselves and the world.

• Make a priority to reprogram your mind in a positive, hopeful, and optimistic manner. It's well worth the effort.

SPIRITUAL ENLIGHTENMENT

*"All of us have mortal bodies composed of
perishable matter but the soul lives forever:
it is a portion of the Deity housed in our bodies."*
— *Flavius Josephus*

There are over 3000 religions in the world — all of them can't be completely right and probably none of them are completely wrong. I recommend having a *personal relationship* with the Creator since "An atheist is a person with no invisible means of support." No one person or religion has the market cornered on "the truth." In the movie *Oh God*, George Burns as God was asked: "Which of the world's religions is the closest to the divine truth?" He replied, "The divine truth is not in a building, or a book, or a story. The heart is the temple wherein all truth resides."

Conventional wisdom advises against discussing religion; however, I've met many persons who are afraid, confused, or disenchanted about God and religion. Thanatologists hold that anxiety about death is a concern for nearly everyone. I believe that fears and misinformation about God and afterlife are at the core of many physical, mental, and spiritual ailments. Thus, I discuss these controversial but vitally important topics.

Willis Harman, Ph.D., author of *Global Mind Change* and *Insight Into The New Age: A Scientific Inquiry Into Consciousness And The Nature Of Reality* describes *esoteric* teachings that show remarkable similarities among various religions. Christianity has esoteric roots, mystical Judaism dates to 2000 B.C., and Sufism is the esoteric branch of Islam. Aldous Huxley termed these core teachings common to many religions the "perennial philosophy." Dr. Harman lists these similarities:

1. "The world of matter and individual conscious-ness — the world of things and animals and people — is the manifestation of a divine ground within which all partial realities have their being."
2. "Human beings are capable not merely of knowing about the divine ground, they can also realize its existence by intuition, which is superior to normal reasoning. This immedi-ate knowledge unites the knower with that which is known."
3. "Humans possess a double nature, a time-bound ego, and an eternal self. This eternal self is the spirit, the spark of divinity within the soul. It is possible for a human being to identify with the spirit — the divine ground — that is, to recognize one's own divine nature."
4. "The life of a human being on earth has only one purpose — to identify with the eternal self and so to come to *unitive* knowledge of the divine ground."

To help you understand my religious orientation, my dad was Catholic and my mother Lutheran; I attended Lutheran services until age 18 when I attended a Nazarene church. I accepted Jesus as my personal savior and have felt His presence in my life ever since. I attended a Methodist theological seminary, my brother is a Baptist, my sister a Presbyterian, and my parents now worship by helping others. I studied and attended Seventh Day Adventist, Church of Jesus Christ of Latter Day Saints, Jehovah's Witness, Universalist-Unitarian, and Christian Science churches. I have studied Judaism, Hinduism, Islam, and other Eastern religions. I currently attend Unity and United Church of Christ (UCC) services.

I believe we are all children of God and a valuable part of the Creation. As Max Muller wrote, "There never was a false God, nor was there ever really a false religion, unless you call a child a false man."

I present this chapter in a spirit of unity and love. Let us remember there is but *one God*. Consider the blind men and the elephant analogy. God is like the huge elephant and we humans are like blind persons trying to describe Him. *Sharing* spiritual viewpoints helps us better comprehend the phenomena of God and life. I'm not advocating a worldwide religion; I do encourage an appreciation and respect of varying viewpoints. Those who worship God in any manner have much more *in common* than not; let's increasingly focus on our *similarities* instead of our differences.

The Nature of God

My parents showed me a beautiful sunset when I was five years old and I told them I thought it "looked like God." Gerald G. Jampolsky, M.D., author of *Love Is Letting Go of*

Fear, co-authored *Love Is The Answer* with Diane V. Cirincione. They write: "It is possible to see God simply as a force that is neither vengeful, judgmental, nor punishing — only loving and forgiving. Being able to experience God as a loving force and a light shining in you and throughout the universe at all times is very different from the childhood concept of a God that many of us have — with a beard, way up in the sky, distant and external, waiting to judge us."

God is Love. God is the greatest phenomena that exists in the universe, encompassing and *being* all that is. God is the Energy and "stuff" of life. Of the phrase "In the beginning was the word," Biblical scholar Dr. R. Errico translates from the original Aramaic: *"Energy of mind was always in existence."* Gurudas describes "the word" as sound wave, movement, and vibration. He says the origin of the universe is vibrational movement as waves of energy lead to the formation of matter. Modern physicists developing the Grand Unified Theory are finding a universe of pure energy forming the very substance of our world. God is the Life Force behind all existence. He/She/It permeates every molecule of the creation.

Yet, God personally and intimately loves each one of us and awaits our return to Him. God is incredibly interested in each of us as individuals. God is as near to us as our breath and is inside you and me. God is like the sun and the various aspects of creation are like rays of sunshine. God is Spirit — equatable with love, energy, universe, life, and nature. Many people could identify with the concept of "the Force" in the *Star Wars* films. God is like that; an all pervasive power that eternally is good, love, peace, and wisdom.

Sincerely ask God for inner guidance and then trust your answers. The word "fear" also can be interpreted as "respect;" God is a power worthy of love and respect but not to be feared. Don't be afraid to talk about, search, and question established beliefs. You certainly won't hurt God's feelings. Don't let differing beliefs, past misconceptions, or semantics keep you from personally knowing the living God that exists within and all around you.

I once had a vision of a huge golden sphere surrounded by an infinite number of tiny golden specks. Each individual speck was connected to the sphere by a tiny golden thread. A closer look revealed that the central sphere contained additional specks or dots. I marveled at this translucent and iridescent golden array as a calm, clear voice or thought said, "This is how God and the Universe are. All life is One and interconnected."

The entire array symbolized God or life. The sphere represented the place of realization that God is All. The specks depicted individual souls — some very close to or inside God and others quite distant. The specks outside the sphere were connected to the central orb and the golden threads were the countless pathways to God. These pathways varied greatly in the route taken toward the sphere. Some were straight shots a short distance away; others were very far away and were linked by winding and tortuous paths.

The important point is that all the dots were, in fact, *connected to the Source*. Viewed from a sufficient distance or perspective, a perimeter could be drawn around the entire assemblage. This was a beautiful vision of how all life is connected to and is part of the magnificent process we call God. From a limited or human viewpoint, the dots seemed separate from the center just as some persons think they are distant from God. But from a cosmic or enlightened perspective, life is one vast unified whole.

The Unity movement states: "God is not a physical man in the sky, for this limits him. God is Spirit, everywhere present, the one and only Spirit, behind, in and through all things, visible and invisible . . . . *There is only one presence and one power in the universe, God the good, omnipotent.*" God is omnipotent, omniscient, and omnipresent; that is, all-powerful, all-knowing, and all-present. Given these truths, what is there to fear?

We're each an intimate and important part of life, beloved by God, and destined for a great and eternal existence. The Supreme Being understands our weaknesses yet *loves us in our brokenness.* Any attempt by us to love or contact God will be instantly recognized and rewarded. Unless we consistently and defiantly resist God, we can't lose. And few — if any — will *forever* reject God, good, love, and peace over evil and disharmony.

God is always and forever in intimate communication with each of us. A common Unity phrase is, "There is no spot where God is not." The Apostle Paul said: "The God that made the world and all things therein, He, being Lord of heaven and earth . . . is not far from each one of us; for in Him we live, and move, and have our being . . . for we are also His offspring" (Acts 17: 24, 27, 28).

Build your life on the spiritual bedrock of a loving God and eternal afterlife. Knowing that we have eternity and Divine love alters our very being. Life on earth looks very different when seen through eyes of strong faith, hope, love, and belief in God. The key ingredient is a personal relationship with the Creator and each of us has that possibility every moment.

Experience the *Ground of Existence* as being inside and all around you. Albert Einstein said: "The most beautiful thing we can experience is the Mysterious . . . to know that what is impenetrable to us really exists, manifesting itself as the highest wisdom and the most radiant beauty which our dull facilities can comprehend only in their most primitive forms . . . this knowledge, this feeling, is at the center of true religiousness."

Space scientists estimate there are more stars in the universe than there are grains of sand on all the beaches of earth. Given the magnitude of the cosmos, is it possible we don't know the final word about God, afterlife, and pre-existence? God doesn't love and direct just a few select persons from one certain religion. The God I'm describing created and maintains the entire universe (Universal Intelligence) *and* each person (Innate Intelligence).

Ram Dass speaks of our brains as being like TV receivers that pick up a limited number of stations. We may only be aware of channels 3, 5, and 7, but there are many other stations that we don't normally detect. The truth is, *there is more to "reality" than can be detected by our five senses.* Hummingbirds can differentiate between eight shades of white that appear the same to us. Animals can hear sounds, for example a dog whistle, that humans can't. These scientific facts should cause us to pause before we make definitive statements about the nature of reality and God.

Einstein proposed the Theory of Relativity that states $e=mc^2$; that is, energy equals mass multiplied by the square of the speed of light. In other words, *energy and mass are transmutable and interchangeable* under certain conditions. Quantum wave mechanic physicists hold that energy and mass are not separate entities but phenomena that overlap in nature. When asked to describe the nature of reality, this theory explains that solid matter has properties of energy or light waves; and, conversely, energy or light waves have properties of solid matter. Read *The Tao of Physics* by physicist Fritjof Capra, Ph.D., for a more detailed discussion of this topic.

TIME science writer Eugene Linden writes: "For much of this century, scientists have known that the comfortable solidity of things begins to break down at the subatomic level. Like the Hindu veil of Maya, the palette from which nature paints atoms proves illusory when approached. From afar, this world appears neatly separated into waves and particles, but close scrutiny reveals indescribable objects that have characteristics of both." The nature of reality is neither solid mass nor pure energy but more an interplay or flow between the two.

Physics and chemistry describe the ephemeral nature of existence: All "solid" objects are largely space, with tiny atoms whirring at high speeds inside this space. When you rest your hand on a table, the molecules and atoms that make up your hand and the table interchange. The most exciting implication of all this is *there is no separation in the unity of life.* Religions have long told us that *God is love and light, permeating all existence.* Now physicists *similarly* describe life as a mysterious interplay between matter, energy, and light. My point? There is more to life than meets the eye. Ninety-nine percent of life is invisible — comprised of spirit and energy. God is universal energy and intelligence; all life is one and unified with this force.

Feeling Closer to God

Since God is all around and within us, it is nonsensical to speak of *getting* closer to God. Yet, some persons don't *feel* close to God or even believe that such a power exists. Others feel they are so sinful or inferior that their chances of being loved or "saved" are remote. Some don't know they are — at the root of their being — eternal spirit and an integral part of the creation. *A magnificent creation and design implies a Master Creator and Designer.* God reveals Itself to all those who truly desire to know the truth. Matthew 7:7 reassures: "Ask, and it shall be given you; seek, and ye shall find; knock, and it shall be opened unto you."

It is God's desire that *all* will come to know Her and the reality of eternal life. Luke 12:32 states, "Fear not, little flock; for it is your Father's good pleasure to give you the kingdom." I Corinthians 15:22 says, "For as in Adam all die, even so in Christ shall *all* be made alive." Since God is all-powerful, this will eventually occur — *without time and space limitations*. Butterworth says, "You can never be separated from God because you are an expression of God, the self-livingness of God." Paul, in I Corinthians 3:16 asked, "Know ye not that ye are a temple of God, and that the spirit of God dwelleth in you?" Speaking of God, Alfred Tennyson wrote, "Closer is he than breathing and nearer than hands and feet."

Some persons spend a lot of money, travel long distances, and practice rigorous techniques to "find God." If these approaches seem right for you, follow them. Ultimately, however, you will find that the object of your search was and always will be inside of and all around you. A famous poet of India, Kabir, after being asked about minute details regarding the path to God, said, "Verily it maketh me smile to hear of a fish in water athirst; if He be near, no path needeth thou at all."

Becoming *enlightened* — really knowing God and our eternal nature — alters our life view in a positive and dramatic way. From an earthly perspective there are a lot of problems and tragedies. The enlightened person feels compassion for all this yet remembers that our time on Earth is but a fraction of eternity. Our four score or so years on Earth are just a drop of water in the ocean of life. Infinity has no beginning and no end. Hope and faith are always warranted so learn your earthly lessons, love each other, and serve God. We can whistle our way through each day, knowing there is much more to life than our present physical setting.

Remember that God is your friend, always there to

help, guide, and comfort. You may have read accounts of persons who lived a pauper's life when, in fact, they had lots of money. We may write them off as eccentrics, but their situation is a good analogy for many of us. All of us are spiritual billionaires, but some of us don't realize it; thus, some persons unnecessarily lead spiritually bankrupt lives. Resolve to increase in awareness of your spiritual riches. In *The Be Happy Attitudes,* Rev. Robert Schuller exclaims, "I'm a child of God. I'm God's idea and God only gets good ideas."

As you become enlightened, you will sense messages of the good news all around you. The whisper of the wind, the babbling brook, the beauty of nature's cycles — all creation sings a song of joy and peace. Some people say they need a miracle to believe in God; with eyes that really see, we realize that *all creation is a miracle.* Plants growing, the birth of a child, planets in balance — every atom is literally a miracle that we too often take for granted. We need to awaken from our earthly stupor and really relish life — like a child experiencing things for the first time. Live life one moment at a time and be as fully aware as possible to realize all the blessings and miracles that are *here now.*

Concept Therapy states: "The very highest states of consciousness and the most supernormal powers have occurred uniformly in the case of those whose conscious thought was most habitually occupied with conceptions of Deity as being omnipotent, omniscient, and omnipresent. It is everywhere. It has all the power and all the knowledge, and it is right with us. When that concept is really operative, great things, much greater things, will begin to happen in our life and in our expression."

Jesus said, "And ye shall know the truth, and the truth shall make you free." (John 8:32) This is the good news of our inner divinity — the reality of God in each of us. Consider the words of Psalms 82:6 (reiterated by Jesus in John

12:34,) "I have said, ye are gods; and all of you are children of the most High." *Internalizing* this good news is crucial for true wellness, self-love, and inner peace. Consider Ephesians 4:6, "One God and Father of all, who is above all, and through all, and in you all." Yes, there is a spark of the divine in each one of us.

Genesis 1:31 tells us that after the Creation, "God saw everything that He had made, and, behold it was very good." Genesis 1:27 states, "So God created man in his own image . . ." Rev. James Elliot, United Church of Christ minister, interprets this as saying that each of us is created with the spirit of God within and that we have the potential to become godlike. *Like God* in that we can become a new creation so filled with the spirit of God that our essential nature changes. Don't let the semantics throw you; we are all one with God. Part of becoming a fully functioning and enlightened human being, then, is realizing and expressing our inner godlike potentials.

Meditate upon this good news and realize the significance of this insight. Salvation, grace, love, and eternal life are there for all of us. Any outreach to God will be met with open arms. God is a much more wise, beneficent, and loving phenomena than She is usually given credit for. *Be here now* — live each moment fully and consciously — and realize your oneness with the Source of all life.

Recall the Biblical story of the "prodigal son" who disobeyed his father and squandered a fortune. The son was living in the "far country" of spiritual ignorance and temporary "separation" from his father. We each have temporarily strayed from the spiritual path and wasted our potentials. Just like the prodigal son, however, we eventually tire of the superficial and yearn to return home. Take heart in the father's response when the son returned; he forgave his son and had a feast prepared. Similarly, the Creator always stands ready to accept, love, and transform us. *Feeling* any closer to God yet?

Jesus and Christ Consciousness

Jesus was an advanced soul who experienced life from the highest levels of Cosmic or Christ Consciousness. He knew the truth of His inseparability from God, saying, "I and my Father are one . . . the Father is in me and I in him." (John 11:30 and 38) The life of Jesus was a beautiful demonstration of the potentials inherent in humans who realize and express their Divine natures. From a Christian perspective, Jesus was that human in whom God was most fully revealed. But the Jesus I know and love has a message and significance for all persons, all religions, and in all times.

Theologians and the world's religions can't agree on the precise meaning of the Christ event, so listen to *your heart and mind.* Leslie Weatherhead, in his wonderful book, *Life Begins At Death*, states, "I have a speculation that Jesus may have been a spirit very highly developed, perhaps through innumerable reincarnations who, as the hymn says, from his throne on high, seeing our miserable plight, offered to come back and take on our flesh in order to help us and bring us to God."

My understanding of who Jesus is involves the concept of "Christ Consciousness." Jesus was a man who demonstrated and taught the Divinity-potential in all humans. He knew about and lived out His inner divinity; He showed how we can be, what we can achieve, and that we live after "death." His greatest gift was bringing the good news of God — that the kingdom of heaven is within and all around us, that we are one with God, and that we can be spiritually reborn for the asking. If we each have a spark of God in us,

Jesus Christ had a large flame. He chose to take on a human birth and suffer so that He could bring a heaven-sent message.

Unity, a 100-year-old worldwide Christian organization, states: "Unity proclaims the divinity of Jesus but goes further and assures that you, too, are a child of God and therefore divine in nature. Jesus expressed His divine potential and sought to show us how to express ours as well. Salvation is then the expanding understanding of one's innate divinity and perfectibility through living the life demonstrated by Jesus."

Jesus Christ, the Light of the world, tried to bring light to the darkness of religious understandings of His day. Jesus the man remembered and developed His inner Christ Consciousness. He achieved a fine balance between the human and divine — a rare but wonderfully instructive feat. "Christ Consciousness" is that aspect of God that teaches and inspires each of us; that level spoke loud and clear in Jesus. He knew His oneness with the Source of Life and taught from that perspective.

Perhaps you've seen religious artworks of persons with a miniature Christ inside their chest. Hindu depictions show a servant of God, Hanuman, in the same position over the heart or fourth chakra. This is the anatomical correlate of Christ actually residing within us. The Christ exists within us just as a holographic fragment contains the whole. The Christ Consciousness that illumined Jesus and other great teachers speaks to each of us as well. In *Oh God*, "God" was asked, "Is Jesus Christ the Son of God?" He answered, "Jesus was my son. Buddha was my son. Mohammed, Moses, you, the man who said there was no room in the inn was my son. And so is the one who charges $11 for steak in this one."

God speaks to all persons in different ways. I don't

believe any one religion has an exclusive understanding of or audience with Jesus. That would limit the love and outreach of God and Christ. Rather, every culture and religion — in differing ways — has and will continue to receive the Christ message. Native American stories describe past visits from a bearded, pale-skinned visitor with holes in his moccasins. He has since been known as the "Greatest Reflection of the Creator" and the "Morning Star Visitor." Jesus is alive today in the spirit, working unceasingly to teach and minister all those in need. This is the *universal significance* of the Christ event.

In Colossians 1:27-28, Paul reminds us of "Christ in you, the hope of glory . . . that we may present every man perfect in Christ Jesus." Oliver L. Reiser, author of *Cosmic Humanism,* wrote, "If there is one thing the Christian mystery sought to teach, it was the divinity within man, the 'Christ-in-you,' undeveloped and unheeded." In Richard Bach's *Illusions,* the reluctant messiah says, "Okay, I'm the son of God, but so are we all; I'm the savior, but so are you! The works that I do, you can do! Anybody in their right mind understands that."

Unity minister Eric Butterworth, author of *Discover The Power Within You* and other excellent books, states: "Christ is a degree of stature that Jesus attained but a degree of potential stature that dwells in every man . . . Every man is a potential Christ. But only a few know this, and an even fewer number succeed in expressing any marked degree of the perfection of the Christ indwelling. It is not that we want to depreciate Jesus. We couldn't do that if we wanted to. We are not pulling Him down to our level, but showing that we can be lifted up to His level." Dr. George Lamsa holds that "in the name of Jesus" means "done by the *method* of Jesus;" that is, realizing our oneness with God just as Jesus did.

Jesus clarified our relationship with God. While some religious models depict humans as continually *working toward* divinity, Jesus taught that we are *already* divine by grace and birthright. In *Life Is For Loving*, Butterworth says, "Man is a spiritual being, created with the same mind as in Jesus Christ. The difference between Jesus and us is that he acted constantly at the level of his divinity while we often act at the level of our humanity. His mission was to help people to turn inward and discover the new world of their infinite potential."

Emilie Cady says: "Oh, how in our ignorance we have mistaken and misunderstood God, in consequence of which we are today pygmies when He wanted to make us giants in love and health and power by manifesting more of Himself through us! . . . this same Christ lives within us that lived in Jesus. It is the part of Himself which God has put within us, which ever lives there, with an inexpressible love and desire to spring to the circumference of our being, or to our consciousness, as our sufficiency in all things."

I attended theological seminary, in part, to reach a clarification of some religious questions. I learned that religious documents from thousands of years ago have been *translated, interpreted differently, added to, deleted from,* and otherwise changed. Given its length, language, and changes, the Bible says many things to different people and is subject to varying interpretations. I agree with the saying, "Take the Bible seriously but not necessarily literally."

One important lesson I learned was the significance of prepositions. Consider the frequently quoted Biblical statements, "For God so loved the world, that He gave His only begotten Son, that whosoever believeth *in* Him should not perish but have everlasting life." (John 3:16) and "I am the way, and the truth, and life; no one comes to the Father, but *by* me." (John 14:6) Two key prepositions, *in* and *by*, are of pivotal importance in interpreting these statements. In earlier Aramaic, Greek, and Hebrew versions, interchangeable prepositions were commonly used. *In* could also have been translated *like*; *by* could be replaced with *as*, resulting in a vastly different meaning.

Now consider the different messages in these sentences: ". . . that whosoever believeth *like* him shall not perish, but have everlasting life" and "no one comes to the Father, but *as* me" (as Jesus did). In other words, when you see reality *like* Jesus did, you understand that the kingdom of heaven is within and at hand. You can then enjoy the unconditional love of God that is ours *now* and throughout eternity.

God wouldn't let the salvation or damnation of the multitudes hinge upon the interpretation of a few prepositions. Jesus repeatedly emphasized that God was like a shepherd who would not let one of his flock be lost. Supreme Beings do not have time or space limitations for their love or forgiveness. Rev. Robert Love, author of *Hell No,* says, "I can affirm that only through Christ does one come to God, for I affirm that the Christ event has universal significance . . . The Christ event touches all people, regardless of our temporal awareness of the faith God has given to all of us . . . I say that God brings all people to himself through Christ."

Butterworth states, "Jesus taught that man lives in two worlds — not in succession, but concurrently. He lives in the world of appearances, the three-dimensional world of form and shape, of time and space — the world where we have fluctuating experiences of sickness and health, of peace and war, of harmony and chaos. But man also lives in a spiritual world as a spiritual being . . . This is that of you that is the perfect idea in the Mind of God. You are simply asleep to this greater self, your innate divinity. Paul says, 'Awake thou that sleepest, that Christ may shine upon thee.' (Ephesians 5:14) And what is Christ but your own divinity . . . it is you at the point of God."

In our heart of hearts — our inner core or true self — we all want to live according to God's will. It takes a *conscious* decision and inner willingness for this conversion to take place. Take a moment, getting quiet within first, and say "yes" to the God and Christ nature within. Fear not; God has a much more sensible and far-reaching plan for the salvation of all than He is sometimes given credit for. The Christ-spirit that so empowered Jesus also exists within all persons, just waiting to be expressed. Butterworth says, "The true hope of mankind is the Christ-Spirit in the heart of all men, which Jesus in His illumined consciousness revealed."

Twenty years ago, I was caught in a severe winter storm. The roads were pure ice and interstate traffic was creeping at 20 mph. My little car spun out of control after I passed a slower moving semitrailer. It continued to spin as the truck — unable to stop — bore down on me. I remember thinking I would probably die and then said, *"Jesus help me!"* My car immediately shot off the road; the semi just missed me and I was unharmed. Believers would call that a miracle and an example of help from a Divine Being who continues to aid and direct us. Skeptics would call it luck. But a persistently spinning object can't instantly change direction without an outside force being exerted. I'm a believer.

Jesus *saved* us from ignorance of our true nature and demonstrated that life continues beyond the grave. He taught us to love and serve each other, to follow our hearts and minds, and not be intimidated by orthodoxy. For nearly 2000 years, the *details* of His message have been changed, misunderstood, and debated. Fortunately, God and the heavenly host continue to communicate the big idea and speak in our hearts. Listen to that voice and open your heart's door to the ever beckoning Christ within.

Prayer

Daily prayer is an excellent way to improve our faith in and relationship with the Creator. The most important aspect of prayer is your sincere desire to commune with God. *Group* prayers, songs, chants, and silent meditations can be even more powerful. We're told that the Father knows our needs even before we ask. As such, *the best prayer is a prayer of thanks* — knowing that God will give us what we *need*. Praying is not a lever with which to manipulate God; you don't have to wake God up or talk Him into anything. Prayer is simply communicating with our Higher Power and giving thanks for the bounty that *always* flows from the Source of all good.

When you pray, enter the "closet" of your inner mind — the quiet space within where you remember you are one with God. A calm and relaxed state is optimal for talking with God and hearing answers or inspiration in return. If prayer is talking to God, then meditation is listening. Spend a few quiet moments after prayer and note the wise and reassuring thoughts that arise from deep within. Since God is part of us — at our innermost true self — prayer is also like talking to ourselves. "Be still and know that I am God." (Psalms 46:10)

The night before I finished the last revision of *Balanced Living*, I felt a profound peace, like I had finally arrived after years of praying, working, and searching. I talked with my wife Michelle about this at length, explaining that I had originally planned to become an M.D.

but that a series of events resulted in my becoming a *D.C.* (Doctor of Chiropractic). I finally felt that these life changes had occurred for a good reason and worked out for the best.

The next morning, I started to complete the last several hours of work on the manuscript. Just as I had done for nearly four years, I turned on the computer and monitor that usually show a blank screen followed by computer codes and prompts. That morning, however, the monitor screen immediately showed a vivid display of royal gold and maroon squares. (The colors on the cover of *Balanced Living* are the closest to these colors I could find.) These colored squares each contained the same two letters. Without reading further, guess what the two letters were. I rubbed my eyes and pinched myself to make sure I wasn't dreaming. The letters were D.C.!

I looked up and said, "Thanks, I needed that," then wondered why we don't receive more signs of hope and faith from above. The answer came in a split of a second as a clear and calm thought:

1. We must first *ask* for help and inspiration from above.

2. We must keep our senses (including our intuition) alert and *perceive* this guidance, remembering it may not come when or how we expect it.

3. We should *give thanks* for this help.

4. We must use it for the betterment of humankind and to the glory of God/Universal Intelligence.

If we *just once* sincerely ask God and Christ to help, it is done; we don't have to keep begging and repeating. Remember the most powerful prayer: "Thy will, not mine, be done." God, as the underlying intelligence and power behind all creation, has the best perspective of what we need.

One excellent prayer is entitled *Prayer for Peace:*
"Lord, make me an instrument of your peace.
Where there is hatred . . . let me sow love.
Where there is injury . . . pardon.
Where there is doubt . . . faith.
Where there is despair . . . hope.
Where there is darkness . . . light.
Where there is sadness . . . joy.
O Divine Master, grant that I may not so much seek to
        be consoled as to console.
To be understood as to understand.
To be loved as to love.
For it is in giving that we receive.
It is in pardoning that we are pardoned.
It is in dying that we are born to eternal life."

In a very real sense, our every thought, word, and deed is our prayer. We can show our appreciation to God by expressing our full potentials in loving and harmonious ways. As we increasingly live one moment at a time, we see life as a dance or play with the Beloved. We can walk hand in hand, in constant communion with the Source of all life. As he prepared to leave on a train, Gandhi was asked by a reporter to send a message to the people. He hurriedly scribbled on a scrap of paper "My life is my message." Similarly, our life can be our prayers — expressions of thanksgiving and demonstrations of our physical, mental, and spiritual abilities.

Heaven: Realizing the Kingdom Within

Heaven has been depicted in various ways by different cultures and belief systems. Earl A. Grollman, author of *Concerning Death: A Practical Guide For The Living,* describes Protestant beliefs as ranging: "from those who do not believe in any afterlife to those who may believe in reincarnation . . . from materialistic conceptions of heaven as a place of golden streets . . . and hell as a place of raging fires to more symbolic concepts of heaven as a spiritual realm of being in harmonious relationship with the eternal and of hell's representing alienation and isolation from the eternal."

Viewpoints concerning heaven include: a personal identity that survives the experience of death; fellowship with God and communion with saints and loved ones; opportunities for growth, spiritual development, and service. The Roman Catholic faith holds that the paschal mystery (the death and resurrection of Christ) is the key for hope. In the resurrection "death is conquered — not only the death of Christ but ultimately one's own death as well."

Jewish beliefs include an acknowledgment of the inevitability of bodily death while recognizing the deathlessness of a person's spirit. There is, Rabbi Grollman continues, "the acceptance that man transcends death in naturalistic fashion. Man is immortal; in body, through his children; in thought, through the survival of his memory; in influence, by virtue of the continuance of his personality as a force among those who come after him; and ideally, through the identification with the timeless things of the spirit. There was postulated a continued existence of the soul after death . . . The soul was the immortal part of man that was independent of the body . . . Before the body comes into being, the soul already exists." In addition to resurrection into heaven, "For others there is the belief in the transmigration of the soul, where human beings after death would enter another body and thus a new life . . . According to the Kabbala, the soul of Aaron was first reincarnated in Eli and then in Ezra."

O. Lazarus, in *Liberal Judaism and Its Standpoint*, summarizes a Reform Jewish attitude toward death: "There is that within us which is immortal and it is not bounded by time and space. It is this, man's soul, as it is called, which continues, so we believe, to live after the death of the body. To it, death is but an incident of life." The Conservative Jewish movement also has beliefs in resurrection and immortality of the soul.

The word "heaven" literally means "expanding." Says Butterworth: "Life is a limitless experience in an expanding universe . . . Life is growth and unfoldment and life is lived from inside out . . . The average person lives his life from outside in. He frustrates his potential when he lets his level of consciousness be determined by what people say, what conditions appear to be, what he reads in the paper . . . It doesn't really matter what happens around you or to you. These things are in the world, and you can overcome the world . . . And you can control your thoughts, for you are the master of your mind — or *you* can be."

Heaven, continues Butterworth, is: ". . . the upper level of man's total consciousness. Jesus said, 'In my Father's house are many mansions' (John 14:2). In other words, there are many levels at which we can experience life. There are numerous upper floors and there is a basement. It may be said that most people live much of their lives in the basement of existence, unaware that there are rooms upstairs for happy and successful living . . . No matter where a man may be or on what level he may be expressing, the Kingdom of God is within him . . . His sin is simply the frustration of his potentiality. He is living in a veritable hell. Interestingly, the word 'hades,' which is usually erroneously translated as 'hell,' literally means 'not to see.' The man in the basement is not able to see the fullness of life. But there is more in him, there is God in him." *The more we realize this good news, the more we can experience heaven within and all around.*

In *Go Toward The Light* by Chris Oyler, Ben — a seven-year-old dying of AIDs — asks his father about the nature of heaven. His dad replies, "We don't know exactly what it looks like. But it will feel like coming home. You know what it's like to get back home after you've been away for a while? You know how good it feels? That's what it will be like — like going home." Five years after a near-death-experience, Howard Storm was often moved to tears when telling of his time with angels of light. "I can't talk about it too much without getting homesick. I can't wait to go home again."

Remember to "seek ye first the kingdom of God and his righteousness; and all these things shall be added unto you." (Matthew 6:33) *Make spiritual balance a priority in your life.* Engage in activities that help you feel closer to God. There are lots of *methods* that can make life seem more like heaven — that help us remember God is inside and all around us. Matthew 3:2 and 4:17 state, "The kingdom of heaven is at hand." Yes, the kingdom of heaven is within. Calm your mind and live in the present moment so you can increasingly realize this good news.

Jampolsky and Cirincione state, "There is a bridge to heaven on earth. Heaven can be found not as a place but a state of mind. It's the experience of oneness with each other and God, of limitless peace, joy, and love." Of that wondrous feeling that we all have experienced, if only for a second, they encourage, "You can choose, right now this minute, to have that one second of heaven on earth."

We need to quiet our cerebral hemispheres once in awhile and feel, as Plotinus wrote, the truth of humans at the center of a "totally supportive universe." Butterworth recommends that we "let go of all tensions and think of

Spirit as streaming, pouring, and rushing into us from all sides . . . God is seeking us!" Quiet the mind, still the drunken monkey, and sense the good news that surrounds you.

Living in the present moment is one key to experiencing heaven. Ken Keyes states, "The past is dead; the future imaginary; happiness can only be in the eternal now moment." Find your spiritual balance and spend a little time each day reminding yourself of the true nature of reality. Above all, remember that you are a beloved child of God; love and forgive yourself just as God does. Then allow your inner potentials to naturally unfold and shine. Goethe said, "As soon as you trust yourself you will know how to live." St. Augustine said, "Love God and then do as you will."

Life ideally leads to growth, love, service to others, hope, faith, wisdom, patience, and forgiveness. This is our real nature and how we can be most of and eventually all the time. Strive to follow Christ's example moment by moment as suggested by Charles Shelton, author of *In His Steps*. Ask yourself, "Is this something Jesus would say, do, or think?" Don't chastise yourself for mistakes; rather, gently and steadily steer a course toward the Divine. With faith, perseverance, and help from above and all around, we can individually and collectively be transformed and experience heaven.

One of the best analogies I've found about our inner state of heaven or hell is told in *How Can I Help?* by Ram Dass and Paul Gorman: "A big, tough samurai once went to see a little monk. 'Monk,' he said, in a voice accustomed to instant obedience, 'teach me about heaven and hell!' The monk looked up at this mighty warrior and replied with utter disdain, 'Teach you about heaven and hell? I couldn't teach you about anything. You're dirty. You smell. Your blade is rusty. You're a disgrace, an embarrassment to the samurai class. Get out of my sight. I can't stand you.' The samurai was furious. He shook, got all red in the face, was speechless with rage. He pulled out his sword and raised it above him, preparing to slay the monk. 'That's hell,' said the monk softly. The samurai was overwhelmed. The compassion and surrender of this little man who had offered his life to give this teaching to show him hell! He slowly put down his sword, filled with gratitude, and suddenly peaceful . . . 'And that's heaven,' said the monk softly."

When asked how one might enter the kingdom of heaven, Jesus spoke of letting our light shine, using our talents, and helping others. We each have a special talent to give God and others. Native American spiritual wisdom speaks of all creation having a "give-away," a special gift to impart at the right time. Service to others helps us feel an inner peace that contributes to experiencing heaven within, now, and forever more.

Service to Others

Ralph Waldo Emerson said, "It is one of the most beautiful compensations of this life that no man can sincerely try to help another without helping himself."

Wishing to learn more about heaven and hell, a seeker was given a tour of each. In hell, people gathered around a huge banquet table with the most scrumptious foods of all kinds. They were all gaunt and starving, however, since they could only eat with very long utensils which they couldn't maneuver into their own mouths. In heaven, the scene was much the same with the same foods and long spoons and forks. Here, however, the inhabitants were well fed and happy, since *they had learned to feed each other.*

Jesus told us, "Inasmuch as ye have done it unto one of the least of these my brethren, ye have done it unto me." Gandhi had inscribed on his tomb, "Think of the poorest person you have ever seen and ask if your next act will be of any use to him." Service to others is an essential component of spiritual balance. The most serene people I know are those who regularly and unselfishly give of themselves. The amazing thing is that these actions are also self-serving; we always get back more than we give.

Rabbi Grollman comments, "When many people die, a *death notice* appears in the press. In reality it is a *life notice* because, but for it, the world would never have known the person had been alive. Only he who has been a force for human goodness, and abides in hearts and in a world made better by his presence, can be said to have *lived*." The Golden Rule admonishes us to "Do unto others as you would have others do unto you." This is the way we should treat each other out of common decency and respect. Since we are all one in a very real sense, what we do to others, we also do to ourselves. What goes around, comes around; we reap that which we sow. *To enjoy the kingdom of heaven, then, provide service to and love one another.*

Some persons feel an inner malaise or emptiness that often is due to a lack of meaning or direction in life. A self-centered life devoid of service *misses the mark* and doesn't feel right. The solution for this problem is simple: *open your heart and see how life calls you into service.* It may be visiting shut-ins, hospital or school volunteer work, senior citizen assistance, boy or girl scouts, donations to charities, church work, animal shelter assistance . . . the possibilities are limitless.

Service to others is an excellent way to grow spiritually and discover our true nature. Albert Einstein said: "A human being is a part of the whole called by us universe, a part limited in time and space. He experiences himself, his thoughts, and feelings as something separated from the rest, a kind of optical delusion of his consciousness. This delusion is a kind of prison for us, restricting us to our personal desires and to affection for a few persons nearest to us. Our task must be to free ourselves from this prison by widening our circle of compassion to embrace all living creatures and the whole of nature in its beauty."

All humanity is one big family — all children of God — all brothers and sisters. Serving others helps us escape the illusion of separateness and remember that we're all in this earthly classroom together. Involvement with others connects us with our higher selves as we transcend selfish ego-centered boundaries. We can then reach a better balance between our egos (temporary personality) and our *higher selves* (our real and eternal natures).

Ramakrishna, a great Indian saint, likened this situation to a coach in which the driver (ego) guides the horses while the owner (higher self) sits quietly inside the coach. Because the driver has never seen the owner, he thinks he is totally in charge. But when the owner gently but firmly makes himself known (enlightenment and awareness of our higher selves), the coachman relinquishes his fantasy and becomes content in the role of servant.

Ram Dass and Paul Gorman in *How Can I Help?* describe this state: "It responds more and more to the call of 'Not my but Thy will, O Lord.' The ego finds joy and relief in attuning to the greater Way of All Things, to the larger harmonies of the universe in which it can find its proper place and need no longer be driven by the insatiable need to control. In surrender to its proper station, the ego finds peace. The higher Self is now freer to guide the work of loving kindness and compassion. The character of service also begins to change."

We all go through tough times now and then. It's immensely reassuring and empowering to know someone cares — someone else is there to listen, share space, and help us onward. Let's try to be there for each other — reach down a little deeper and show we care. When done on a worldwide basis, we can meet the challenge to realize and establish heaven on earth. Remember the "expanding" meaning of heaven; we increasingly enjoy heaven within when we *expand our centers* to include others and their needs. Sometimes we look at all the world's problems and feel helpless and hopeless: "What can *I* do?" The truth is: *Each of our efforts are enough.* As we each do our share, the world's problems will be addressed.

Ram Dass and Gorman conclude, "Helping becomes an act of reverence, worship, gratitude . . . Mother Theresa, for example, bending to hold a dying leper, sees there only 'Christ in a distressing disguise.' She's not 'helping a dying leper,' she's loving God, affirming in whomever she's with universal qualities of perfection and beauty . . . We work on ourselves, then, in order to help others. And we help others as a vehicle for working on ourselves . . . Gradually, as our practice continues, the fact of our unity becomes more real and powerful to us than the belief in our separateness." We "come to see, with undeniable certainty, that who we are is Spirit, beyond form . . . separateness is seen to be a creation of mind. All really is One."

United we stand. Let us stand together as God's children — all across the world — and unite in action to address the problems of the world. Unified, we will win the battle against war, crime, ignorance, prejudice, drugs, disease, loneliness, and starvation. As we realize the power of service and cooperation, no problems will be too big to solve, no goals too high to reach.

Remembering Who We Are

C. S. Lewis said that God is in the business of creating little gods. Eastern religions speak of the "maya" or *illusion* that we are just physical beings; under this illusion, we suffer and worry a lot, especially when death, sickness, and tragedies occur. Knowing and remembering *the truth* — that we are spiritual beings and eternal souls — helps our faith during tough times. An excellent model for children of all ages was discussed in *Go Toward The Light*. Our spirits are like our fingers — always present whether we are wearing gloves or not. We slip gloves (our bodies) on at birth and off at death, but our eternal selves are always there — just as our fingers exist independently of the glove. Make a game using this model to help children — especially those who are dying — *remember* their true nature.

As Dr. Wayne Dyer reminds us, "You are a spiritual being having a human experience." Or, as an unknown author put it: "Know this, O man, sole root of sin in thee; Is not to know thine own divinity!" I know it's hard to comprehend that one's *real self* is eternal soul or spirit. Remembering this takes hope, faith, and daily reminders. Even though we can't see the spiritual realm, it exists. Take heart from these words from "The Little Prince" by Antoine de Saint-Exupery, "It is only with the heart that one can see rightly; what is essential is invisible to the eye."

Robert Browning says it well:

"Truth is within ourselves, it takes no rise from outward things, whate'er you may believe.

There is an inmost center in us all, where truth abides in fullness; and around, wall upon wall, the gross flesh hems it in, this perfect, clear perception — which is truth.

A baffling and perverting carnal mesh binds it, and makes all error; and to know rather consists in opening out a way whence the imprisoned splendor may escape, than in effecting entry for a light supposed to be without."

The Prologue to Eric Butterworth's book, *Discover The Power Within You*, states: "According to an old Hindu legend there was a time when all men were gods, but they so abused their divinity that Brahma, the chief god, decided to take it away from men and hide it where they would never find it. Where to hide it became the big question. When the lesser gods were called in council to consider this question," they suggested burying man's divinity deep in the earth, in the deepest ocean, or on the highest mountain. "Then Brahma said, 'Here is what we will do with man's divinity. We will hide it deep down in man himself, for he will never think to look for it there.' Ever since then, the legend concludes, man has been going up and down the earth, climbing, digging, diving, exploring, searching for something that is already in himself. Two thousand years ago a man named Jesus found it and shared its secret; but in the movement that sprang up in His name, the Divinity in man has been the best kept secret of the ages."

One tool for increasing awareness of *who you really are* is to develop the "*watcher* state of consciousness." In a relaxed state, visualize your real or eternal self standing on a bridge, overlooking the river's flow that is your life. See your life's events, not as an attached and emotional participant, but as a calm and objective "watcher." Oriental artworks have beautifully depicted an old wise person who stands on a bridge and watches, impassively and with understanding, the flow of water below. You can increasingly relate to the authentic self within you — that realized being inside who observes all and says, "Ah so. So it is."

Each moment and learning experience on earth is exquisitely designed to teach and transform us. Avoid a constant judgment of "this is good and desirable" or "this is bad and unwanted." Rather, develop an acceptance of the hills and valleys of life. Remember, one of the "secrets" to enjoying inner peace is to live in the moment fully. Living with *present time consciousness* means avoiding preconceived expectations of how things will be. Expectations set us up for disappointment whereas being open to the present moment allows us to experience life to the fullest. Set your goals and work toward them; be open, however, to unexpected or uncontrollable changes and see what blessings might be therein. Confucius said, "Everything has beauty but not everyone sees it."

The enlightened person realizes that accidents happen, tragedies occur, and things change. And yet, we can remain composed, full of faith, and hopeful through all of this. Pictures or carvings of the Buddha often show a look of equanimity, realizing how life is and seeing with eyes of infinite understanding. His grin has been called "the smile of unbearable compassion." Feel the hurts, cry the tears, and experience the temporary setbacks that are part of a human existence. *At the same time, look beyond the illusion* and remember that God is All; there is nothing to worry about and nothing to lose. This is the cosmic perspective that, balanced with our humanity, transforms us into enlightened beings.

Trust yourself and trust God; fear is the opposite of faith and keeps us from realizing our true nature. In *Emmanuel's Book,* Emmanuel says, "There is not a heart that exists in your human world that, if it were assured of safety would not open instantly. It is all an issue of fear." Humanity's collective consciousness is evolving beyond basic survival, pleasure, and power needs. More and more persons are developing the upper chakras or energy centers of love, planetary consciousness, higher wisdom, and cosmic consciousness. There's a *balance* to be reached as we increasingly identify with our true nature while honoring our humanity.

One useful model is that *our eternal selves choose life events purposely and consciously* in between life stages or incarnations. I say "model" because we don't know for sure and our understanding of the universe is limited. Our souls may choose certain events in the next life or dimension in order to learn specific lessons. Suppose that our souls do go through a series of life experiences for good reasons. Just as we go through elementary, high school, and college educations, we likewise benefit from life's gradational lessons. Our eternal selves may have some consciousness-raising to do — some work on the rough edges before they can completely appreciate or experience God. Our inner selves may need to learn patience, empathy, or humility; each may thus select a particular life experience that aids soul growth in a deficient area.

Rabbi Weiner, authority on the Jewish Kabbala, states: "It is said that before a person is born, he carries a light on his head which enables him to see from one end of creation to the other. Perhaps that means he is given a full picture, a preview of all the things that are going to happen to him in life ahead . . . Then he is told that he must choose, for choice is always one of man's sacred gifts from the Creator, and the final choice is his. If, then, the answer is 'yes' — the Angel of Forgetfulness touches him on the center of the upper lip, he forgets everything he saw, and he is born." Roderick MacLeish, in *Prince Ombra,* says "This is why we are born with a cleft on our upper lip and remembering nothing of where we came from."

The soul may choose an earthly life with mental or physical handicaps or tragedies. From our limited earthly perspective, these are unfortunate and undesirable events. From a *higher or cosmic* viewpoint, temporary pain and suffering are well worth increased spiritual growth. A paralyzed person learns many lessons that a fully mobile person wouldn't. Blind persons "see" life differently because of their impaired vision. The death of a child may inspire, improve, and bring others closer to God.

This cosmic perspective lends *hope* and a greater meaning to the seeming tragedies of life. I'll never forget one patient in a hospital emergency room. A little boy had been hit by a truck; it was his first day of kindergarten and he was the only child of young parents. He vomited as we worked on him and I could see the alphabets from his noontime meal of soup. Despite hours of resuscitative care, he passed on. I saw his parent's faces as the doctor told them the news. Afterwards, several doctors and other staff wept openly and hugged each other.

I went outside and cursed God and the world. How could a loving God allow a little boy to die so tragically? What kind of world was this where innocent persons die and suffer? Similar events motivated me to search for answers to the ultimate questions in life. From a higher or *enlightened* perspective, his death had many important meanings. It brought the hospital staff closer together and broke through their usual calloused approach. It affected and stimulated me, and others I presume, to seek answers and meanings about death and suffering. His life and death continue to have meaning as I write about it 20 years later.

Consider the *possibility of greater meanings in and lessons from earthly tragedies.* Perhaps we do choose challenging events in life in order to aid soul growth. From a spiritual perspective, death and suffering are worthwhile and meaningful if they bring just one soul closer to God. This is hard to see at the time of tragedy but has real significance when viewed from a broader perspective. God didn't cause the truck to hit the boy, but thank God we can grow and learn even from such tragedies. Work at realizing your true nature — who you really are — and observe how the universe seems more and more perfect.

Evil

Did you ever notice that the words "evil" and "devil" are "live" and "lived" spelled backwards? Indeed, the existence of evil is largely a result of life "lived backwards," contrary to our true nature. Some persons believe in a personified and literal devil; others — myself included — view evil more figuratively. In either case, remember that evil has no real power in the light of good or God. Theologian Karl Barth's notion of evil was "nothingness."

Nigel Wright, author of *The Satan Syndrome*, states, "Evil is that power at work in the world about which nothing good should be said or thought. For this irrational, absurd and destructive power, human beings should entertain nothing but scorn." Theologian Ted Peters says, "The question as to whether or not the devil exists as a personal being I take to be diversionary. What is theologically decisive is that sin and its fruits of cruelty grow out of our own souls when we are ravaged by anxiety rather than nourished by faith in God."

Unity, Christian Science, Universalist-Unitarian, and other more liberal denominations deny the existence of any significant power or presence opposed to God. They acknowledge the *appearance* of evil in the world, but ascribe these to man's ignorance and erroneous use of God's laws of life. *Science and Health* by Mary Baker Eddy defines devil and evil synonymously: "a lie; error; the opposite of truth." Evil does not exist as a separate power just as darkness is not a power opposed to light. There is only one power — the power of God and love.

Butterworth says, "Personalizing evil as the devil is the 'great cop-out of history' — it's easy to blame evil acts on the influence of satan. The Aquarian Gospel states that the only devil is the lower self of man. The savior and demon selves are both within us — exalt the former and dethrone the latter. The devil and burning fires are both the works of humans — only man can dissipate them."

Other religious views maintain that satan has a major impact on earthly events by influencing and possessing people. Still others are somewhere between these two viewpoints — unsure of the literal or figurative nature of satan. In my opinion, the concept of satan has been given too much emphasis. Past overemphases about our sinful nature and the power of satan have underestimated the power of good and God. If any personified evil does exists — in a major evil power or lesser spirits or both — God and Christ are more powerful and always triumph over evil. Since God is everywhere, all-powerful, and all-knowing — where is there room for any significant or lasting evil?

Some persons cite tragedies and heinous crimes as proof of satan's existence. But most tragedies are due to forces of nature or inappropriate actions by humans. I believe that, ultimately, all apparent tragedies will make sense and result in a greater good. God doesn't cause tragedies and doesn't always stop them; He does, however, always love and care and can turn hardship into victory.

During a 1985 near-death-experience (NDE), university professor and now minister Howard Storm asked angels why earthly suffering and evil aren't stopped by Higher Powers. The answers included:

1. Humans have free will and God allows us to choose even when we are wrong;
2. Humans learn from their errors and a greater

       good results from those teachings;

   3. Higher Powers *do* stop many acts of ignorance and violence but — like rangers stopping forest fires — sometimes can't stop them all in time;

   4. "Premature" or seemingly tragic deaths are a way for enlightened souls to come home to God.

All persons will eventually realize their inseparability from God and live in harmony. The good news of eternal life and oneness of all creation help me accept and deal with life's *temporary* evils and tragedies. I hope it helps you, too. Earthly life involves suffering, sickness, tragedy, injustice, and eventually death. Even so, the viewpoints we've been discussing can help us cope with these tough times. Keep marching forward with hope and faith, knowing that God is always there helping and guiding you.

One of humanities biggest "evils" is not realizing its true identity as part and parcel of God. Our biggest "sin" is the mistaken concept of ourselves as worthless sinners; "sin" = Superstitious Ignorant Negation. Dr. Errico translates "sin" as "to miss the mark" or make a mistake. What should we do when we realize our sin? *Repent* — which can be translated as *quit it* and *change*. When you make a mistake or miss the mark, change and do better. It's as simple as that. Don't confuse the issue by giving any attention to the nonexistent or relatively meaningless concepts of satan/devil/evil. Rather, *keep your heart and mind on God and Christ and your optimal spiritual unfolding.*

Genesis 1:27 and 31 describe that after creating the Earth "God created man in his own image . . . God saw everything that he had made, and, behold, it was very good." That includes you and me! In *Autobiography of a Yogi*, Paramahansa Yogananda says, "The man form is higher than the angel form; of all forms, it is the highest. Man is the highest being in creation, because he aspires to freedom." Hebrews 2:6-7 states, "What is man, that thou art mindful of him? . . . Thou madest him a little lower than the angels . . ." A little higher, a little lower; as bald as I am, I'm not going to split hairs. Either way, a human being is a lofty calling. Jesus said to the multitudes, "Ye are the salt of the earth . . . ye are the light of the world." (Matthew 5:13-14) Humans are not hopeless sinners, and God would not allow any evil to hamper His plan of salvation for all.

I want to share a "mini-miracle" that occurred in relationship to this last point. As I was finishing the last draft of *Balanced Living*, something kept encouraging me to add the scripture about the high calling of human beings and our near-angelic nature. I had looked in the Concordance of my Bible but couldn't find the passage. The day before I mailed the last revision to my publisher, something told me to look one more time. The closest I could find (in the Concordance) was a passage about angels in Hebrews 2:16 on page 1159 of my grandpa Marsh's old King James Version.

That wasn't it and I was about to give up when a strong inner thought or feeling encouraged me to look on the right lower portion of the preceding page. My skeptical self said, "Right. There are over 1200 pages of small print. Am I supposed to look at each page until I find it?" The intuition continued so I glanced at page 1158 and there it was in Hebrews 2:7! This is just one example of how I believe I am directly helped and guided from above on a regular basis. God, Christ, and the heavenly host are always ready to assist and direct if we ask for help and use it for the betterment of humankind.

It is only fitting that a discussion of evil turns to a focus upon the hope of God and Christ. Good and God are all powerful and ultimately really all that exist. As James 3:11

asks, "Doth a fountain send forth at the same place sweet water and bitter?" Don't give the concepts of evil or devil any energy or a second thought. Rather, focus on good and God and live a victorious life of balance and goodness. Doing this renders evil to its rightful nonexistent state. Turn on the light and the darkness disappears instantaneously; similarly, evil vanishes when we let our lights shine and affirm the sovereignty of good, God, and Christ.

During his NDE, Rev. Storm's soul or consciousness temporarily left his body and encountered other spirits. These entities encouraged him to follow them, and Howard found himself in utter darkness. Resisting these "shadow or dark spirits," he was mentally and physically attacked and forced to continue further into the darkness. These *evil-acting* spirits immediately disappeared, however, when Howard prayed for help from God. He was instantly rescued from the darkness when he said, "Jesus, help me!"

This is a true-life example of how weak and confused evil powers are, especially when confronted with the love, light, and power of God. Persons who truly desire to know their Creator and do what's right should have nothing to fear from evil spirits. Would a loving earthly father allow a less powerful and evil person to tempt and torture his beloved children? Of course not. How much more must our Heavenly Father love and protect us? Don't seek or acknowledge evil in any form; rather, focus on good and God.

Hell

I once worked with a young patient who had attempted suicide. "Hank" had put a shotgun under his chin and pulled the trigger just as the barrel jerked forward. Hank's face was blown off but he was still very much alive. He could hear but was blind and couldn't talk. He had lost his nose, eyes, and most of his face. What would or could you say to a person like this? I was in theology school at the time and was also working in suicide and crisis counseling. I spoke to Hank and let him know that we cared and tried to reassure him that he would be okay. He wrote, as best a recently blinded person could, "God, help me. I'm in hell."

Indeed he was. Hank still faced the same problems that plagued him in the first place. In trying to escape by suicide, however, he had increased his problems many times over. He had created an outward physical hell that matched his previous inner one. I think about Hank and his self-imposed hell from time to time. Did he ever learn that heaven was always accessible and an open-ended possibility for him?

"There are several major theories about hell," says Rabbi Grollman. "Hell has been seen by some as the place or realm of everlasting torment for those who have rejected the offer of salvation by God in Jesus Christ. Others cannot believe that a God of love would condemn persons forever, and therefore any punishment in the hereafter is remedial and disciplinary so that ultimately all are restored . . . Others cannot believe that, even though sin deserves punishment, hell and the satanic will coexist with God throughout eternity; therefore they affirm that there is no immortality of evil and everlasting torment, that all evil will be annihilated."

Dr. Errico says that in the original scriptures, hell was never a *place* but was used idiomatically to mean a feeling of torment — if you do something wrong, you regret it. When you do something right, you feel good — like being in heaven. He contends the descriptive idioms heaven and hell have been erroneously converted to literal physical places. In *The Awakened Life*, Dr. Wayne Dyer describes the importance of reprogramming our minds since *thoughts are antecedents of actions.* He says that Jesus taught us to avoid sinning by thought, word, and deed — not to avoid going to hell — but to prevent the negative effects of these. We hurt and hold *ourselves* back when we sin; that results in a temporary punishment or hell until we change for the better.

I personally believe any hell is temporary, self-induced, and a state of mind or consciousness. The concept of an eternal and fiery hell has already delayed too many personal relationships with God. Tired of life being like hell? Open your heart and mind; repent and ask for Divine assistance. Change for the better. Then experience the reality of a loving God who has always been waiting patiently for you.

Rev. Robert Love, Methodist minister and author of *Hell No*, uses Biblical, philosophical, and historical facts to make a strong case against an *eternal* place of torment. He asks: "Would a loving God consign any of His children to eternal damnation? Can I experience a God whose love knows no limits while keeping hell in my heart? Can we preach a God of unlimited love while having to hold open a place in our hearts for hell? If God wills that none perish, and he is all-powerful, why would he not save all? . . . If we define hell as a place where people are *eternally* separated from God, such a place does not exist."

He continues: "Why does the concept of the salvation of all find us resisting it, instead of seeking a way for it to be? . . . I do not claim that the person cannot say 'no' to God and goodness in a temporal and temporary way . . . But all creation will eventually recognize God's lordship. We were created in God's image . . . Human will cannot forever say 'no' to God because we cannot forever contradict our nature . . . In only one place — Matthew 25:31-46 — is the crucial element of *eternal* punishment mentioned. In all of those that remain, we could read them to apply to punishment for evil that is not eternal."

Rev. Love concludes: "The church has preached that hell is a place where one is separated from God, while maintaining that God is everywhere . . . If God is everywhere, there is no place of separation from God . . . God loves sinners while hating sin . . . Why does the church find it so hard to believe that God can separate people and evil, and restore his life to us? . . . The message of Christianity is that God refuses to allow evil (including lack of faith and unbelief) to have the last and eternal word . . . Nowhere in the Bible or in Christian theology do I find a God who seems at all willing to stop his search for even one. Time is one of God's creatures, and time will not catch God's purpose unfulfilled."

Unity minister J. Sig Paulson points out that some religions "scare the hell out of people to try to get them to heaven." Emilie Cady holds that some persons are afraid to make a decision for Christ or to know God because of misunderstandings fostered by churches that use an "accept or suffer in hell" theology. John Bradshaw, ex-Catholic priest and author of *Homecoming*, tells of parochial school nuns showing him pictures of hell and saying, "This is where your soul will be if you sin." Yes, the archaic and mistaken concept of an eternal hell has kept too many persons from knowing their Heavenly Father.

The notion of hell belittles and blasphemes God. What earthly father would intentionally pass — even for a moment — his child's finger through a flame? Consider the Biblical story of the shepherd who leaves 99 sheep to find the one that was lost. Jesus said, "For the Son of man is come to save that which was lost . . . Even so it is not the will of your Father which is in heaven, that one of these little ones should perish." (Matthew 18:11 and 14) The Bible clearly states God's will: "The Lord . . . not willing that any should perish, but that *all* should come to repentance." (II Peter 3:19) If *God* wills it, it shall be done.

A burning hell is an analogy or instructive story. For example, consider Luke 16: 23-24 about the rich man in hell. My King James Version plainly states: "Parable of the rich man and Lazarus." This is a *symbolic* description of how painful a life devoid of spiritual growth is. Dostoevsky said, "I am convinced that the only Hell which exists is the inability to love."

The Rev. Richard McBrien, theologian at Notre Dame, said the Roman Catholic Church has moved from a negative view of persons — that the human race is damned and only a relatively few will be saved — to a perspective that mankind is "essentially a saved community from whom a few may be lost." Hell is no longer a part of the Jewish afterlife. Sin, in the Jewish perspective, "is atoned for in this life through repentance and the experience of death itself." Origen viewed hell as a place of spiritual separation from God; his "universalist" view claimed that hell's purpose was *remedial* and that hell's sinners could be reclaimed. Martin Luther and John Calvin believed that hell was a figurative description of alienation from God. Eastern Orthodoxy views hell allegorically.

Newsweek writer Kenneth L. Woodward states: "Today, hell is theology's H-word, a subject too trite for serious scholarship . . . heaven and hell are no longer thought of as different locations, with separate zip codes, but radically opposed states of intimacy with and alienation from God . . . Hell, then, is not a place created by a God bent on getting even, but the alienation we choose for ourselves. Heaven, on the other hand, is for lovers — of others and God. 'Thou hast made us for Thyself,' wrote Saint Augustine nearly 17 centuries ago, 'and our hearts are restless; till rest in Thee.'"

The word "hell" is translated from "sheol" and "gehenna"

and can also be interpreted as pit, grave, or death. We all die physically and to our immature spiritual natures, but that's not an eternal hell. To inherit the kingdom of heaven — and escape "hell" — we must die and be reborn spiritually. We "die" to our old nature like a caterpillar dies before it becomes a butterfly. Our new nature, more like God, replaces our former self. Evil simply cannot coexist with or experience God. Evil goes to hell — dies — just like darkness "dies" when light is turned on.

One of my senior citizen patients recently passed on. "Ruth" was a jewel of a person — always loving, helpful, and thoughtful. She had attended the same church for 60 years and rarely missed a service. We had discussed death and dying since she was clearly approaching the time of transition. The last time I saw her, I had a feeling she would pass on soon; I remarked that God would be glad to receive such a beautiful soul. She earnestly replied, "I sure hope so. I hope I don't go to that other place!" And I thought, "How sad that even a person like Ruth isn't assured of God's love and grace." How many others similarly fear, wonder, and worry about "going to that other place?"

God always stands ready to receive *all persons* in love and forgiveness. Truly repent and open yourself to the reality of love and mercy that *is* God. Pray and meditate on these things; then decide for yourself whether the God you know needs an eternal hell in His loving plan. As you let go of fears of hell, feel a new freedom within. Love, respect, and know God because He deserves respect, but you no longer need fear eternal punishment. *Let this message of joy heal you physically, mentally, and spiritually.* See life through the eyes of the beloved child of God that you are. No longer fearing "not making the heavenly team," you can now blossom into a beautiful and vital part of the creation.

Suffering

An old Chinese proverb says: "You cannot prevent the birds of sorrow from flying over your head, but you can prevent them from building nests in your hair."

Buddha taught that the cause of suffering is selfish desire. When we excessively desire or *must have* something, we set ourselves up for suffering. Ken Keyes, in *A Handbook To Higher Consciousness*, speaks of downgrading our desires into *preferences*: "Happiness happens when your consciousness is not dominated by addictions and demands — and you experience life as a parade of preferences." It's okay to prefer to be healthy, have nice material possessions, and loving family and friends. But we can do without them if necessary and don't desperately need to have them. *Don't put all your eggs in one basket.* If one person, cause, or thing is your whole life, you are setting yourself up for suffering when change occurs. And, paradoxically, *change* is one of the *constants* in life.

When we have strong needs, we are overly attached to the object of our desires. Our attachments create an inner anxiety: "What if my new car gets a scratch? What if my spouse leaves me? What if my nice home burns down? What if my children neglect me later in life?" *The mind with excessive attachments continually suffers and worries.* This self-created suffering disappears when we realize that external things are of transient importance.

An enlightened being remembers that God is All and doesn't store up treasures vulnerable to moths, rust, or thieves. Sure, we all would like to have a pleasant and comfortable external world. A life of balance usually will result in inner *and* outer prosperity. When hard times occur, however, the realized person is equal to the challenge. So seek the kingdom first; external trappings are icing on the cake but not necessary for happiness.

Have you ever tried to hold sand in a tightly clenched fist? The sand trickles through all sorts of cracks between the fingers. Try holding your opened but slightly cupped hands together and notice how much more you can hold. We eventually lose what we try to smother or desperately own. People and possessions are around you to enjoy in a balanced way. We don't own them, however, and they are all subject to change, decay, and death.

The death of a loved one is especially hard to accept and understand, but a cosmic perspective helps us see the light at the end of the tunnel. Remember, we can't really be separated; there is nowhere to go since all creation is really One. The departed one has merely passed over and dropped the body. The spirit or soul is always vibrantly alive. The love that exists between you never dies and is one of the constants of life. You can sense and talk to a departed one. Eternal life is a reality for all of us; try to remember this truth as you work through the grief. Keep your faith and hope strong and clear.

I know it's hard, especially when our understanding of all this is yet fragile. Even with a strong faith, there is a transition time of sadness and feeling alone. The great Tibetan teacher Marpa, weeping after the death of his son, was approached by a student who said, "I don't understand. You teach that all this is illusion, created by the clinging and desire and resistance. Yet there you are weeping. If all this is illusion, why do you grieve so deeply?" Marpa replied, "Yes, everything here is an illusion. And the death of a child is the greatest of these illusions."

Elisabeth Kübler-Ross, M.D., author of *AIDS: The Ultimate Challenge* and other excellent books on death and dying, described the five stages of grieving: *Denial* occurs first as we "can't believe it has really happened." A second stage is *anger* as we regain our energy but feel powerless to change the tragedy; we may feel anger toward God, life, or the person who died or left us. Next is *bargaining* as we try vainly to reverse the loss. *Depression* follows as we realize that the loss is real and we mourn. Finally, *acceptance* occurs as we realize it's over, we can't change it, and get on with life.

These stages don't necessarily occur in order and a person may go back and forth between stages before reaching acceptance. Similar stages of grieving may occur after divorce; broken relationships; and physical, mental, or sexual trauma.

To mourn for awhile is a natural part of the grieving process. After a time, however, the balanced and realized being continues on with life. The earthly plane has a certain amount of tragedy built into it, and our human hearts accordingly hurt and ache. Our realized selves, however, can look at all this with an enlightened perspective. The sun seems to vanish each night, but *in reality* the earth's rotation only makes it *seem* so. Similarly, suffering may seem catastrophic but in reality can be a blessing. When we see past appearances, we realize the sun is always shining as is hope, life, and joy.

Bernie Siegel, M.D., says, "Afflictions heal and adversity opens you to a new reality." He calls these apparent setbacks "spiritual flat tires — unexpected events that can have positive or negative outcomes, depending on how we respond to them." Nonagenarian Ralph Von Aling said it well, "I find that most of my problems in life proved to be blessings in disguise." Nietzsche pointed out, "That which does not kill me, makes me stronger." In *You Gotta Keep Dancin'*, Tim Hansel says, "Pain is inevitable, but misery is optional." There is an *intensity* accompanying suffering that makes us reach deep within ourselves and learn important lessons.

Edgar Cayce taught that we can learn by meditating and being in tune with the Spirit or we can graduate from "the school of hard knocks." Thus, although there are less painful ways to learn, suffering can be an excellent teacher. The advanced soul even *welcomes* suffering as it shows where he or she is still attached. This leads us to the paradoxical statement that "suffering is grace." When you know God is All and want to be as close to that level of consciousness as possible, everything — including suffering — can be a vehicle for spiritual growth. Thus, if various sufferings help us grow stronger spiritually, bring them on. It's not being a martyr or a masochist; if suffering comes along, though, the realized being uses even that to grow.

Ram Dass tells of visiting a friend who was dying of pelvic cancer. He initially tried to talk with her about spiritual growth through suffering, but she didn't want to hear any of it. During a later visit, he just sat quietly, centering on a calm inner place where he could feel both compassion and clarity about her predicament. As she lay writhing in pain, she turned to him and whispered, "I've never felt so peaceful in my life. At this moment, I wouldn't be anywhere else in the universe."

I have seen similar transformations accompany severe and chronic suffering. "Harold," the emphysema patient I mentioned earlier, was initially very demanding and negative. Two years later, a few months before his death, he was patient, thankful for small favors, and appreciated the few positive aspects in his world. He had learned to focus on the positive and appreciate the little things in life.

Emmanuel says that suffering and strife are a perfect backdrop for soul growth and asks: "If this world were a perfect place, where would souls go to school? Do not weep for the limitations that you see existing in your world.

Those limitations are there for a purpose . . . View your world as a transient place where souls choose to come because this is what they have selected as their mode of learning to the most minute detail . . . There is an overall plan of which you are not aware and to which you can only contribute by being who you are, doing your best, seeking your higher truth, and following your heart . . . You are learning."

After years of suffering in a German prison camp and being separated from his family, Dr. Victor Frankl wrote: "I only knew one thing which I'd learned well by now. Life goes very far beyond the physical person of the beloved. It finds its deepest meaning in his spiritual being, his inner self. Whether or not he is actually present, whether or not he is still alive at all seems somehow not to be of importance."

Harold Kushner, author of *When Bad Things Happen to Good People*, speaking of terminal diseases and death by forces of nature, stated: "Laws of nature don't make exceptions for nice people. Expecting God to spare good people from pain is like expecting a bull not to charge you because you're a vegetarian." Rabbi Kushner views religion as "a way of seeing the world" and tells dying persons and grieving families, "God is on your side. And if you take down the barriers of fear and guilt, then God will give you the strength to lead the last days of your life with grace . . . will you be able to recognize that the ability to love and forgive are the weapons God has given us to live fully, bravely, and meaningfully in this less than perfect world?"

In *You'll See It When You Believe It*, Dr. Wayne Dyer states: "I have a very strong belief that everything that comes into your life is supposed to, and every condition of your life is part of the perfection of it, and there's a blessing in all of it, and that there are no accidents, that it's a perfect — absolutely, totally perfect — universe." Jampolsky and

Cirincione say, "To live in love is to be an eternal optimist. It's to believe that there are no accidents, no coincidences, that everything that happens to us is according to God's plan and provides the lessons that God would have us learn."

Kübler-Ross says: "Life naturally begins when the soul, the entity, enters the physical body to start a new existence in the physical world. We are here to grow, to learn, to have all the experiences that the physical world can offer. And when we have passed all the tests, we are allowed to graduate and return back to our original home."

Dr. Carl Sagan says that if just *one atom* were taken out of the universe, the whole thing would collapse. Consider the magnitude of this universal organization and lawfulness; I believe a similar perfection exists in every detail of human life. From *a limited human viewpoint*, there are accidents, tragedies, and disasters. From a *universal perspective*, it's all grace — all creation growing closer to God. God is at work in all events — "good" or "bad;" what seems bad *now* will make sense someday. Keep your heart and mind on the *big picture*, especially during a personal tragedy. Perhaps those who die young have learned their earthly lessons more quickly than the rest of us. *They can go home again*, awaiting and helping those left behind. Remember: trust God, don't be misled by appearances, maintain your faith and hope, and keep trying. You can't lose.

In the movie *Oh God*, John Denver asked "God:" "If you're so involved with us, how can you permit all the suffering that goes on in the world?" George Burns as God replied, "I don't permit the suffering — you do. Free will. All the choices are yours . . . you can love each other, cherish and nourish each other, or you can kill each other." It's not God's will that tragedies occur. God *is* total health, goodness, love, peace, and harmony. A Being with these attributes does not decree tragedies upon people. People often cause tragedies upon others or themselves. Thank God that He uses even tragedies and disasters to aid spiritual growth.

Another cause of suffering is the law of karma; that is, *we reap that which we sow.* If we touch a hot stove, we get burned. If we commit transgressions against others, we sometimes must suffer or learn from the consequences of our actions. I say "sometimes" because we can neutralize negative karma by *truly repenting and changing* inside. The Old Testament taught "an eye for an eye and a tooth for a tooth," but in the New Testament, Jesus taught that forgiveness and redemption are available for the sincere asking.

We don't have to burn in the temporary "hell fires" of karmic retribution. Repent, realize your divine nature as a child of God, start living right, and make up for your misdeeds. Remember that we personally suffer the most when we hurt others. Our every thought, word, and deed has a cosmic "boomerang" effect. Right living is its own best reward since "what goes around comes around."

There are higher purposes in life that make earthly sufferings meaningful and worthwhile. Joseph's suffering started a chain of events that eventually led to saving Israel. What *seemed* like a string of misfortunes resulted in a *greater good.* Dr. Frankl uses the term *supra-meaning* and offers the following analogy. Would an ape, being used to develop a miracle drug, understand the need for and meaning behind being punctured and experimented upon? Its limited intelligence could not understand that its suffering was meaningful and important. Frankl then asks, "And what about man? Are you sure that the human world is a terminal point in the evolution of the cosmos? Is it not conceivable that there is still another dimension possible, a world beyond man's world; a world in which the question of an ultimate meaning of human suffering would find an answer?"

I had been wondering and praying about why God allows suffering and doesn't prevent tragedies. Soon after that, our cat killed a bird and stood there with the bird in its mouth, looking at me. I love my cat *and* the birds, but I don't like the cat killing birds. Caging the cat would protect the birds but limit the cat's freedom. Even if I could protect the birds in my yard, what about all the other cats that kill birds in the world? I can't protect and control every cat and bird in the world. Perhaps this is like *God's predicament;* He loves all of creation but doesn't like some of our actions. He doesn't restrict our freedom or interfere when we make poor choices. But God is always watching, teaching, and loving — knowing that everything will be okay in the long run.

The world's seeming tragedies — like cats killing birds — are part of life and nature. Do everything possible to right the wrongs of life while working from a place of trust and hope. Remember that God is all-powerful and ever-present yet intensely personal and loving. There is a Divine intelligence and perfection throughout the universe. It may not seem that way to us but that is our goal: not to *set* things right so much as *see* things rightly. The word "disaster" literally means "without the astra or world of thought and spirituality." That is, disaster arises when we don't think or see rightly. An enlightened perspective of hope and faith will keep you going when you don't think you can take another step.

Polarities

One key to understanding life is to acknowledge and accept the polarities in our world. Although all life is truly One, *at the same time*, every facet of life can involve extremes. Consider the opposite ends of the spectrum in every aspect of life. The fire that warms us can burn our houses down. Water necessary for life can drown us. Love and hate, war and peace, good and bad, birth and death — these terms are often used as if they belong together. In a sense they do; although they are opposites, they are part of the overall scheme. Each point along the spectrum has important lessons to teach. We each are periodically challenged to accept, learn from, and deal with these extremes.

In the drought of 1988, the grass was brown, water levels dropped, and rationing measures were implemented. Crops suffered, animals died, and fires raged out of control. I resolved to never complain about rain again. When it finally rained, our family ran in it and cheered; the message that came to me at that moment was "Into every life a little rain must fall." Rainy days and seemingly negative events have value and a purpose. All the phases of life have their unique contributions to make and add to our earthly experience. Live each moment fully and trust God that everything happens for a reason and has a lesson to impart.

The drought helped me realize the importance of polarities — they all exist for a good reason. We wouldn't appreciate good and love as much without the contrasting qualities of bad and hate. Polarities gives us an opportunity to choose and experience varying extremes. How can we *freely* choose good over evil and love over hate until we have experienced both? I noticed that those persons who grumbled the most about the drought and heat also complained after the rains and cool weather returned. *It's not the polarities that are the problem, then, but how we view and react to them.*

In the movie *Oh God, Book II*, a little girl asked God, "Why do bad things happen?" He answered, "That's the way the system works . . . Have you ever seen an up, without a down? A front, without a back? A top, without a bottom?

You can't have one without the other. I discovered that if I take away sad, then I take away happy, too. They go together . . . If somebody has a better idea, I hope they put it in the suggestion box." Universal laws — like forces of nature and polarities — allow an organized and predictable cosmos. If they constantly made exceptions, they wouldn't be universal.

Spiritual enlightenment empowers our heartfelt work to correct injustices, heal wounds, and help as much as possible. At the same time, remember that God is in His heaven and all is right with the world. These two different world views — there are problems to correct *and* it's all perfect — are both simultaneously true. Working to reduce suffering while realizing that suffering can be an instructive lesson — that's the fine line a realized being walks. Acknowledge the polarities of life and flow through your changes with as much love, faith, and understanding as possible. "To everything there is a season, and a time to every purpose under the heaven." (Ecclesiastes 3:1)

Afterlife

We each have wondered, "What happens after I die? Is this all there is? If there is an afterlife, what is it like, and will I make it there?" In *The Denial of Death*, Ernest Becker, Ph.D., wrote, "The idea of death, the fear of it, haunts the human animal like nothing else, it is a mainstream of human activity." Henry Ward Beecher's deathbed words were, "Now comes the Great Mystery."

A Parable of Immortality by Henry Van Dyke neatly sums up my beliefs about afterlife: "I am standing upon the seashore. A ship at my side spreads her white sails to the morning breeze and starts for the blue ocean. She is an object of beauty and strength, and I stand and watch until at last she hangs like a speck of white cloud just where the sea and sky come down to mingle with each other. Then someone at my side says, 'There she goes!' Gone where? Gone from my sight — that is all. She is just as large in mast and hull and spar as she was when she left my side and just as able to bear her load of living freight to the place of destination. Her diminished size is in me, not in her. And just at the moment when someone at my side says, 'There she goes!' there are other eyes watching her coming and other voices ready to take up the glad shout, 'Here she comes!'"

This is a beautiful analogy for things not yet seen or fully understood. Recall the many aspects of life that we cannot perceive or understand that yet are very real. Buckminster Fuller stressed that 99 percent of who and what human beings really are is invisible; thus, only one percent of our true being can be detected by the five ordinary senses. Even the mother brontosaurus, in the children's movie *Land Before Time*, knew this: "Some things you see with your eyes; others, you see with your heart." There is a leap of faith involved with afterlife beliefs. If the saying "seeing is believing" is true, then some people will have to wait and see for ourselves. There is, however, a growing body of information suggesting the existence of an afterlife. And, paradoxically, "believing is seeing" may be a more accurate description of how things work.

Most of us perceive life under the influence of an illusion or dream. Earthly life is like a play, a temporary manifestation of energy in the mind of the Cosmic Dreamer God. "Row, row, row your boat gently down the stream. Merrily, merrily, merrily, merrily, life is but a dream." When we realize we're like actors playing various roles in God's production, the entire game changes. We realize the wisdom of I Corinthians 16:55: "O Death, where is thy sting? O Grave, where is thy victory?"

Enlightenment doesn't automatically accompany physical death although dying can teach important lessons. The most surprising lesson to many persons is that we don't really die. Dying is more accurately termed "passing on" or "leaving the body," like a snake sheds its skin. Chief Seattle of the Dwamish tribe said, "There is no death, only a change of worlds." We pass on from one realm to the next, from one body to another type or perhaps no body at all. Dying is like walking through a door into another room. Emmanuel says, *"Death is completely safe* and is like taking off a tight shoe."

Cycles in nature serve as a paradigm for *life's phases*. Read *Hope for the Flowers* by Trina Paulus; the caterpillar apparently dies in the wintry cocoon only to emerge a transformed butterfly in the spring. What we call death is merely a change in our outward appearance as the inner self moves relentlessly toward the Source of all existence. In the northern climes, winter's illusion of death is followed by spring's rebirth. Similarly, each cycle of life is important and part of the master plan.

Cyclical life stages sounds a lot like reincarnation or transmigration of the soul. There certainly seems to be some recycling mechanism — giving us another try — operant in the cosmos. Remember the more than two billion galaxies in the universe? That's just part of God's creation, part of the majestic and complex splendor of the cosmos. Isn't it conceivable that in this vast framework there are other life forms, dimensions, planes of existence, and life stages? Might there be other possibilities besides just one earthly life, then either heaven or hell?

Dr. Leslie Weatherhead, minister and author of *Life Begins at Death*, states, "Can Christians believe in reincarnation? I think they can. That is to say, I don't see anything in this theory which contradicts the Christian position. In our Lord's time, it was part of the accepted beliefs of everybody. Indeed, it was accepted by the Christian church until 553 when the Council of Constantinople rejected it by a very narrow majority. And after all, five hundred million Buddhists and Hindus accept the idea of reincarnation. To brush away an idea tenaciously held by such an enormous number of our fellows, including some very great saints and scholars, seems to me a thing one should hesitate to do."

Consider, for example, the implications of the questions asked in John 9:22 and Matthew 16:13-14. Other evidence suggesting a cyclical afterlife include geniuses, child prodigies, and persons with knowledge of places they've never been or of people they've never met.

Great thinkers throughout the ages have believed in reincarnation, including: Origen, St. Augustine, St. Francis of Assissi, Plato, Cicero, Pythagoras, Schopenhauer, Hume, Goethe, A. Conan Doyle, Emerson, William Blake, Whitman, Longfellow, Tennyson, Browning, Kipling, Benjamin Franklin, Voltaire, Henry Ford, and Thoreau.

Reincarnation is just one *model* for trying to understand what may occur before and after our earthly life. *Transmigration of the soul* is perhaps a more accurate term and doesn't involve coming back as an animal or a plant or even back to Earth necessarily. I don't believe that a long series of lives is obligatory; salvation through grace and realizing/expressing the divinity within can abbreviate the need for additional schooling.

Suggested readings for additional information about reincarnation include: *Life Begins At Death* by Dr. Leslie Weatherhead; *World Beyond* and *Here and Hereafter* by Ruth Montgomery; *There Is A River* by Thomas Sugrue; *Many Mansions* by Gina Cerminara; *Twenty Cases Suggestive of Reincarnation* and other works by Ian Stevenson; *Discover The Power Within You* by Eric Butterworth; *Reincarnation: A New Horizon in Science, Religion, and Society* by Sylvia Cranston and Carey Williams; and *Reincarnation: The Second Chance* by Sybil Leek.

The terms "preexistence, birth, life, death, afterlife, and rebirth" are misleading; they are each just phases in eternity. Did the eternal self of you start with your human birth? I think not. A Church of Jesus Christ of Latter Day Saint's Publication, *Combination Reference*, by Eldin Ricks lists several scriptural passages that indicate premortal existence. These include Ecclesiastes 12:7; Jeremiah 1:4-5; Zechariah 12:1; and John 9:1-3. The objective of these references, he writes, is "To show that this life is another stage in an eternal purposeful journey." As Ralph Von Aling puts it, "We are Spiritual Beings, encased in a cloak of flesh. Birth and Death are but two commas in our eternal existence." Another term for death is "graduation" — graduating into the next realm.

Will your spiritual inner self die when the body stops functioning? Again, no. Past, present, and future are human concepts that limit our understanding of the eternal now moment. Birth and death are only two points along the eternal spectrum of life. The reality of life is *infinity* with no beginning and no end. Says William Wordsworth in *Ode: Intimations of Immortality:* "Our birth is but a sleep and a forgetting: the Soul that rises with us, our life's Star, hath had elsewhere its setting, and cometh from afar; Not in entire forgetfulness, and not in utter nakedness, but trailing clouds of glory do we come . . . "

Most persons have read or heard of "out-of-body" or "near-death experiences" (NDE). Drs. Kübler-Ross, Raymond Moody, and Ken Ring are three of the better known authors about these phenomena. Dr. Moody wrote *Life After Life, Reflections on Life After Life,* and *The Light Beyond.* Dr. Ring is the author of *Life at Death* and *Heading Toward Omega* and started IANDS — the International Association For Near-Death Studies. Other recommended works include: *A Collection of Afterlife Research Findings* by Craig Lundahl; *Recollections of Death: A Medical Investigation* by Michael Sabom, M.D.; *The Return From Silence* by Scott Rogo; *What Survives? Contemporary Explorations of Life After Death* edited by Gary Doore, Ph.D.; and *Closer to the Light* by Melvin Morse, M.D. (about children's near-death-experiences).

I first heard of NDE's as a youngster after my uncle Cliff Marsh had such an experience. His car had been hit by a semi, and he nearly died from multiple and severe injuries. He experienced being in a meadow of lush green grass and hearing beautiful music. He described an accelerated awareness — everything was more brilliant than usual — and it was so peaceful that, except for his family, he didn't care if he came back. Like most persons who have out-of-body experiences, he didn't fear death afterwards and was completely assured about the afterlife.

Dr. Moody describes a typical case: "A man is dying and as he reaches the point of greatest physical distress, he hears himself pronounced dead by his doctor. He . . . feels himself moving very rapidly through a long, dark tunnel. After this, he finds himself outside of his own physical body . . . Soon, other things begin to happen. Others come to meet and help him. He glimpses the spirits of relatives and friends who have already died, and a loving, warm spirit of a kind he has never encountered before — *a being of light* — appears before him." Dr. Ring speaks of the NDE as "representing an individual's direct personal realization of a higher spiritual reality . . . a glimpse, albeit a brief one, of a transcendental domain of preternatural (supernatural) peace and beauty."

NDE evidence points convincingly to continued existence with the soul or consciousness surviving bodily death. Persons who survive near-death have described events taking place outside the hospital room while they were clinically dead. For example, one patient described a car wreck that occurred while her heart and lungs had stopped. After being successfully resuscitated, she gave a detailed account of the accident that her spirit saw while floating about near the hospital. Such stories are common and are termed "tennis shoe stories" since NDE'ers often describe an item — like an old tennis shoe — that is on top of the hospital. How else would these patients — who were brought to the hospital by ambulance — know such details except by continued existence and awareness beyond physicality?

Elisabeth Kübler-Ross, M.D., described being visited by a recently deceased patient. This patient's spirit visited to dissuade Dr. Kübler-Ross from abandoning her work during a time of discouragement. The "dead" patient also wrote a note to her minister who had worked closely with them. Handwriting analysis showed a positive identification with earlier samples written by the patient when she lived on earth. I thank Dr. Kübler-Ross for her pioneering work in furthering our knowledge about the continued existence of human life. Since then, others like Bernie Siegel, M.D., have reported contacts from "deceased" patients.

Chris Oyler asked the director of home-nursing what to expect at the time of death of her son: "They say there's a warm feeling that comes over them, and that they can feel their spirits leaving their bodies and being lifted up. They usually see a light . . . it's always a light that is beckoning them. They feel torn. They want to follow the light, but they don't want to leave the people they love behind. The best thing you can do for Ben is to let him know that it's okay to leave you. And that you love him."

Mrs. Oyler described the moments just after Ben passed on: "The room was full of Ben. He was all around us everywhere. Warm and loving. He was lingering for a moment to say good-bye. To tell us not to worry, that there wasn't anything to be afraid of, and never was."

A year and a half after Ben's death, Chris realized, "You never stop being a mother, even when your child is gone. You carried that child inside you, and you participated in the miracle of life when that child was born. And you know that all that energy and love cannot just vanish without a trace."

During my years of working in hospitals, I had the opportunity to be around many persons just before, during, and after they died. I sometimes spoke afterwards with patients who were successfully resuscitated. The majority did not recall anything, but several individuals reported classic experiences: a white light at the end of a tunnel, friends and loved ones there to greet them, sweet music, the presence of God or Jesus, being told their time on earth was not yet over, and a lasting certainty about the afterlife.

Several older patients have reservedly but lucidly told me, "I wouldn't tell many people about this but last night I was visited by my late husband. He stood right there by the foot of the bed, smiled, and told me I would see him again." Often, this patient would expire within the next day or two. Reports of this type were usually by females and involved a visit by their departed spouse or parent. These patients were oriented and totally coherent. They were excited about their experience but hesitant to tell others for fear of ridicule or being thought they were "crazy."

A 1984 National Opinion Research Council found that 67 percent of all adult Americans claim they've had some "psychic" experience. More persons are becoming open-minded about these experiences that lend hope and a growing understanding of life after life. Increase your faith and understanding about continued existence after death. As your belief in afterlife increases, your experience of life can improve dramatically. *How would you live if you knew for a fact* that your soul or spirit — the real you — didn't die? How would humanity change if we really knew that life is eternal, afterlife is a fact, and death is nothing to fear? We have eternity to live, love, learn, and serve others. Find joy in each moment, do what is right, and honor God as you *enjoy eternity.*

Onward to the Future

Cataclysmic earth changes have been predicted by sources as diverse as fundamentalist Christians and New Age psychics. Destructive forces of nature, the anti-Christ, nuclear holocaust, AIDs — there are a lot of ways our apple cart could get upset. Except . . . you and I know that our *true* selves can't be destroyed. Swami Rama, author of *Yoga And Psychotherapy* and founder of the Himalayan International Institute of Yoga Science and Philosophy in Honesdale, Pennsylvania, was asked if he was concerned about a disastrous end of the world. He smiled gently and replied, "Your world may end but mine cannot."

Build your house on a bedrock of faith and an inner knowledge of the Creator within. Life may change drastically in the future. Cataclysmic changes aren't preordained but could occur unless we individually and collectively evolve in consciousness. Recall the story of the wise man and the boy with the bird in his hand; similarly, the future is in our hands. *It is as we would have it.*

Dr. Ken Ring describes prophetic visions by persons with NDE's. Common elements of a world preview include: *geographic* changes — earthquakes, volcanic activity, land and pole shifts, and catastrophic weather; *socioeconomic breakdown* — famine, social disorder, and economic collapse; *nuclear war* — usually the extreme threat rather than actual atomic holocaust; and a subsequent era of *global peace* and brotherhood. Persons with NDE's were told these were "necessary purgations effecting the transformation of humanity into a new mode of being." Cataclysmic events were seen as "transitional rather than ultimate. They would be followed by a new era in human history, marked by human brotherhood, universal love, and world peace."

Lazaris, a spirit speaking through Jach Purcel, says: "There will be catastrophes, yes, but they will not destroy our world as some tell you . . . Weather all over the world will seem stranger . . . there will be technological disasters — plane crashes, train wrecks, toxic spills and leaks . . . Though there will be regional distress and even tragedy, there will not be wholesale destruction. You will continue and there is a future . . . you are making tremendous progress . . . when you step back and look at the progress of humankind over several thousands of years — even over several hundreds of years — you can see the progress. There is great hope in your world and there is greater success coming . . . In your world there are many who detract and constrict. Yet there are those exceptional people. And it only takes one."

After her NDE, one woman related, "I was informed that mankind was breaking the laws of the universe and as a result of this would suffer. This was not the vengeance of an indignant God but rather like the pain one might suffer as a result of arrogantly defying the law of gravity." The coming catastrophes were "an inevitable educational cleansing of the earth. Mankind, I was told, was being consumed by the cancers of arrogance, materialism, racism, chauvinism, and separatist thinking." But in the end she saw "calamity turning to Providence."

An A.R.E. (Association for the Advancement of Realization and Enlightenment) speaker summarized Edgar

Cayce's views: "If there are severe earth changes then they will have been brought on by mankind's refusal to acknowledge and to allow the Spirit — the force of God — to move into and be the center of our lives and to be of service to our fellowman. This is the lesson that we need to learn. This is what we need to start applying in our daily lives. If we don't do it, these earth changes may definitely occur but there is no reason for them to occur if mankind will change."

That makes sense. An optimist always see potentials for growth, improvement, and positive change. I believe we humans will *wake up* to our true nature and increasingly address the problems that stem from unenlightened thoughts, words, and deeds. When we remember that all persons are brothers and sisters and act accordingly, the problems of the world will automatically be corrected. In *The Politics of Love*, Leo Buscaglia says that others tell him, "You're advocating loving everyone, that's unrealistic." To this, Leo replies, "Well, whom do you suggest I discard and for what reason? How can I help but love you, you're me!"

We shape the future through our individual and collective thoughts, words, and deeds. Remember the glass of water question — is it half full or half empty? There is no right answer, but I personally favor the positive or thankful viewpoint, appreciating what is versus what isn't. Why not believe in and work toward the most optimistic and hopeful scenarios?

We can help establish heaven on earth. With the ever-present guidance from above and right actions, utopia living can be a reality. Don't think it's all up to you; that's asking for rapid burn out. We each are individually important, however, in making our contributions. A Native American story of the creation depicts God as the Master Potter at the wheel of life. Each of us is a vessel cast by the

Creator; we can show our worth and gratitude to the Creator by being a *useful vessel.* "What you are is God's gift to you — what you make of yourself is your gift to God."

Consider small communities where people help each other during times of need; when someone's home burns down, the community mobilizes and contributes lumber, labor, and products to correct the problem. Grandma makes food for the workers while Junior picks up nails dropped by the carpenters. Similarly, each person plays a vital part in the worldwide scheme of things. Dr. Victor Frankl says, "Everyone has his own specific vocation or mission in life . . . Therein he cannot be replaced, nor can his life be repeated. Thus, everyone's task is as unique as is his specific opportunity to implement it." United, we *can* solve the earth's problems.

Human potentials and resources are unlimited when we use *possibility thinking* and focus on creative solutions. Look at the great success of "Habitat for Humanity," this great example of people working together with an emphasis on self-responsibility and quality. A belief in *abundance* opens doors for new inventions, ideas, and techniques. *Humankind has everything they need to solve all the problems of the world right now!* This was one of the late Buckminster Fuller's main messages.

Look at the technological advances in the last 100, 50, and ten years; why can't these improvements accelerate even more quickly and be oriented toward practical solutions of world problems? We can stop starvation and poverty on earth *now* if we make it a priority. We have the ability to feed the world — only distribution and political problems stand in the way. The superpower standoff is over; it's way past time to focus our money, time, and technology toward *peace-time* applications.

We feed birds throughout the winter, and I noticed

that on mild days, only one redbird couple uses the feeder. The dominant birds usually maintain their territory; during severe winter storms, however, there are as many as 12 redbirds at the feeders. They apparently *waive* their usual rules during times that threaten survival. Humans, too, have strong instincts for survival and protectionism; but sometimes, our judgments clouded by fear and greed, we forget that we are all children of God. Some of our brothers and sisters are suffering and dying; perhaps we too could waive our past caveman-like ways and share our resources. There's plenty for all.

Why can't we solve all our problems — quickly, thoroughly, and lovingly? Butterworth says, "The law is, 'It is your Father's good pleasure to give you the kingdom' (Luke 12:32). God is all-sufficiency — your instant, constant, and abundant supply . . . Thus any limitation must be a limitation in thought, in the faith that shapes the substance . . . The wealth of the universe will be yours to the degree that you can see it and see yourself using it." Consider the miracle of feeding 5000 with five loaves and two fishes; Jesus taught the possibility of abundance and prosperity for *all.*

In *Life And Teaching Of The Masters Of The Far East,* Baird T. Spalding writes, "Jesus recognized that the one in Christ Consciousness knows no limitation. He . . . looked to God as the source and creator of all and gave thanks for the power and substance right at hand to fill every want . . . God is holding the ideal perfect world in mind in every detail and it is bound to come forth as a heaven or perfect home where all His children, all His creatures, and all His creations may dwell in peace and harmony. This is the perfect world that God saw in the beginning and the one He is thinking into existence right now, and the time of its manifestation lies in our acceptance of it."

Regarding the return of Christ, consider that each generation since his death has believed theirs would be the time for His second coming. When Jesus said He would return, His followers made ready for it. Nearly 2000 years later, some are still sure the time is near. Theologians who specialize in "eschatology," or end events near the second coming, can't agree on a literal versus a figurative interpretation. Could it be that Jesus meant a return and triumph in *Spirit*, available anytime, anywhere, and for all persons in all lands?

Megatrends 2000 by John Naisbitt and Patricia Aburdene points out, "Just before the last millennium, in the 990's, most sources report a popular belief that the world would come to an end in the year 1000 . . . Over the course of history, in addition to the years 500 and 1000, the millennium has been set at 1260, 1420, 1533, (the fifteenth centennial of Christ's death), 1843, 1844, 1845, 1847, 1851, and 1914." It's as if humankind collectively wishes for a rapid and external solution to earthly problems. How about a collective effort — with God's help — at responsibly solving our own problems?

They conclude: "Humanity will probably not be rescued *deus ex machina* either in the form of a literal Second Coming (the fundamentalist expectation) or by friendly spaceships (the New Age version). Though we will be guided by a revived spirituality, the answers will have to come from us . . . The meaning of that great symbol the millennium depends entirely on how it is interpreted. It can mark the end of time or the beginning of the new. We believe the decision has already been made to embrace its positive side. Within the hearts and minds of humanity, there has been a commitment to life, to the utopian quest for peace and prosperity for all, which today we can clearly visualize."

Perhaps there will be a literal and physical return of

Jesus some day. Until then — and even if it never happens in the *outer* — examine your *inner* self and find Christ patiently waiting. Remember the scene of Jesus, lantern in hand, knocking on a door at night? This is a beautiful depiction of how God, Christ, the heavenly host, and your inner self with its divine potentials stand ready to illuminate the darkness. "Knock and it shall be opened unto you. Seek and you shall find." So it's a win-win situation. Realized or saved persons can experience the spiritual reality of Jesus right now and if He physically returns as well.

Again, Hope

Isn't life interesting? Our earthly experience is an exquisitely designed curriculum for human students. Let's learn our lessons quickly and well; see beyond the illusions and problems as you realize your inner potentials and dreams. We each are a miracle, created and beloved by God. We each are special; like snowflakes, no two persons are alike. We each are here for a reason and have untold talents and abilities. For all this, I sense hope.

Dr. Weatherhead asks, "May it be that our relationship to God is not a relationship of, for example, ants on an ant-heap, with a superior being looking down upon them and trying to keep interested in their doings? May it not be that the illustration of the brain is closer to the truth, that is to say, that we are to God as the cells of our brains are to us; that we are in a very real sense part of Him and that He is expressing His life through us and that each one of us therefore is precious to Him . . .?" I believe so and for these truths, I see hope.

We receive help and direction from God and heavenly assistants — angels, masters, and saints. *A Book of Angels* by Sophy Burnham relates inspiring stories of encounters with spiritual beings who help us along the way. Hindu teachings describe the "Boddhisatva," a highly developed spiritual entity who comes back to earth to teach and guide others. Some persons have had contact with these celestial beings or feel a real kinship with them.

My grandma Pitstick was a great soul — always positive, cheerful, and interested in the other person. Shortly before she died, she told me: "Mark, I've prayed to Saint Josephine and asked her to help you. She has always been there for me, especially during the tough times. If you ever need direction, call for her." This spiritual entity was as real to Grandma as I was. Organized churches have long taught that angels and saints give guidance from above. Given our vast universe, why can't there be diverse types and numbers of beings to aid our growth and unfoldment? Pray for all guidance to be from God and Christ and in the spirit of love, and you can't go wrong.

In the prologue of *Emmanuel's Book*, we are reassured: "This earth plane is neither the beginning nor the end of your existence. It is simply a step, a schoolroom. My friends, let me impress upon you how solidly you are planted in eternity, how brilliantly you can shine in your own physical world, how possible it all is, how beautifully the Plan is designed. In God's Plan no soul is alone. No soul is ever lost."

No, my friends, we're not in this alone. We have our amazing inner potentials; we have each other on earth as helpmates and friends. We have higher beings of various types to directly help and guide. And always operating through these levels is the Supreme Being. For all this, I feel *hope* no matter what our temporary station in life may be. As Kenneth Caraway said, "There is no box made by God nor us but that the sides cannot be flattened out and the top blown off to make a dance floor on which to celebrate life."

Look for signs of spiritual awakening. These include:

- a tendency to think and act spontaneously
- a loss of interest in judging other people and yourself
- a loss of ability to worry
- frequent, overwhelming episodes of appreciation
- contented feelings of connectedness with others and nature
- frequent attacks of smiling
- an increased susceptibility to the love extended by others and the uncontrollable urge to pass it on.

In the past, Native American youth would go through a *vision quest*; they spent several days alone in nature, searching for their vision from the Great Spirit. After that, when problems or conflicts would arise, tribal leaders would ask, "What is your vision and how does this problem relate to your purpose in life?" We each have a special purpose; get in touch with your *inner vision* and use these goals to stay centered as you journey down life's path.

Joseph Campbell said, "If you follow your bliss, you put yourself on a kind of track that has been there the whole while, waiting for you, and the life you ought to be living is the one you are living."

Ruthie and Verena Cady were conjoined twins who shared a single heart and died at age seven. From an earthly perspective, what a tragedy. From a higher consciousness, their short lives were beautiful demonstrations of how nothing stops God from making triumph out of sadness. Says their mother Marlene, "There are those people who say, 'Oh, how tragic' . . . I always tell these people that the only tragedy is their interpretation of the girls' situation because obviously Ruthie and Verena are happy kids . . . They could find happiness in things you'd never even think of looking at. That's the big message I hope people get from their lives: Appreciate what you have."

A few months before passing on, Verena calmly remarked, "I think that pretty soon we're going to die. But don't worry, Mom. God told me He'll make sure everything's all right." At their funeral service, their father Peter said, "Inhale Ruthie and Verena's spirits, and exhale any sorrow you may feel at their passing." These two souls taught us a lot. Remember, even in the midst of apparent tragedy, God works for good and teaches us hope!

While photographing daffodils growing up through the snow, I realized the wisdom of looking at life through the eyes of an artist all the time. That is, *look for the beautiful, the interesting, the miraculous, and the unique.* Selectively focusing on the beautiful and positive in life raises our consciousness; *really see* the divine order and the beauty of the universe. Watch the movie *Awakenings* and notice how vibrant and exquisitely beautiful *all life* seemed to Leonard after being freed from his catatonia. There's always something special to appreciate if we would only open our eyes, ears, hearts, and minds.

How wonderful life is and how much better it will become as more of us realize our eternal and spiritual nature. Keep a lofty perspective and remember who you really are and where you are going. *Your eternal self — soul, spirit, and inner divinity — is the real you.* Bank on it. Be inspired by this truth and follow your dreams, hopes, and inner visions. Trust in God and yourself — you're not a worthless sinner. God has no time or space limitations for all to come to Him. Until we know God, we suffer in a self-imposed "hell" of isolation from the Divine and our true nature. As soon as we say "yes" to God, our lives fill with love and light and become more like heaven.

ACTION STEPS

• If you haven't already done so, take a moment and earnestly invite God and Christ to the forefront of your life. Having made that conscious decision, resolve to live as you know you should.

• Find a home church or worship group to aid your spiritual growth but remember that your personal relationship is most important. Some persons have been turned off by organized religions and do better with individual worship approaches, like walking in nature and talking with God.

• Whatever your methods, benefit from regular spiritual renewal and communing with God. A cane or willow basket becomes brittle and can break unless it is periodically dipped in water. In the same way, our spirit is revitalized and our faith restored with prayer, meditation, and fellowship.

• Write down sayings or quotations that are meaningful for you and review these to increase your faith.

• Remember that God understands diversity and individuality — He or She created it — so follow your heart and worship God as you feel moved to do.

• If you have religious questions, take advantage of the many resources available to address these issues. Use books, tapes, and services of various spiritual teachers as needed.

• Remember your eternal nature and that you were created in God's image. Let this good news vitalize your body and soul and let your light shine!

EPILOGUE

This is not the end but the beginning of a new and better life if you want it. Some of this information may be new or seem strange to you. Don't you feel, though, that many of us are ready — even overdue — for a change? You *can* achieve optimal physical health, self-actualization, and spiritual enlightenment. That's a sizable undertaking but you now possess the information to proceed. Implement your changes slowly but steadily, following an inner flow and doing it *your* way. You can enjoy a greater quality and quantity of life. Life can be much richer and fuller for a relatively small expenditure of time and effort.

Remember, the solutions to all of your problems can be found with a little study, effort, and faith. Read widely and listen to educational and inspirational audio and video-tapes. Fill your heart and mind with motivational and positive messages on a regular basis. Only *you* can create your own heaven on earth and your contribution to the collective effort is vital. Leo Buscaglia tells of a Buddhist teacher who said, "To know and not do is really not to know." Now you know. I hope you do what's needed so you can discover how great life can be.

I call for *generalists* in all professions to guide and teach those who desire optimal holistic health. Health care providers who can combine scientific, mental, and spiritual realms can help direct health consumers toward their fullest potentials. I'll be among them — teaching, writing, practicing, and living life to the fullest. Together, we can do it. Now it's up to *you* to use this information. Do you really want to be vitally alive and at peace?

Refer back to *Balanced Living* as needed; read and use the various resources discussed. Review your notes and the information you highlighted while reading. Remember, this is the compilation of 20 years of education, clinical experience, seminars, and intense searching. So don't be overwhelmed by the immensity of the project; just jump in, get your feet wet, and start changing at a moderate pace. List some goals for this week; take Action Steps today and start to discover the real and glorious you. Become a health nut and a self-actualized person. Devote a few hours each week toward educating yourself and practicing healthy lifestyle habits; it will pay enormous physical, mental, and spiritual dividends.

Realize and release your full potentials and watch your life and world improve. Steven W. Hawking, Ph.D., author of *A Brief History Of Time,* states, "The more you understand the nature of things, the closer you are to the mind of God." Now you should understand much more about the nature of things. Yes, we can transform our lives and the world into a literal heaven on earth. Remember, the Earth walk is short; use it wisely. Realize your fullest potentials, let your light shine, and let's get started.

RESOURCES

PHYSICAL BALANCE

International Health Foundation
(Lendon H. Smith, M.D., program)
(for information about books, tapes, and
health care products)
2233 S.W. Market St. Dr.
Portland, OR 97201-2429

Optometric Extension Program
(eye doctors using vision therapy)
2912 S. Daimler St.
Santa Ana, CA 92705
714-250-8070

St. Helena Hospital and Health Center
(Dr. John McDougall's programs)
P.O. Box 250
Deer Park, CA 94576
800-358-9195 (outside CA); 800-862-7575 (inside CA)

Dr. Bernard Jensen
(books and tapes on holistic healing)
24360 Old Wagon Road
Escondido, CA 92027
619-749-2727

The Preventive Medicine Research Institute (PMRI)
    (Dale Ornish, M.D., program)
    1001 Bridgeway, Box 305
    Sausalito, CA 94965
    800-328-3738 or 415-332-2525

For a mail order source for vegetable and fruit juicers,
The Program for Better Vision, lumbar support cushions,
    cervical pillows, shower and drinking water filters,
    LifeSign program to stop smoking, and other natural
    health aids: (associated with Tom Ferguson, M.D.,
    founder of *Medical Self-Care* magazine)
        SelfCare Catalog
        5850 Shellmound Ave., Suite 390
        Emeryville, CA 94662-0813
        1-800-345-337

Health & Healing
    (Julian Whitaker, M.D., program)
    C/O Phillips Publishing, Inc.
    7811 Montrose Road
    Potomac, MD 20854
    800-777-5005
    clinic phone number 800-283-0158
    (4321 Birch, Suite 100
    Newport Beach, CA)
    714-583-7666 (referral number for doctors
    using this program in your area)

CHIROPRACTIC

The American Chiropractic Association
    1701 Clarendon Blvd.
    Arlington, VA 22209
    703-276-8800

International Chiropractic Association
    1110 N. Glebe Road, Suite 1000
    Arlington, VA 22201
    703-528-5000

World Chiropractic Alliance
    2950 N. Dobson Rd., Suite 1
    Chandler, AZ 85224
    1-800-347-1011

Chirp Inc.
    (to locate D.C.s using the
    Pierce-Pettibon method in your area)
    209 Richland Ave.
    Dravosburg, PA 15034
    412-469-2000

NUTRITION

The Juiceman
    (for fruit & vegetable juicing information)
    655 S. Orcas; P. O. Box 80587
    Seattle, WA 98108
    800-800-8455

American Dietetic Association
     (national organization)
     216 West Jackson Blvd., Suite 800
     Chicago, IL 60606-6995
     800-877-1600

La Leche League International
     9616 Minneapolis Ave., Box 1209
     Franklin Park, IL 60131
     708-455-7730

Ann Wigmore Foundation
     (nutritional healing with raw foods)
     196 Commonwealth
     Boston, MA 02116
     (617) 267-9424

Dr. Kurt Donsbach, D.C., Ph.D.
     (clinics and information)
     Hospital Santa Monica
     Rosarito Beach [Playa Rosarito]
     Baja California, Mexico and/or
     Hospital San Agustino
     Bulevar Agua Caliente
     Tijuana, Baja California Norte, Mexico
     619-428-1146; 800-359-6547

Gerson Institute
     (for *HEALING* newsletter, books, tapes, and
     Gerson Therapy Center)
     P. O. Box 430
     Bonita, CA 91908
     619-267-1150

Bio-Zoe, Inc.
>   (for publications and nutritional
>   supplements from Gary Todd, M.D.)
>   112 Academy St.
>   Waynesville, NC 28786
>   800-426-7581; 704-456-3505

PSYCHOLOGICAL

Nightengale-Conant Corporation
>   (mail order source of audiotapes)
>   7300 N. Lehigh Ave.
>   Chicago, IL 60648
>   800-323-3938

ECaP (Exceptional Cancer Patients group
>   started by Bernie Siegel, M. D.)
>   1302 Chapel St.
>   New Haven, CT 06511
>   203-865-8392

SPIRITUAL

Rev. Robert E. Love
>   (author of *Hell No*)
>   To obtain this book, write:
>   Box 9
>   Prospect Hill, NC 27314

A.R.E. (Association for Research and
>   Enlightenment — Edgar Cayce)
>   67th Street & Atlantic Ave., Box 595
>   Virginia Beach, VA 23451

International Association for Near
    Death Studies (IANDS)
    Box 7767
    Philadelphia, PA 19101

Unity School of Christianity
    (source of multimedia publications)
    Unity Village, MO 64065S

SEVA Foundation
    (a service foundation
    for those wanting to help others)
    108 Spring Lake Dr.
    Chelsea, MI 48118-9701
    313-475-1351

Hanuman Foundation
    (book and tape library for works by Ram Dass)
    524 San Anselmo Ave., #203
    San Anselmo, CA 94960
    800-248-1008

Elisabeth Kübler-Ross
    (Life, Death and Transition Workshops)
    South Route 616
    Head Waters, VA 24442
    703-396-3441

REFERENCE LIST

I

J

K

L

M

SELECTED BIBLIOGRAPHY

Abrahamson, E. M., M.D. *Body, Mind, And Sugar*. New York: Avon Books, 1977.

Anderson, Mark, and Bernard Jensen, D.C., Ph.D. *Empty Harvest*. Garden City Park, NY: Avery, 1990.

Bach, Richard. *Illusions*. New York: Random House, 1977.

______. *Jonathan Livingston Seagull*. New York: Avon Books, 1970.

______. *One*. New York: Morrow, 1988.

______. *The Bridge Across Forever*. New York: Morrow, 1984.

Ballentine, Rudolph, M.D. *Diet & Nutrition: A Holistic Approach*. Honesdale, PA: The Himalayan International Institute, 1978.

Becker, Ernest, Ph.D. *The Denial Of Death*. New York: The Free Press, 1973.

Benson, Herbert, M.D., *The Relaxation Response*. New York: Avon Books, 1976.

Bradshaw, John. *Homecoming*. New York: Bantam Books, 1990.

Brazelton, T. Berry, M.D. *Toddlers And Parents*. New York: Delacorte Press, 1976.

Brody, Jane. *Jane Brody's Good Food Book*. New York: Norton, 1985.

Brownell, Kelly D., Ph.D. *Making A Weight Loss Program Work: The LEARN Program*. Dallas: Brownell & Hager Publishing Co., 1989. [For more information: 1555 W. Mockingbird Lane, Suite 203; Dallas, TX 75235-5018 (214)-637-1100]

Burnham, Sophy. *A Book Of Angels*. New York: Ballantine Books, 1990.

Buscaglia, Leo. *Born For Love: Thought For Lovers*. New York: Random House, 1992.

______. *Living, Loving, & Learning*. Thorofare, NJ: Slack, Inc., 1982.

Butterworth, Eric. *Discover The Power Within You*. New York: Harper & Row, 1968.

______. *Life Is For Loving*. New York: Harper & Row, 1973.

Caplan, Theresa and Frank. *The Early Childhood Years*. New York: Perigee Books, 1983.

Capra, Fritjof, Ph.D. *The Tao Of Physics*. New York: Bantam Books, 1975.

Castenada, Carlos. *The Teachings Of Don Juan*. New York: Pocket Books, 1968.

Cerminara, Gina. *Many Mansions*. New York: NAL-Dutton, 1988.

Cheraskin, E., M.D., D.M.D., and W. M. Ringsdorf, Jr., D.M.D. *Psycho-dietetics*. New York: Bantam Books, 1974.

Chopra, Deepak, M.D. *Quantum Healing*. New York: Bantam Books, 1989.

Clason, George S. *The Richest Man In Babylon*. New York: Bantam Books, 1982.

Cousins, Norman. *Anatomy Of An Illness*. New York: Bantam Books, 1979.

______. *Head First: The Biology Of Hope*. New York: Dutton, 1989.

Dass, Ram. *A Miracle Of Love*. New York: E. P. Dutton, 1979.

______. *Be Here Now*. New York: Crown Publishing, 1971.

______. *Grist For The Mill*. Santa Cruz, CA: Unity Press, 1976.

______. *Journey Of Awakening: A Meditator's Guidebook*. New York: Bantam Books, 1978.

______. *The Only Dance There Is*. Garden City, NY: Anchor

Press, 1974.

______, and Paul Gorman. *How Can I Help?* New York: Alfred A. Knopf, 1985.

DeRoeck, Richard E., D.C. *The Confusion About Chiropractors*. Danbury, CT: Impulse Publishing, 1989.

Diamond, Harvey and Marilyn. *Fit for Life*. New York: Warner Books, 1985.

______. *Fit for Life II: Living Health*. New York: Warner Books, 1987.

______. *Your Heart — Your Planet*. Santa Monica, CA: Hay House, 1990.

Dobson, James, Ph.D. *Dare To Discipline*. Wheaton, IL: Tyndale House Publishers, 1970.

Donkin, Scott, D.C. *Sitting On The Job*. Boston: Houghton Mifflin, 1989.

Donsbach, Kurt, D.C., Ph.D. *Dr. Donsbach's Guide To Good Health*. New York: Pocket Books, 1985.

Douglas, Ben, M.D. *Ageless: Living Younger Longer*. Brandon, MS: Quail Ridge, 1990.

Dryburgh, Robert, D.C. *So You're Thinking Of Going To A Chiropractor*. New Canaan, CT: Keats Publishing Inc., 1984.

Dufty, William. *Sugar Blues*. Radnor, PA: Chilton Book Co., 1975.

Dyer, Wayne, Ed.D. *Gifts From Eykis*. New York: Pocket Books, 1983.

______. *Pulling Your Own Strings*. New York: Avon Books, 1978.

______. *The Awakened Life*. [audio tapes]

______. *The Sky's The Limit*. New York: Pocket Books, 1980.

______. *What Do You Really Want For Your Children?* New York: Avon Books, 1986.

______. *You'll See It When You Believe It*. New York: Avon, 1990.

______. *Your Erroneous Zones*. New York: Avon Books, 1977.

Eaton, S. Boyd, Marjorie Shostak, and Melvin Konner. *The Paleolithic Prescription: A Program Of Diet And Exercise And A Design For Living*. New York: Harper & Row, 1988.

Eddy, Mary Baker. *Science And Health*. Boston: The First Church of Christ Scientist, 1875.

Ellis, Albert, and Robert A. Harper. *A Guide To Rational Living In An Irrational World*. N. Hollywood, CA: Wilshire, 1975.

Emmanuel. *Emmanuel's Book*. New York: Friend's Press, 1985.

Forman, Robert, Ph.D. *How To Control Your Allergies*. Atlanta: Larchmont Books, 1984.

Frankl, Victor E., M.D. *Man's Search For Meaning*. New York: Pocket Books, 1959.

Fredericks, Carlton, Ph.D. *Low Blood Sugar And You*. New York: Constellation International, 1969.

Freeman, Arthur, and Rose DeWolf. *Woulda, Coulda, Shoulda: Overcoming Regrets, Mistakes, And Missed Opportunities*. New York: Morrow, 1989.

Fromm, Erich. *The Art Of Loving*. London: Unwin Publications, 1987.

Fuller, Buckminster. *Critical Path*. New York: St. Martin's Press, 1981.

Gerson, Max, M.D. *A Cancer Therapy — Results Of 50 Cases*. Barryton, NY: Station Hill Press, 1990.

______. *HEALING — The Gerson Journal*. (See Resources.)

Gibran, Kahil. *The Prophet*. New York: Alfred A. Knopf, 1967.

Golbecks, The. *American Wholefoods Cuisine*. New York: New American Library, 1983.

Goleman, Daniel, Ph.D. *The Varieties Of The Meditative Experience*. New York: E. P. Dutton, 1977.

Graedon, Joe, R.Ph. *The People's Pharmacy*, rev. ed. New York: St. Martin's Press, 1989.

Green, Elmer and Alyce. *Beyond Biofeedback*. New York: Dell Publishing Co., 1977.

Grinder, John, and Richard Bandler. *Reframing: Neuro-Linguistic Programming And The Transformation Of Healing*. Moab, UT: Real People, 1982.

Grollman, Earl A. *Concerning Death: A Practical Guide For The Living*. Boston: Beacon Press, 1974.

Gussow, Joan D., and Paul D. Thomas. *The Nutrition Debate*. Palo Alto, CA: Bull Publishing Co., 1986.

Hansel, Tim. *You Gotta Keep Dancin'*. Elgin, IL: Cook, 1986.

Hansen, Mark Victor. *Dare To Win*.

Harman, Willis, Ph.D. *Global Mind Change*. Indianapolis: Knowledge Systems, Inc., 1988.

_____. *Insight Into The New Age: A Scientific Inquiry Into Consciousness And The Nature Of Reality*. [audio tapes]

Hawking, Steven W. *A Brief History Of Time*. New York: Bantam Books, 1988.

Hedrick, Lucy. *Five Days To An Organized Life*. New York: Dell, 1990.

Henning, Joel. *Holistic Running*. New York: The New American Library, Inc., 1978.

Hill, Napoleon. *Think And Grow Rich*. New York: Fawcett Crest, 1960.

Hollender, Jeffrey. *How To Make The World A Better Place*.

Huggins, Dr. Hal. *Why Raise Ugly Kids?*

Hutschnecker, Dr. Arnold A. *The Will To Live*.

Huxley, Aldous. *Doors Of Perception*. New York: Harper Collins, 1963.

Imrie, David, M.D., and Lu Barbuto, D.C. *The Back Power Program*. New York: Wiley, 1990.

Inlander, Charles B. *Medicine On Trial: The Appalling Story Of Ineptitude, Malfeasance, Neglect, And Arrogance*. New York: Pantheon Books, 1989.

James, William, Ph.D., M.D., LL.D., Litt.D. *The Varieties Of Religious Experience*. New York: Macmillan, 1985.

Jampolsky, Gerald G., M.D. *Love Is Letting Go Of Fear.* Millbrae, CA: Celestial Arts, 1979.

______. and Diane V. Cirincione. *Love Is The Answer.* New York: Bantam Books, 1990.

Jensen, Bernard, D.C., Ph.D. *Food Healing For Man.* (See Resources.)

______, and Mark Anderson. *Empty Harvest.* Garden City Park, NY: Avery, 1990.

Johnson, John H. *Succeeding Against The Odds.* New York: Warner, 1989.

Jourard, Sidney, Ph.D. *The Transparent Self.* New York: Van Nostrand Reinhold Co., 1971.

Joy, W. Brugh, M.D. *Joy's Way: A Map For The Transformational Journey.* Boston: Houghton Mifflin Co., 1979.

Kaplan, Robert-Michael, O.D. *Seeing Beyond 20/20.* Hillsboro, OR: Beyond Words Pub., 1987.

Katzen, Mollie. *The Moosewood Cookbook.* Berkeley, CA: Ten Speed Press, 1977.

Kelder, Peter. *Fountain Of Youth.* Gig Harbor, WA: Harbor Press, Inc., 1989.

Kelner, Hall, and Coulter. *Chiropractors — Do They Help?* Richmond Hill, Ont., Canada: Fitzhenry & Whiteside Ltd., 1986.

Keyes, Ken. *A Handbook For Higher Consciousness.* St. Mary, KY: Living Love Publications, 1972.

______. *The Hundredth Monkey.* St. Mary, KY: Vision Books, 1981.

Kostrubala, Thaddeus, M.D. *The Joy Of Running.* New York: Pocket Books, 1984.

Kowalski, Robert. *The 8 Week Cholesterol Cure.* New York: Harper Collins, 1990.

Kübler-Ross, Elisabeth, M.D. *Death: The Final Stage Of Growth.* Englewood Cliffs, NJ: Prentice-Hall, Inc., 1975.

______. *On Death And Dying.* New York: Macmillan, 1969.

______. *Questions And Answers On Death And Dying.* New

York: Macmillan, 1974.

______, and Mal Warshaw, M.D. *AIDS: The Ultimate Challenge.* New York: Macmillan, 1988.

Kunin, Richard A., M.D. *Mega-Nutrition.* New York: New American Library, 1981.

Kushner, Harold. *When Bad Things Happen To Good People.* New York: Avon Books, 1983.

La Leche League International Staff. *La Leche League International Cookbook.* Franklin Park, IL: La Leche International, 1981.

______. *The Womanly Art Of Breastfeeding*, 4th rev. ed. New York: NAL-Dutton, 1983.

Lair, Jess, Ph.D. *I Ain't Much, Baby — But I'm All I've Got.* New York: Doubleday & Co., Inc., 1969.

Lappe, Francis Moore. *Diet For A Small Planet.* New York: Ballantine Books, 1982.

______. *World Hunger, Twelve Myths.* New York: Grove Press, 1986.

Lazarus, O. *Liberal Judaism And Its Standpoint.* London: Macmillan, 1937.

Leboyer, Dr. Frederick. *Birth Without Violence.* New York: Alfred A. Knopf, 1975.

Leek, Sybil. *Reincarnation: The Second Chance.* New York: Bantam Books, 1974.

Love, Rev. Robert. *Hell No.* Hicksville, NY: Exposition Press, 1976. [Out of print; see *Resources* for author's address.]

Lundahl, Craig. *A Collection Of Afterlife Research Findings.*

Mandell, Marshall, M.D. *Allergy, The Unrecognized Cause Of Physical, Mental, And Psycho-somatic Illness.*

Maslow, Abraham, Ph.D. *Motivation And Personality.* New York: Harper & Row, 1970.

McDougall, John, M.D. *McDougall's Medicine — A Challenging Second Opinion.* Clifton, NJ: New Win Publishing, 1986.

______. *The McDougall Plan.* Clinton, NJ: New Win Publishing, Inc., 1983.

______. *The McDougall Program*. New York: NAL-Dutton, 1990.

Mendelsohn, Robert, M.D. *How To Raise A Healthy Child In Spite Of Your Doctor*. New York: Ballantine Books, 1987.

Miller, Emmett E., M.D. *Feeling Good; How To Stay Healthy*.

Montgomery, Ruth. *Here And Hereafter*. New York: Fawcett Crest, 1968.

______. *World Beyond*. New York: Fawcett Books, 1985.

Moody, Dr. Raymond. *Life After Life*. Atlanta: Mockingbird Books, 1975.

______. *Reflections On Life After Life*. Atlanta: Mockingbird Books, 1977.

______. *The Light Beyond*. New York: Bantam Books, 1989.

Morse, Melvin, M.D. *Closer To The Light*. New York: Ivy Books, 1991.

Naisbitt, John, and Patricia Aburdene. *Megatrends 2000*. New York: Morrow, 1990.

Ornish, Dean. M.D. *Dr. Dean Ornish's Program For Reversing Heart Disease*. New York: Ballantine Books, 1990.

Ornstein, Robert E. *Healthy Pleasures*. Reading, MA: Addison-Wesley, 1990.

Ostrander and Schroeder. *Superlearning*. New York: Dell Publishing Co., 1979.

Oyle, Irving, D.O. *The Healing Mind*. Millbrae, CA: Celestial Arts, 1979.

Oyler, Chris. *Go Toward The Light*. New York: NAL-Dutton, 1990.

Pauling, Linus, Ph.D. *How To Live Longer And Feel Better*. New York: Avon Books, 1987.

Paulus, Trina. *Hope For The Flowers*. Mahwah, NJ: Paulist Press, 1992.

Prather, Hugh. *Notes On Love And Courage*. New York: Doubleday, 1977.

______. *Notes To Myself*. New York: Bantam Books, 1976.

Price, Dr. Weston. *Nutrition And Physical Degeneration*, 9th ed. San Diego, CA: Price-Pottenger, 1977.

Pritikin, Nathan, M.D. *The Pritikin Diet*. Out of print. See new edition: ______, with Patrick M. McGrady, Jr. *The Pritikin Program For Diet And Exercise*. New York: Bantam, 1980.

Rama, Swami, et al. *Yoga And Psychotherapy*. Honesdale, PA: The Himalayan International Institute, 1976.

Rapp, Doris, M.D. *Is This Your Child?* New York: William Morrow & Co., Inc., 1991.

Reiser, Oliver L. *Cosmic Humanism*. New York: Gordon & Breach, 1975.

Reuben, David, M.D. *The Save Your Life Diet*. New York: Random House, 1975.

R. H. J. *It Works*. Marina del Rey, CA: DeVorss & Co., 1980.

Ricks, Eldin. *Combination Reference*. Salt Lake City, UT: Desert Book, 1979.

Ring, Dr. Ken. *Heading Toward Omega*. New York: Morrow, 1985.

______. *Life At Death*. New York: Morrow, 1982.

Robbins, Anthony. *Unlimited Power*. New York: Fawcett Columbine, 1986.

Robertson, Donald S., M.D. *The Snowbird Diet*.

Robertson, Laurel, et al. *The New Laurel's Kitchen*. Berkeley, CA: Ten Speed Press, 1986.

Rogo, Scott. *The Return From Silence*.

Sabom, Michael, M.D. *Recollections Of Death: A Medical Investigation*.

Salinger, J. D., *Nine Stories: Teddy*. New York: Bantam Books, 1953.

Satter, Ellyn, R.D., A.C.S.W. *Child Of Mine: Feeding With Love And Good Sense*. Menlo Park, CA: Bull Publishing Co., 1986.

Scala, James, Ph.D. *Making The Vitamin Connection*. New

York: Harper & Row, 1985.

Schiedermayer, David L., M.D. *Life And Death Decisions*.

Schuller, Rev. Robert. *Success Is Never Ending, Failure Is Never Final*. New York: Bantam Books, 1990.

______. *The Be Happy Attitudes*. Waco, TX: Word Book Publishers, 1985.

______. *Tough Times Never Last, But Tough People Do!* New York: Bantam Books, 1984.

Schwartz, David J., Ph. D. *The Magic Of Thinking Big*. N. Hollywood, FL: Wilshire Book Co., 1959.

Schwartz, Jack. *Human Energy Systems*. New York: E. P. Dutton, 1980.

Seiderman, Arthur, O.D., et al. *20/20 Is Not Enough*. New York: Knopf, 1989.

Selye, Hans, M.D. *The Stress Of Life*. New York: McGraw-Hill, 1956.

Shelton, Charles. *In His Steps*. Waco, TX: Word Book Publishers, 1988.

Siegel, Bernie, M.D. *Love, Medicine, & Miracles*. New York: Harper & Row, 1986.

______. *Peace, Love, And Happiness*. New York: Harper & Row, 1989.

Simonton, O. Carl, M.D., Stephanie Matthews-Simonton, and James L. Creighton. *Getting Well Again*. New York: Bantam Books, 1978.

Smith, Lendon H., M.D. *Encyclopedia Of Baby And Child Care*. New York: Prentice-Hall, 1972.

______. *Feed Your Kids Right*. New York: McGraw-Hill, 1978.

______. *Feed Yourself Right*. New York: McGraw-Hill, 1982.

______. *Happiness Is A Healthy Life*, New Canaan, CT: Keats Publishing, Inc., 1992.

______. *Hyper Kids Workbook*. Santa Monica, CA: Shaw/Spelling, 1990.

______. *Improving Your Child's Behavior Chemistry*. New York: Prentice-Hall, 1984.

BIBLIOGRAPHY   361

_____. *The Children's Doctor*. 1969. [Out of Print.]

_____. *Vitamin C As Fundamental Medicine*. Tacoma, WA: Life Sciences Press, 1988.

Spalding, Baird T. *Life And Teaching Of The Masters Of The Far East*. Marina del Rey, CA: DeVorss & Co., Publishers, 1955.

Stare, Frederick J., M.D., Ph.D., Robert E. Olson, M.D., Ph.D., and Elizabeth M. Whelan, M.P.H., Sc.D. *Balanced Nutrition*. Holbrook, MA: Bob Adams, Inc. Publisher, 1989.

Stevenson, Ian. *Twenty Cases Suggestive Of Reincarnation*. Charlottesville, VA: University Press of Virginia, 1980.

Sugrue, Thomas. *There Is A River*. Virginia Beach, VA: ARE Press, 1989.

The EarthWorks Group. *50 Simple Things You Can Do To Save The Earth*. Berkeley, CA: EarthWorks Press, 1989.

Thie, John., D.C. *Touch For Health*. Pasadena, CA: TH Enterprises, 1987.

Thomas, Lewis, M.D. *The Medusa And The Snail*. New York: Bantam Books, 1979.

Tice, Louis, *New Age Thinking*. [audio tapes]

Todd, Gary, M.D. *Acquiring Optimal Health*. (See Resources.)

_____. *Nutrition, Health, And Disease*. West Chester, PA: Whitford Press, 1985.

Tracy, Brian. *Getting Rich In America*.

Von Aling, Ralph. *Well-Being Through Conscious Evolution*. Sugarcreek, OH: Schalabach Printers, 1990.

Waitley, Denis, Ph.D. *Being The Best*. Nashville: Oliver-Nelson, 1987.

_____. *10 Seeds Of Greatness*. Old Tappan, NJ: Fleming H. Revell Co., 1983.

_____. *The Psychology Of Winning*. Chicago: Nightengale-Conant Corp., 1979.

_____. *The Subliminal Winner*. [audio tape series]

Walker, N. W., D.Sc. *Guide To Diet And Salad*. Phoenix:

O'Sullivan, Woodside & Co., 1980.

Watts, Alan. *Meditation.*

______. *The Book On The Taboo Against Knowing Who You Are.* New York: Vintage Books, 1972.

Weatherhead, Leslie D. *Life Begins At Death.* Nashville, TN: Abingdon Press, 1989.

Weil, Andrew, M.D. *Health And Healing.* Boston: Houghton Mifflin, 1985.

Wellness Encyclopedia. Wellness Letter. Eds. of University of California, Berkley. Boston: Houghton-Mifflin, 1991.

What Survives? Contemporary Explorations Of Life After Death. ed. Gary Doore, Ph.D.

Whitaker, Julian, M.D. *Reversing Heart Disease.* New York: G. Putnam & Sons, 1988.

Wigmore, Ann, N.D. *Rebuilding Health With High Enzyme Living Foods.*

Wilk, Chester, D.C. *Chiropractic Speaks Out.* Park Ridge, IL: Wilk Publishing Co., 1976.

______. *Everything You Should Know About Chiropractic.* Park Ridge, IL: Wilk Publishing Co., 1980.

Williams, Roger J., Ph.D. *Biochemical Individuality.*

Williams, Wendy. *The Power Within.* New York: Harper Collins, 1990.

Wright, Nigel. *The Satan Syndrome.* Grand Rapids, MI: Zondervan, 1990.

Yogananda, Paramahansa. *Autobiography Of A Yogi.* Los Angeles: Self-Realization Fellowship Publishers, 1974.

Ziglar, Zig. *Courtship After Marriage.* New York: Ballantine Books, 1992.

______. *Raising Positive Kids In A Negative World.* New York: Ballantine Books, 1989.

______. *See You At The Top.* New York: Pelican, 1984.

INDEX

A

Chemical stress, 23, 35, 38

Chemicals and foods, 23, 148, 174, 186-187

Children's exposure to TV, 168, 243-244

Chiropractic care, 74, 77, 89, 97-143, 190

Cholesterol, 85, 146, 150-153, 168

Cigarette smoking, 42, 52, 54, 61-62, 125, 146-147, 170, 186, 188-189, 207, 239, 253

Cleansing crises, 28-32, 67, 192, 194

Clinical ecologist, 189-191

Colds or flu, 28, 31-32, 35, 67, 191, 194

Collateral circulation, 82

Colon cancer, 25, 154, 175

Commitment, 249-251

Concept Therapy, 268

Congestion, 24, 27, 30, 69

Constipation, 25-26, 37, 64-65, 83, 137, 153-154, 180

Control from Within: A Nine-Step Program to Stop Smoking, 50

Corrective chiropractic care, 100, 102, 104, 106-107, 111-113

"Costo-vertebral" subluxations, 120

Council of Constantinople, 314

Counseling, 221-222

Creative laziness, 205

Cruciferous vegetables, 62-63

D

Dairy products, 26, 62, 68, 145-147, 151, 157, 161, 173-175, 180, 190-192, 195

Decongestant preparations, 37

Degenerative joint disease (DJD), 88, 91, 93, 106, 121, 159

Dehydration, 36, 65

Depression, 40, 51, 83, 145, 155, 158, 208-209, 220, 231, 233, 235

G

H

I

O

P

R

ABOUT THE AUTHOR

Dr. Mark R. Pitstick holds three degrees: a premedical B.S. in zoology, an M.A. in clinical psychology, and a Doctor of Chiropractic degree. He also received graduate theological training while majoring in pastoral counseling.

In addition to his busy private practice, Dr. Pitstick is a frequently requested speaker. He has addressed hundreds of groups at schools, universities, clubs, churches, and industries. His *Balanced Living* Seminars© combine speaking, slide presentations, music, small group work, and demonstrations.

Dr. Pitstick is a member of several professional organizations, the Kiwanis Club, and the United Church of Christ. He has received an Outstanding Young Man of America award. He and his wife, Michelle, a licensed dietician, have two daughters, Faith and Rae Lynn.

For additional information about *Balanced Living* Seminars©, write or call the Balanced Living Chiropractic Center, 35 N. Plaza Boulevard, Chillicothe, Ohio 45601; phone number: (614) 772-4476.

BALANCED LIVING: Realizing Your Fullest Potentials

For additional copies of *Balanced Living*, telephone TOLL FREE 1-800-356-9315 or FAX TOLL FREE 1-800-242-0046. MasterCard/ VISA accepted.

To order *Balanced Living* directly from the publisher, send your check or money order for $16.95 plus $3.00 shipping and handling ($19.95 postpaid) to: Rainbow Books, Inc., Order Dept. 1-T, P.O. Box 430, Highland City, FL 33846-0430.

For QUANTITY PURCHASES, telephone Rainbow Books, Inc., (813) 648-4420 or write to Rainbow Books, Inc., P.O. Box 430, Highland City, FL 33846-0430.